Accessory Apartments
in
Single-Family Housing

Accessory Apartments in Single-Family Housing

by
Martin Gellen

Published in the United States of America
by the Center for Urban Policy Research
Building 4051–Kilmer Campus
New Brunswick, New Jersey 08903

Library of Congress Cataloging in Publication Data

Gellen, Martin.
  Accessory apartments in single-family housing.

  Includes index.
  1. Housing, Single family—Conversion to accessory apartments—United States.
2. Accessory apartments—United States. I. Title.
HD7287.6.U5G45   1985   333.33'8   85-149
ISBN 0-88285-105-5

Contents

List of Exhibits   vii

Acknowledgments   xi

Introduction   xiii

Chapter One
House Conversion and the Accessory Apartment   1

Chapter Two
Supply, Production, and Demand   29

Chapter Three
Space Standards and Social Change   57

Chapter Four
The Problem of Exclusive Single-Family Zoning   103

Chapter Five
Neighborhood and Environmental Impacts of
Accessory Apartment Conversions   133

Chapter Six
Promotion and Control
of Accessory Apartment Conversions   177

Conclusion   197

Index   201

List of Exhibits

Chapter One
1.1   An In-Line Expandable House   9
1.2   Third Bedroom Addition   10
1.3   Custom-Designed Expandable House   11
1.4   Garage Conversion   12
1.5   Garage Conversion and Addition   13
1.6   Split-Level Home   15
1.7   Expansion Potential of a Split-Level House   16
1.8   Marcel Breuer Exhibition House, Garden of the Museum of Modern
        Art, New York City 18, 19
1.9   The Techbuilt House 20, 21
1.10 The Flexabilt House 22, 23
1.11 A Life Cycle Home with Accessory Apartment   24
1.12 Expandable House with Accessory Apartment   25

Chapter Two
2.1   Components of Housing Inventory Change, U.S. 1890-1980 ..   32
2.2   Additions to the Supply of Rental Housing by Type of Addition and
        Urban Location, U.S. 1950-1980   34
2.3   Additions to the Housing Inventory by Means Other Than New
        Construction by Type, United States, 1973-1980   35
2.4   Distribution of New, Converted, and Unchanged Dwelling Units by
        Urban Location, Size and Year Moved In, United States 1973-1980.   37
2.5   Size of Structure and Occupancy Characteristics by Urban Location
        and Tenure, Same Units Before and After Conversion, United
        States, 1973-1980 ....   38, 39

2.6   Estimated Total Accessory Apartment Conversions, United States,
      1973-1980 40

2.7   Conversions and Mergers in the Housing Inventory, Dwelling Unit
      Characteristics, United States, 1973-1980 42

2.8   Conversions and Mergers in the Housing Inventory, Household
      Characteristics, United States, 1973-1980 43

2.9   Conversions and Mergers in the Housing Inventory by Year Moved
      into Dwelling Unit, United States 44

2.10 Estimated Annual Losses from the Housing Inventory, United
      States, October 1973 to October 1980 46

2.11 Owner-Occupied Households by Urban Location, Household Type
      and Component of Inventory Change, United States, 1973-1980 ... 48

2.12 Renter-Occupied Households by Urban Location, Household
      Composition and Component of Inventory Change, United States,
      1973-1980 49

2.13 Median Household Size by Tenure and Component of Inventory
      Change, United States, 1950-1980 50

2.14 Condition, Quality, and Size of New, Unchanged, and Converted
      Dwellings by Urban Location, Tenure and Component of Inventory
      Change, United States, 1973-1980 51

2.15 Rents and Incomes of Households in New, Converted, and
      Unchanged Dwellings by Urban Location, Tenure, and Component
      of Inventory Change, United States, 1973-1980 52

Chapter Three
3.1   Size of New Homes, United States, 1950-1980 59
3.2   Owner-Occupied Dwellings by Number of Rooms, 1950, 1980 60
3.3   Average Household Size, United States, 1970-1980 62
3.4   Distribution of Households by Size, United States, 1790-1980 63
3.5   Median Age of Once-Married (Never Divorced) Mothers at Selected
      Stages of the Family Life Cycle and Estimated Number of Years
      Between Selected Events for Women Born 1880-1959, by Decade
      of Birth 64

3.6   Changes in Mean Family Size, Mean Members Less than 18 Years
      and Mean Members 18 Years and Older, United States, 1948-1978 . 65

3.7   Distribution of Households by Household Types, United States,
      1940-1983 68

3.8   Median Rooms and Rooms Per Person by Size of Household,
      Renters and Owners, United States, 1970 70

3.9 Minimum Space Required for Basic Household Activities by Number of Persons in Household 72

3.10 Actual and Expected Space Consumption Over the Family Life Cycle for a Typical Home Owner 76

3.11 Percentage Distribution of Non-Farm Families by Rooms Per Person and Age of Head, United States, 1955 77

3.12 Household Composition of Sample in the Northern California Community Study by Tenure 84

3.13 Space Standards and Thresholds for Measuring Underutilization by Household Size 85

3.14 Owner-Occupied Dwellings With and Without Surplus Space by Household Composition, Northern California, 1977 86

3.15 Linear Probability Regression Model of Space Utilization in Owner-Occupied Single-Family Dwellings, Northern California, 1977 88

3.16 Underutilization Thresholds as a Function of Space Standards 91

3.17 Estimates of Underutilized Housing at Varying Space Standards by Tenure of Occupied Dwelling Units, United States, 1950, 1970, 1980 92

3.18 Panel A: Underutilized Dwellings by Household Sizes and Tenure Panel B: Change in Number and Percentage of Underutilized Dwellings by Household Size @ Maximum Space Standard Threshold of 3.0 Rooms Per Person: 1950-1980 .... 94, 95

Chapter Five

5.1 San Leandro, California 134

5.2 Change in Population by Age, San Leandro, California, 1960-1980 135

5.3 Change in the Distribution of Households by Size, San Leandro, California, 1960-1980 136

5.4 Percentage Distribution of Total Population by Age, Washington Manor, San Leandro, California, 1960-1980 137

5.5 Percentage Distribution of Dwellings and Households by Size, Washington Manor, San Leandro, California, 1960-1980 138

5.6 Typical Single-Family Homes, Washington Manor, San Leandro, California 142

5.7 Additions and Alterations, Washington Manor, San Leandro, California 143

5.8 Accessory Conversion Site Plans, Washington Manor, San Leandro, California 144

5.9   Second-Story Additions, Washington Manor, San Leandro, California 145

5.10 Duplex Addition, Washington Manor, San Leandro, California ... 147

5.11 Garage Conversions, Washington Manor, San Leandro, California 148

5.12 Converted House, Washington Manor, San Leandro, California .. 149

5.13 Projected Incidence of Vehicles Under Varying Density Assumptions, Washington Manor, San Leandro, California 152

5.14 Off-Street Parking Capacity, Washington Manor, San Leandro, California 153

5.15 Front-Yard Parking Pads, Washington Manor, San Leandro, California 154

5.16 Demographic Composition of Households, Broadmoor District, San Leandro, 1980 155

5.17 Lot and Building Sizes, Broadmoor District, San Leandro, California 156

5.18 Subdivision Plan, Broadmoor, San Leandro, California 157

5.19 Typical Single-Family Homes, Broadmoor, San Leandro, California 158-60

5.20 Additions to Garage, Broadmoor, San Leandro, California .. 161, 162

5.21 Additions to Existing Housing, Broadmoor, San Leandro, California 164, 165

5.22 Accessory Apartment Attic Convrsion, Broadmoor, San Leandro, California 166

5.23 Double-Wide Driveway, Broadmoor, San Leandro, California.... 167

5.24 Double-Wide Driveway with Extension, Broadmoor, San Leandro, California 168, 169

5.25 Projected Vehicular Densities Under Varying Conversion Rates, Broadmoor District, San Leandro, California 170

5A.1 Multiple Regression Model of Vehicle Density, San Leandro, California, 1980 175

Chapter Six

6.1   San Francisco Bay Area Poll on Legalizing Accessory Apartments, November 1983 178

6.2   Attitudes Toward Housing Development of Respondents to Poll on Legalizing Accessory Apartments, San Francisco Bay Area, 1983   179

Acknowledgments

Many people helped this project along from inception to completion. George Lefcoe of the Lincoln Institute and Don Terner, former Director of the California Department of Housing and Community Development, gave strong encouragement to this work and intellectual direction as well. Some of the ideas in this book came out of discussions with a number of housing activists and planners in California including Brad Inman, Dan Marks, Ruth Schwartz, Bert Verrips, Dick Morton, Ilene Weinreb, John Landis, and Judy Chess. Discussions with Pat Hare during his numerous visits out West provided important insights into the politics of legalization. I would also like to thank the students from my housing and community development studio at the University of California, Berkeley, who helped prepare the case studies. Thanks also go to the students in Peter Bosselman's Environmental Simulation Laboratory at Berkeley, who developed a simulation model of one of the case studies in order to examine the visual impacts of conversions on neighborhood form.

Financial assistance for parts of this research came from the Committee on Research of the University of California, Berkeley. Mel Webber of the Institute of Urban and Regional Development at Berkeley also provided assistance.

I would also like to thank Roger Montgomery, Michael Stegman, Marsha Ritzdorf, and Steve Barton who reviewed earlier drafts and provided valuable criticisms. J. Michael Marriner designed the graphics for this book, including the house plans. Landscape architect Clare Watsky shot and processed all the photographs and also contributed important insights about the functional and esthetic relationships among garages, yards, and streets in single-family neighborhoods.

Finally, I would like to thank my wife, Robin Jones, an accomplished city planner who gave emotional support and provided valuable intellectual insights at critical junctures in the writing of this book.

Introduction

This book examines accessory apartment conversions as an emerging trend in American housing. It also assesses their potential as an instrument of local and national housing policy.

As the reproduction cost of housing has increased, consumers have begun to make more intensive use of existing dwellings. Accessory apartment conversions represent one form of this response. An accessory conversion does not involve the complete remodeling of a house into flats or small housekeeping units. The extra unit is created by converting part of a primary dwelling or by adding one or more rooms to a structure. It is "accessory" in the sense that it is subordinate in size, location, and appearance to its companion principal unit. Single-family houses have the greatest potential for accessory apartments. Many already have a basement, attic, shed, workshop, or garage which can be easily converted into a separate dwelling space; others have the land or space for adding a new unit.

Conversions of the housing stock are as old as housing itself. At various times in the history of modern cities conversions have provided a large share of additions to the housing inventory. Today they have regained prominence as a source of supply. Over half a million accessory apartments were added to the nation's housing stock by conversion and remodeling between 1973 and 1980. This represented close to 21 percent of all private unsubsidized rental construction for that period, up from less than 9 percent in the previous decade.

Until recently house conversions have been viewed as a form of substandard accommodation appropriate only for the poor: in times when housing costs and family incomes fell out of balance, several families would crowd into a subdivided structure originally designed to hold only one household. Accessory apartment conversions cannot be characterized in this way today. The addition of an accessory apartment to a one-family dwelling does produce a two-family house, but it will not lead to the overcrowding and other undesirable effects associated with increased density. This is because the meaning of the word "family" has changed. Households are much smaller today, and fewer households have children in them. Of those with children, fewer also have the full complement of two parents. As a result, the underlying relationships among building types, tenures, and residential lifestyles as we have known them in the past are unraveling, and the old indicators of density no longer have the same meaning they once did.

Evidence of this change can be found in new construction, where average dwelling and lot size have been declining since 1978. This is only partly a response to the constraints of higher financing and land costs. It also represents an adjustment to the smaller average household size of the new American "family." The downsizing of the existing American home by the creation of accessory apartments reflects a similar reordering of space standards to accommodate a population of smaller households with fewer children. The adjustment process has been slower in the existing single-family stock, however, because of institutional arrangements such as the fixed-payment mortgage and exclusive single-family zoning.

Because we have so many small households today it is possible to create additional housing units out of surplus space in large single-family houses, and to do so without forcing the kind of sacrifice in space standards or liveability which past generations associated with house subdivision. Between 12 and 18 million dwellings in the United States have surplus space that might allow accessory conversion. Clearly, not all of these houses can or will be adapted. Some owners will have neither the need, the desire, nor the resources for undertaking the required improvements. However, even if only 15 percent of these dwellings were converted over the next ten years, the average production of rental apartments would be increased by 150,000 units. This would be enough to eliminate most of the shortfall in rental apartment production predicted for the 1980s.

Although accessory apartments can help meet some of the nation's housing needs, they are not entirely without problems. Some of these are environmental problems: physical alterations that are out of character with the design and appearance of surrounding structures, or increased intensity of land use, which in turn can cause other problems such as greater parking and traffic. This book discusses these problems and suggests methods for their control.

Other problems are cultural and ideological. The accessory apartment in a single-family house deviates from the image of housing, family, and neighborhood that prevails in American culture. It symbolizes a change in the way the single-family house is used and the kinds of people who live in it. These changes clash with the traditional meanings attached to the categories of residential zoning. American land-use regulation has been based on an implicit judgment about the ordering of land development, and a central tenet of this ordering is that single-family houses should be separated from apartments. Today this ordering is under great stress. The structure of the family and the economics of housing which underlay this traditional ordering have changed. New lifestyles and forms of ownership are emerging rapidly, but people's beliefs about housing and family are slow to change. If we are to encourage the creation of accessory apartments in single-family houses—even on a limited basis—we must rethink the concept of the exclusive single-family district and re-examine the rationales for excluding duplexes and accessory apartments from it.

This book contains six chapters, the first two of which lay the groundwork for the policy arguments that follow. Chapter One introduces the accessory apartment and defines it as a form of housing and a type of conversion. It also considers the architectural and technological characteristics that make modern houses suitable for accessory conversions. Chapter Two quantifies the qualitative observations of the first chapter. It presents estimates of conversion activity in the United States, including accessory conversions. It also examines evidence on the physical condition and cost of accessory apartment conversions as well as who owns them, who creates them, and who lives in them.

The remaining chapters deal with policy issues. Chapter Three considers the causes and incidence of under-utilized housing and assesses its conversion potential. Since 1950 average household size has fallen faster than average dwelling size; consequently, the number of homes that contain ''surplus'' space has been rising. This chapter also looks at the social changes that account for this phenomenon and presents evidence on the incidence and estimates of the number of households with surplus space in their dwellings.

Chapter Four deals with zoning constraints on accessory-apartment conversions. It scrutinizes the rationales used by city planners and the courts to justify exclusive single-family zoning. As the meaning of the word ''family'' has changed and new forms of ownership have emerged, these rationales have become less compelling. The final sections of the chapter consider the case for relaxing controls on two-family dwellings and accessory apartments in exclusive single-family districts, and review some recent developments in zoning law that may create the opportunity to do this.

Chapter Five, a case study of an aging California suburb, investigates the immediate physical impacts of accessory conversions in single-family neighborhoods. It considers the potential effects on the physical form of neighborhoods, assesses parking problems, and looks at various ways of relieving them.

Chapter Six, the final chapter, looks at different approaches to the promotion and control of accessory conversions. It considers how local housing market conditions and environmental concerns combine to determine the approach to promotion and control that a community will adopt. It also discusses the problem of illegal units and examines the extent to which building codes represent a barrier to legal conversion. The chapter concludes by discussing a new and different approach to residential zoning: controlling density by regulating ''building envelopes.'' In contrast to traditional zoning, this approach would allow more complete adaptation of the housing inventory to the new dimensions of family and householding that are emerging in our society today.

1

House Conversion and the Accessory Apartment

There are two ways in which one can adjust the housing stock to respond to an increased or changing demand for separate dwelling units: by erecting new buildings, or by adapting existing structures through merger, conversion, addition, or rehabilitation. The second form of adjustment arises because housing, although it is a durable good and fixed in place, is also highly malleable. In residential buildings the utility core and the structure, especially the outer shell, constitute the basic elements of durability. On the other hand, the interior fixtures and finishings—walls, partitions, appliances, and the various types of fittings and fixtures that link appliances to the mechanical systems—can be adjusted to a wide variety of uses, subject only to the precautions that must be taken to minimize the risk of fire and other hazards.

Malleability has its limits, which are not so much technical as economic and environmental. Investment costs and returns determine if and how much adaptation will be done to a building, but the basic variables of economic feasibility are influenced by environmental and cultural constraints. The uses to which any building is put will depend upon the uses of surrounding structures and the design of streets and infrastructure. Adaptation most often occurs in places where the social and physical environment itself is changing. In this sense, building adaptation does not occur at random in a city; it is usually part of a process of social change that in its course alters the spatial structure and physical form of the city.

Conversion is a form of building adaptation through which additions are made to the housing inventory. It can involve subdividing an existing dwelling unit into two or more units, or adding a dwelling unit to an existing residential structure without changing the size or quality of the pre-conversion units, or adapting part or all of a nonresidential building to residential use. Conversion expands the supply of housing available for consumers without adding new structures to the housing stock, or in the case of residential conversions from nonresidential uses, without increasing the scale of the urban physical plant.

This is an important point. Too often conversion is thought to cause overcrowding by packing more people into the same or fewer units. This is an error.

Conversions are a genuine substitute for new construction. They provide separate dwelling units when it is uneconomic or otherwise unfeasible to build new structures, and when structures with under-utilized space are readily available. Such under-used spaces may be abandoned warehouses or storefronts, parts of houses like basements, attics, or garages, or complete houses designed for much larger families but located in neighborhoods that attract students, single persons, and couples. Conversions can be a way to use existing structures more efficiently, especially when economic and social change lead consumers to pare down their space needs.

Conversion Types

The many different types of conversions may be classified according to the nature of the pre-existing structure and what happens to it as a result of conversion. The distinctions are important, because some types of conversion are parts of a broader process of land-use succession, whereas others are more temporary in nature and form. There are four basic types of residential conversions: a) use-conversions, b) conversions from group quarters, c) structural conversions, and d) accessory conversions.

The first type, a use-conversion, involves converting a structure from nonresidential to residential use, that is, conversion to residential use of a structure and site that were not originally designed or intended for residential use. Examples include lofts, warehouses, and storefronts. Housing produced by nonresidential conversions generally departs from conventional standards of what a dwelling should look like and the type of facilities it should contain. Open space may not be easily provided on such sites. Off-street parking may be unavailable or difficult to install. The health and safety problems of adapting industrial buildings may also require expensive if not specialized remodeling techniques. The location of most nonresidential structures may not contain a "residential neighborhood" in the conventional sense of the term, or access to public services and facilities that are usually available in residential zones, such as schools, churches, and convenience shopping. Older cities are an exception, however. Most of them contain districts developed before modern zoning in which residential, industrial, and commercial uses were often mixed together; these cities still have some schools, churches, and other cultural facilities readily accessible even in areas that are heavily devoted to commercial and industrial uses. Another exception would be residential conversions of public facilities such as schools, which are often located in areas zoned strictly for residential use.

The second type, the conversion of group quarters—dormitories, transient hotels, long-term care facilities, or hospitals—is also a use-conversion and involves the same problems of adaptation. Conversions of this type differ from conversions of commercial or industrial buildings because structures designed as group quarters are already divided into sleeping rooms. Because their kitchen, social areas, and sometimes bathing facilities were designed for common use and set apart from each unit, converting group quarters to conventional dwelling units also requires extensive remodeling and redesign. Sleeping rooms must be merged in order to create units with separate kitchens and bathrooms. Common kitchens and bathrooms as well as other common areas—such as dining rooms—must either be removed or retrofitted for other purposes—for example, swimming pools, exercise gyms, or entertainment rooms. Because group quarters have a large amount of space devoted to common facilities, it is usually less expensive to convert them into some form of congregate housing, or condominium development, where recreation or other services constitute an important part of the housing package.

The third type, the residential structural conversion, involves the creation of more units by a major remodeling of a residential building. This includes the conversion of a single-family house into a duplex or the transformation of a large old mansion into a three-plex or four-plex, with one or more units per floor. For this type of conversion the interior of the structure is redesigned and the original unit is cut up in order to create new units of roughly equal size. Probably the most common example of this type is the conversion of two-story single-family houses which contained a central entry hall. Hundreds of thousands of these were built in American cities during the first quarter of the twentieth century. Many with small entry halls were cut up into separate upstairs and downstairs units. The larger houses with spacious halls could accommodate two units per floor.[1]

The extent to which older single-family homes are subdivided depends on the relative supply and demand for small rental units and single-family homes in any particular area. This type of conversion is sometimes spurred on by zoning changes that permit higher densities in a district once devoted to single-family houses. On the other hand, a strong demand for home ownership (like that witnessed during the last decade) can make these marginal properties valuable once again as owner-occupied single-family dwellings regardless of the zoning. When that is the case, many will be restored to their original state. Mergers may also occur if demand becomes skewed toward larger families with multiple earners, as is common in cities with large populations of foreign immigrants, especially Hispanics.[2]

The fourth type, the accessory conversion, involves the addition of a unit to a residential structure in a way that does not fundamentally alter the internal layout or plan of the existing dwelling or dwellings. Accessory conversions vary considerably depending on the type of structure, its age and design, and the size and configuration of the lot. They can occur in single-family houses as well as multiple-unit buildings. Examples include the conversion of a basement or attic, or perhaps of a sunroom, porch, or guest room. Sometimes the conversion of a small section of a house will also require adding other rooms by building an extension to the existing structure. Accessory conversions can also be achieved by adding another floor to the original structure.

The key point about an accessory conversion is that the primary unit remains the larger one and retains the predominant location in the structure. Many accessory conversions are nonstructural and can often be easily merged back into their associated primary dwelling. Unused rooms within or adjacent to a dwelling can frequently be turned into an accessory apartment. This may require only blocking off a doorway, or adding a partition wall to converted space to create a separate bedroom. Restoring the accessory unit to its original use will still be possible with minimal investment and work. Walls within the existing primary unit are rarely removed or new ones installed except when the conversion involves additions to the building. Nevertheless, even when such structural work is necessary the resulting changes should not fundamentally alter the suitability of the primary unit for occupancy by the type of household for which it was originally designed.

Residential conversions of both types—structural and accessory—involve not so much a change in the type of use as a change in the intensity of an existing use. This is often thought to mean packing more people into a fixed amount of housing space when the real price of housing increases; something like this occurred during World War II.[3] But residential conversions can also involve the adaptation or recycling of surplus space in occupied dwellings. This will occur when individual household size declines toward the end of the family life cycle, or when the average household size in the population falls and residential population densities fall with it. This can make individual houses or entire neighborhoods of houses, which were originally designed for occupancy by large families, "socially obsolete"; because of their size and layout, they are not easily adjusted to the domestic needs of smaller families and may prove too time-consuming and expensive to maintain in their original form.

The "In-Law" Apartment

Although accessory conversions can occur in almost any kind of residential structure, the most common type of accessory conversion is the "in-law" apartment. This is a small dwelling unit converted out of surplus space either in a single-family dwelling or in a structure adjacent to it on the same property. It is "accessory" because it is *subordinate* to the primary unit in size, location, appearance, and occupancy.

Both a duplex and a single-family house with an accessory apartment contain two units that can be occupied by two separate households, but the relationship between the two units is quite different in each case. An accessory apartment is rarely greater than one-third the size of the primary unit with which it is associated, whereas a duplex conversion divides a house into two separate units of roughly comparable size. Although an accessory conversion may subtract from the amount of living space available within or adjacent to the primary dwelling, what is usually subtracted is "marginal space"—"spare rooms" or nonhabitable spaces such as basements or sheds—the loss of which does not alter the basic functional characteristics of the main dwelling. The size and layout of the common rooms—kitchen, bathrooms, living rooms, and dining areas—remain the same.

Most accessory apartments are quite small—often consisting of one or two rooms. Because of their location in former basements or attics and the improvised character of their design, the articulation of separate rooms may be weak. Quite a few are single-room units, but these sometimes have as much square footage as larger two- or three-room units because owners who install them tried to save money by avoiding the installation of wall for a separate bedroom or kitchen.

An accessory unit is also subordinate to the primary unit in terms of its location on the property. It is often tucked away somewhere at the rear of the building, in a basement or an attic with an entrance that is not clearly visible from the street. Even when part of the original structure is expanded in order to install the secondary unit, the addition is frequently placed at the rear where it does not dramatically alter the physical form of the building.

Owners of houses with secondary units want them to be unobtrusive, if not invisible, because most are installed illegally without building or use permits. But even where this is not the case, subordination in size and location also reflects their intended function as an accessory dwelling—a separate suite of rooms for occupancy by one or two persons—the presence of which does not prevent the intended use of the primary unit as a single-family house.

This subordinate status and function of the accessory apartment raises the question whether it is really a separate dwelling unit and should be treated by local planning authorities as such. Many accessory apartments do not conform to the standard Census Bureau definition of a housing unit:

> A housing unit is a house, an apartment, a group of rooms, or a single room occupied or intended for occupancy as separate living quarters. Separate living quarters are those in which the occupants live and eat separately from other persons in the building and which have either (1) direct access from the outside of the building or through a common hall that is used or intended to be used by the occupants of another unit or by the general public, or (2) complete kitchen facilities for the exclusive use of the occupants. The occupants may be a single family, one person living alone, two or more families living together, or any other group of related or unrelated persons who share living arrangements except [as group quarters].[4]

According to this definition a separate housing unit exists if its occupants prepare and eat food separately from others in the building and if the unit has either a separate entrance or complete kitchen facilities for their exclusive use. This provides enough leeway for various types of informal arrangements of space and facilities that can function as accessory conversions and yet be designed to prevent discovery and avoid prosecution under zoning laws. Many illegal accessory apartments are therefore likely to be "borderline" housing because they have some of the characteristics of a separate dwelling unit but not all.

One characteristic that might sometimes be missing is a kitchen. Interestingly, the census definition is somewhat ambiguous on this point. It does not require that a housing unit have kitchen facilities, but when a separate entrance is missing, the presence of kitchen facilities becomes the primary criterion. "Complete kitchen facilities" are defined as follows:

> A unit has "complete kitchen facilities" when it has all three of the following for the exclusive use of the occupants of the unit: (1) an installed sink with piped water, (2) a range or cookstove, and (3) a mechanical refrigerator. All kitchen facilities must be located in the structure. They need not be in the same room. Quarters with only portable cooking equipment are not considered as having a range or cookstove. An icebox is not included as a mechanical refrigerator. The kitchen facilities are for the exclusive use of the occupants when they are used only by the occupants of one housing unit, including lodgers or other unrelated persons living in the unit. When a structure consists of only one housing unit, all equipment located inside the structure is classified, by definition, "for exclusive use."[5]

Most zoning laws similarly define a separate dwelling unit by the presence of a separate kitchen; however, this is usually taken to mean the presence of a kitchen stove only.

These definitions have become obsolete because of innovations in domestic technology which make possible preparations of meals at home without "complete kitchen facilities." Portable microwave and convection ovens that can bake and broil have become extremely sophisticated with the development of new types of heating elements and microelectronic controls. Most are inexpensive, take up little space, and require only electricity to operate. Supermarkets normally stock a wide variety of prepared foods and "TV dinners" designed for use with such equipment. In addition, the spread of restaurants serving inexpensive fast foods and "quick cuisine" also make unnecessary the provision of food storage and preparation facilities in small apartments; a few cabinets and a microwave may suffice.

The census definitions are also difficult to apply to accessory apartments in single-family dwellings because the physical and functional boundaries that separate a secondary and a primary unit may sometimes be ill-defined by the occupants of each. A single-family house, for example, could contain a room or set of rooms with a separate entrance and with limited cooking and food storage facilities, but the rooms may not be used functionally as a separate dwelling unit. As long as these quarters are occupied by someone who is "related" to the primary household and considered by the primary household to be one of its members, these rooms will not be functioning as a separate dwelling unit.

Much of the difference in theory between an accessory apartment and a duplex is not a question of whether part of a structure can be used as separate living quarters; it is more a question of the type of occupancy involved. A duplex will ordinarily contain two units of roughly equal size and equally prominent placement on a lot. The two units together can be rented or owned by separate households. Each unit can in effect have different owners if the duplex were subdivided as a condominium. A single-family house with an accessory apartment could never be a condominium, each unit of which is owned by different households. One of the units must always be rented, even though the owner might choose to live in the accessory unit. This could happen in the case of a widow who wanted the income earned from renting out the main part of the house, or a young married couple burdened with a large mortgage.

Subordination in terms of occupancy is sometimes taken to mean occupancy by a secondary or sub-family related in some way to that occupying the primary unit. This meaning corresponds to the popular notion of the accessory unit as an "in-law" apartment. That term is short for "mother-in-law" and refers to a situation where the two units on the property are occupied by a single though extended family, with a married couple living in the primary unit and an elderly parent occupying a rear-yard cottage or basement apartment.

This popular belief about the use of accessory apartments goes back to the first half of the twentieth century, when American families were faced with the problem of supporting elderly parents. Average life expectancy had risen dramatically after 1880 because of improvements in diet and medical treatment. Longevity increased more for women than for men. Because women married younger than men and were subject to lower mortality rates, they tended to outlive their husbands by about ten to fifteen years.[6]

After the death of their husbands, however, most women lacked sufficient savings to support themselves and were forced to abandon their households and move in with children or relatives. This practice was common before the advent of Social Security and the emergence of private pension plans after World War II, both of which made it possible for women to maintain their own households after the retirement or death of the primary wage earner. Paul Glick has estimated that as late as 1950 about 58 percent of women aged 65 and older who had no spouse present lived with families of their kin, especially children. This percentage had been gradually declining since 1910 and started dropping sharply during the 1940s.[7] By 1970 it had fallen to around 29 percent, and further to 18 percent by 1980.[8]

There is little evidence to support this explanation for the origins of accessory apartments. The widow or mother-in-law who moved in with her children rarely needed or wanted a separate apartment.[9] She probably slept in the "spare" bedroom that could be found in most middle-class homes.[10] Moreover, demographic studies indicate that extended family members other than children or spouses were rarely parents of the family head or of the spouse; they were usually unmarried sisters, brothers, or other relatives. Furthermore, the cost of installing a separate secondary unit for a family member could not easily be justified financially.

There is a grain of truth, however, in the notion that the accessory apartment was a response to the financial problems of old age. It was the desire on the part of widows and retired couples to stay in their own homes rather than move in with their children that gave rise to the accessory apartment. This trend was made possible in part by the spread of home ownership. A combination of habit, pride of ownership, and low occupancy costs gave most home owners who reached retirement strong incentives to hold on to their houses. To do this, however, sometimes required renting out part of the house to help meet general household expenses, maintenance costs, and property taxes. If the drop in income that occurred at retirement did not reduce the living standards of an elderly couple, the effects of inflation on a fixed pension benefit would eventually do so. Hence taking in boarders or subdividing their houses became a necessity for many who wished to stay in their homes after retirement.

Evidence from studies about boarding indicate that this practice was common among owners of all classes in the past. Modell and Hareven have shown in their work on household composition in late nineteenth-century Boston that between one-third and one-half of all households that took in boarders were over the age of 40. The decision to do so was associated with the departure of children from households.[11] Glick's study of family composition in the 1940s and 1950s shows the same pattern.[12] Moreover, Glick found that the proportion of home owners who occupied one-unit detached dwellings decreased with the age of the household head; between 40 and 55 it fell by 8 percent. He attributed the drop to owners who converted parts of their homes after their children had grown up and departed.[13] Chapter Two presents some evidence in support of this view from the U.S. Census *Components of Inventory Change*.

Adaptability of Modern Single-Family Houses

According to the conventional view the perfect candidate for duplex conversion is a large, older home which because of age or location is no longer in demand as an owner-occupied single-family house. This is not true of accessory apartment conversions. They can be found in older homes as well as modern ones. Many remain owner-occupied even after conversion. According to the United States Census about 78 percent of all residential conversions in suburbs between 1973 and 1980 occurred in owner-occupied single-family houses. Slightly more than 55 percent of these structures were built after 1950 and 26 percent after 1960.[14]

EXHIBIT 1.1
An In-Line Expandable House

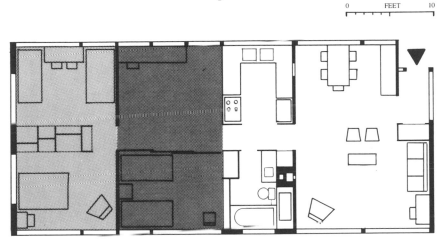

Source: House and Home, 1952

Modern single-family houses offer more opportunities for accessory apartment conversion than do older homes. Some have the potential for room additions which could function as accessory units, and many already contain such additions. Modern construction methods and design and site planning techniques have made postwar homes more adaptable and flexible in this regard than homes of earlier vintage. Some of these technical innovations include modular construction, prefabricated panelized walls, floors, and roofs, layouts with "multi-purpose" zones, attached garages, and double-wide lots.

Most modern single-family homes have in fact been designed to be altered as family composition and the space needs of their occupants change. This is particularly true of homes built during the 1950s. "Expandable houses" were introduced as a response to the housing demand pressures brought on by changes in marriage and fertility behavior which first began occurring in the 1940s. Although the two-child family was still the norm, more women were having their first child earlier in marriage and having a second and often a third soon thereafter. The average time between births therefore decreased sharply.[15] This meant that family size grew considerably faster than family income and also faster than the ability of a married couple to afford the purchase of a larger house. As the children grew up, space needs increased again just before puberty when each child required a separate bedroom. Because household income was increasing more slowly than family size, a move to a larger house would be delayed for many years.[16]

The "expandable" house was a solution to this problem. It was a two- or

EXHIBIT 1.2
Third Bedroom Addition

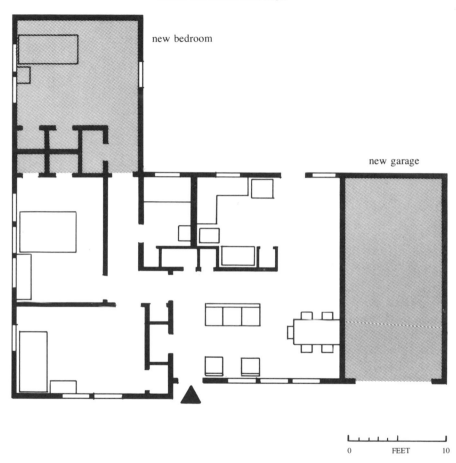

new bedroom

new garage

```
L__I__I__I__I__J
0          FEET          10
```

Source: House and Home, 1951

three-bedroom dwelling placed on a lot large enough to accommodate a house with four bedrooms and one or two extra rooms. The expandable house became popular in part because modern subdivision practices on inexpensive suburban land had increased residential lot sizes and particularly lot frontages. The typical lot of a single-family house built before World War II was 40 feet wide by 100 feet long; hence, pre-war homes were usually long, deep, two-story structures, their full bulk rarely observable from the street. Narrow side yards and the front- and rear-yard requirements of zoning laws usually made it almost impossible to expand this type of house.[17]

The introduction of the 60- and 70-foot frontage in postwar suburban subdivisions led to a radically different dwelling configuration. The postwar subur-

EXHIBIT 1.3
Custom-Designed Expandable House

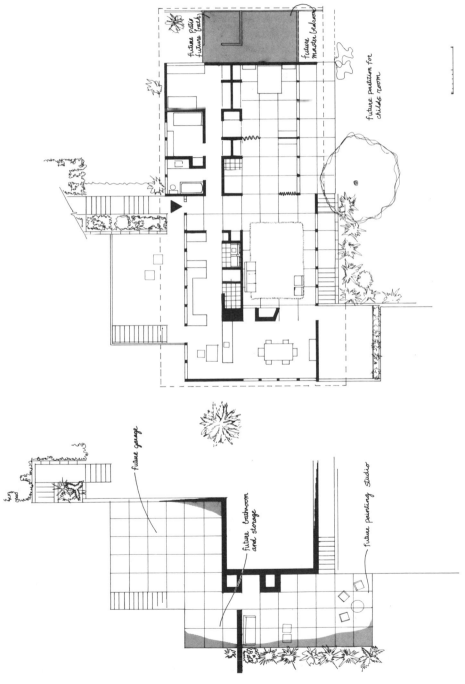

Source: Franklin, Michigan, house by Edward P. Elliot, A.R.I.B.A., Architect, and Edward A. Eichstedt, Landscape Architect, 1952

EXHIBIT 1.4
Garage Conversion

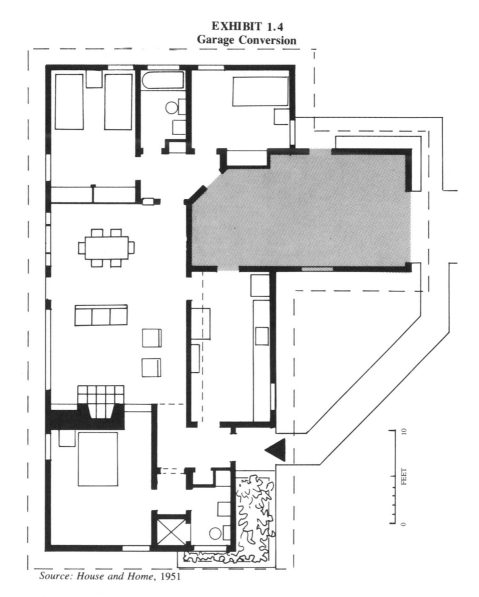

Source: House and Home, 1951

ban house was wide instead of deep. On a 70-foot by 130-foot lot, for example, it was possible to put a house which was 28 feet deep and 32 feet wide with a 13-foot garage attached to one side or detached and located behind the house.[18] This type of structure initially contained 1000 or 1200 square feet of living area and could provide as much as 2000 square feet when fully expanded. An example is shown in Exhibit 1.1. This is an "in-line" plan. The basic house contained only one bedroom. The two bedrooms—separated by a storage wall—were added later. In Exhibit 1.2, both the garage and third bedroom were to be added after

EXHIBIT 1.5
Garage Conversion and Addition

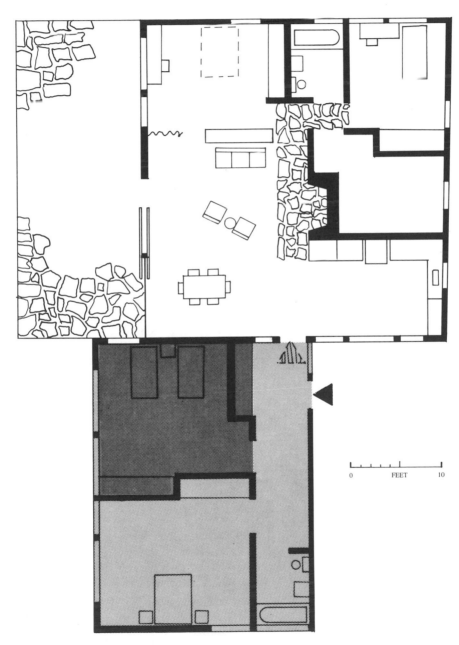

Source: House and Home, 1952

the house was occupied. In this plan, a closet becomes a hallway to the new bedroom, and the door framing was already in the exterior wall, roughed in at the time the house was built. The expandability feature was not just confined to "starter" homes; by the mid-fifties it had also become a normal part of more expensive custom-designed houses (see Exhibit 1.3).

Attached garages were also prime candidates for house expansion. Because the garage was located at the front of the house, was easily accessible from within the house, and was equipped with water, sewer, and utility service, it was the simplest and cheapest type of conversion to make for a family that needed extra living space. Many newly built single-family houses in the 1950s came with attached carports instead of closed garages. It was assumed that as family income rose, the home owner would eventually install a complete garage using plans provided by the builder at the time of purchase. These plans frequently included instructions for future conversion to other uses.[19]

A typical example can be found in Exhibit 1.4. This plan makes the rear third of the garage a passageway between the kitchen and the two junior bedrooms on the right. The space is perfectly designed for conversion to a playroom, workshop, or studio. There is also a separate service entrance on the right-hand side, which makes it possible to partition off one or both of the junior bedrooms into a separate apartment. The garage can be replaced with an open carport at the side of the house.

In the next plan (Exhibit 1.5), the garage is to be completed after the house is purchased and occupied. At some future time a third bedroom is supposed to be added between the garage and the house, and the garage itself is converted to a fourth bedroom and bath. A carport could also be added at the side adjacent to the garage. The garage was designed so that it could easily be converted into an accessory apartment, if the owner wished to do so.

Because expandability made small homes more marketable, builders began to erect single-family homes in the 1950s that could be expanded upwards. Floor joists were installed above the ceiling and reinforced studs on the ground floor so that the second story could be added later on. Sometimes these second stories were partially built as "expansion attics," with plans so that the owner could convert them into full rooms.[20] Expansion attics were a common feature of the famous Levitt houses of the 1950s. The Levitts believed that the attic was the "cheapest, most natural expansion space there is." The only major expense required for finishing the attic was a lift dormer on the shallow slope of the roof. One of the most popular Levitt models had a full attic that ran the width of the house with a glass window in the gable end to admit light.

The basement also served a similar function. In American middle-class homes before World War I the basement was planned primarily as a storage area and as live-in space for servants. With the rise in the cost of domestic labor during World War I and the introduction of labor-saving domestic appliances in the 1920s, the basement shrank in size and lost out to the need for garage space for car storage.[21] When the number of children per family increased during the baby

EXHIBIT 1.6
Split-Level Home

Source: House and Home, 1954

EXHIBIT 1.7
Expansion Potential of a
Split-Level House

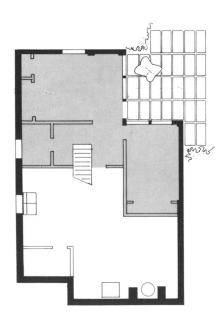

Source: House and Home, 1956

boom, basements were reintroduced, but primarily as unplanned, general-purpose areas. Most often they provided not only storage but also cheap extra living space, which could be used as an additional bedroom, a guest room, or a recreation or family room.

The "all-purpose room" was a common feature of the split-level house. Since the 1920s most single-family houses had been built with two zones: a day zone (living room, kitchen, and dining area) and a night zone (bedrooms). This implied a two-story structure or a rectangle divided across the middle in the case of a one-story structure. Houses built after World War II contained three zones: a day zone, a night zone, and an "all-purpose" zone, which included a family room, storage area, and a utility room (see Exhibit 1.6). The split-level house was thus a three-zone house with each zone located on a different level. It was the most compact and economical of all modern houses and could easily fit on small lots. What made it even more efficient was that the all-purpose zone could be converted easily to additional bedroom space, to a family or recreation room, or to a small "in-law" apartment. Exhibit 1.7 contains an example where space in the lower level of the house (shaded-in areas in the plan) was provided for a family room and an extra bedroom to be completed at the discretion of the owner at some future date. Because of these advantages, split-level houses became extremely popular in the 1950s throughout the northeastern and mid-Atlantic states.[22]

Aware of the tremendous social and private savings that adaptable houses might provide, a number of architects extended the concept of adaptability beyond merely the problem of space needs associated with the child-bearing and child-rearing stages of the family life cycle. With modern building materials and construction techniques it was possible to make houses adaptable for all stages of the family life cycle so that married couples need only buy and live in one house for their entire adult lives.

A rather sophisticated example of this concept can be found in Marcel Breuer's famous Exhibition House, built in 1949 in the garden of the Museum of Modern Art in New York City. The Breuer house was explicitly designed to be altered as family size and composition changed over the life cycle. Rooms could be added as the family grew, and some of them could be adapted to different uses as the children and parents aged (see Exhibit 1.8).

The first part of the plan—the living-dining area, the kitchen, the two bedrooms, and the playroom—was designed for the early stages of family growth, when children are young and parents need to be near them. The bedroom labeled "guest room" in the plan functions as the parents' bedroom during this period. During the middle years of the family cycle, when the children are older and the parents want more privacy, the second part of the plan—garage, bedroom, bath, and dressing area—was to be built. The sleeping room downstairs was then supposed to become the guest room or an extra sleeping space. Later still, if parents, as they aged, found stairs tiring or if an older son or daughter needed to feel more independent and wanted a private entrance, this bedroom-apartment could be

EXHIBIT 1.8
Marcel Breuer Exhibition House, Garden of the
Museum of Modern Art, New York City

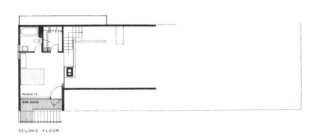

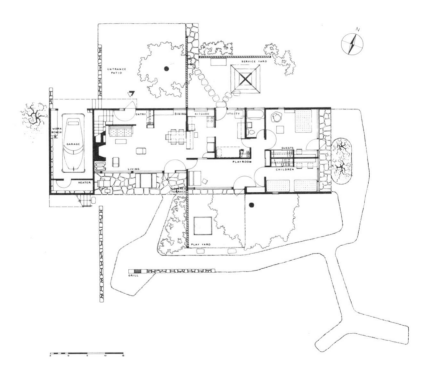

easily adapted for that purpose. The bedroom suite up above had a separate entrance off a sundeck that could be reached by a stairway on the side. It could be
used for rental purposes after the family had decreased in size.

EXHIBIT 1.8 (continued)

Source: Museum of Modern Art, New York City. Photographs courtesy of ESTO, New York

Carl Koch's Techbuilt House was similarly designed as a genuine "life cycle" dwelling. Koch's concept of the "life cycle" house was inspired by Frederick Gutheim's study of the modern family.[23] Koch stretched the idea of adaptability to its limit. He designed a house that would both expand and contract and therefore could be adapted to each stage of the family life cycle. The Techbuilt House had two floors. Koch himself described it as an "attic on top of a basement."[24] Whereas a conventional house sits on the ground, the Techbuilt House was dropped 3 feet 6 inches into the ground, which allowed full use of the foundation to enclose living space. The upper floor was built as if it were an attic, except that 5-foot high walls were placed around the attic under the eaves; this made the entire upper floor usable. To make use of it, no dormers were needed as in the case of the Levitt house (see Exhibit 1.9).[25]

The building itself was essentially complete at the beginning; no additions to exterior walls, foundation, or the plumbing system were required once the house was built. Koch used "industrialized" construction techniques, including stressed-skin plywood panels for the interior walls. Prefabrication made it possible to complete all construction except the interior finish in six days. Practically

EXHIBIT 1.9
The Techbuilt House

Plan 1

Lower Floor   Upper Floor

EXHIBIT 1.9 (continued)

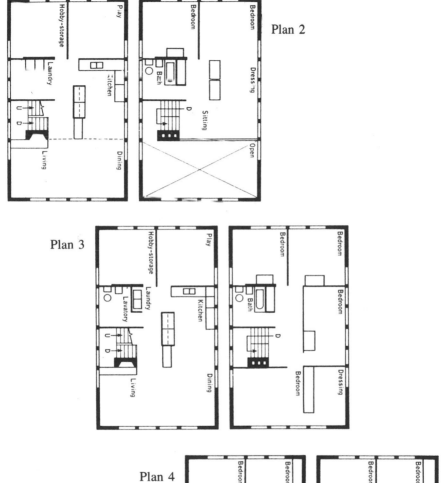

Plan 2

Plan 3

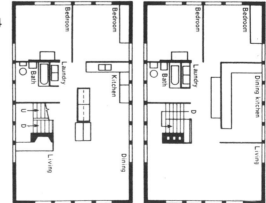

Plan 4

Source: Techbuilt, Inc., Fairhaven, Massachusetts

EXHIBIT 1.10
The Flexabilt House

Plan 1

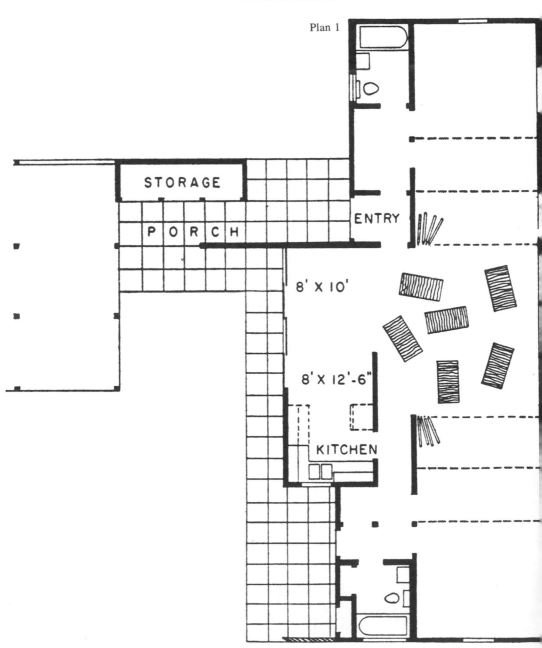

STORAGE

P O R C H

ENTRY

8' X 10'

8' X 12'-6"

KITCHEN

EXHIBIT 1.10 (continued)

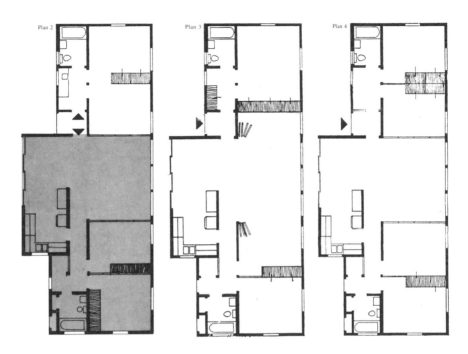

Source: House and Home, 1954

everything inside was flexible; only the stairs, the bathrooms, the chimney, and four load bearing posts were fixed. Up to five bedrooms and a second bathroom could be added one at a time as needed. (The heavy lines in the plans in Exhibit 1.9 indicate plumbing walls for the kitchen and two bathrooms.) Rooms could be created merely by installing paneled walls or merged by removing them; hence the interior layout could be altered as the occupants chose and as their space needs changed. The Techbuilt House was not an architectural fantasy. Koch helped to establish a company called Techbuilt, Inc. which built several hundred homes in the New England area during the 1950s. The houses were priced at $7.50 per square foot for 2000 square feet. The conventional builder's house at the time cost about $10 per square foot and a custom built home about $15 per square foot.[26]

Koch envisioned the house working in the following manner. For the early years of the family life cycle part of the interior of the lower floor of the house was completed to serve as a living-dining room and kitchen combination, but a large section remained unfinished. On the second floor was a single large area comprising a bedroom, sitting room, dressing room, and bath. This section was built as a balcony overlooking the living-dining area below to the right (see

EXHIBIT 1.11
A Life Cycle Home with Accessory Apartment

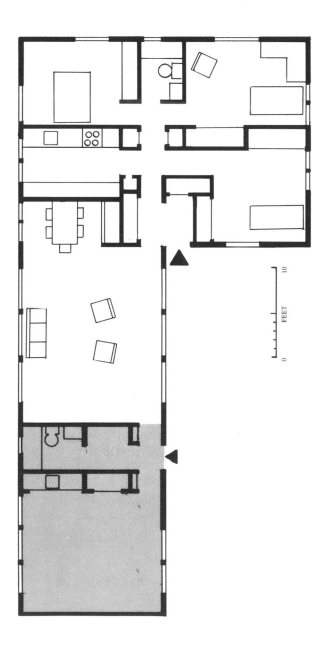

Source: House and Home, 1954

EXHIBIT 1.12
Expandable House With Accessory Apartment

Source: Arco Publishing, New York City

Exhibit 1.9, plan 1). During the child-rearing years the sitting and dressing rooms could be converted into two bedrooms, and the unfinished space downstairs could be completed as playroom, hobby room, and storage area (plan 2). Laundry appliances for the expanding family could also be attached to the plumbing wall below the upstairs bathroom. In the years when the family would be at its peak size the floor of the bedroom-balcony was to be extended across the house to form a bedroom and dressing area for the parents, while the former two bedrooms might be divided into as many as three (plan 3). In the fourth and final stage, when the children left home and the parents reached retirement, the house could be divided into two separate two-bedroom apartments by adding a kitchen to the second floor and converting the parents' bedroom and dressing area into a living-dining area (plan 4). The upstairs apartment would be occupied by the original couple and the downstairs one rented. If the house were eventually sold to a young family the downstairs apartment could be merged back into the primary unit and the cycle reinitiated. The only major conversion expense would be the cost of installing the upstairs kitchen during the fourth stage.[27]

Conventional builders have experimented with various forms of adaptable single-family housing by incorporating these designs and construction principles in their product. During the 1950s Frank Robertson of San Antonio, Texas, for example, designed and produced the "Flexabilt Home."[28] Robertson, who had been in the home-building business for nearly 25 years and had sold second and third homes to veterans with growing families, was inspired to build his Flexabilt Home after the marriage of two of his three children. At that time he realized that his own house, built for a family of five, was unsuitable for only his wife and himself.

The Flexabilt House is based on an elongated plan with a 12-foot wide living space open from end to end, with its service areas and plumbing arranged out of the way along one side (see Exhibit 1.10). At half a dozen points, rooms can be created by installing specially designed "mobile wall" space dividers, including wall panels that can be unstacked and pivoted into place to form a partition and "stub" wall panels that can be set in place to fill smaller gaps. In addition, the house comes with special bookcase or wall-shelf units and six storage modules to be used as closets that can be rolled on castors to any place in the house and adjusted to fit snugly to floor and ceiling. All of these movable parts can be installed by the home owner without any carpentry or special tools. Robertson built several hundred of these houses in and around San Antonio.

Plan 1 is the basic house. The dotted black lines are tracks for partitions; arrows point to four possible locations for storage walls. In plan 2 the young married couple can close off the main part of the house (shaded area), rent one part of it, and live in the other. With the arrival of children the entire house is occupied by the family and arranged with two and later three bedrooms (plan 3). As the family grows a fourth bedroom can be added by installing a partition (plan 4). When the children move away the parents can reduce the number of bedrooms (as in plan 3), or return to a small house with a rental unit (plan 2).

Even when such novel construction methods and designs were not used, the principle of adaptability was incorporated in other ways to allow expansion and contraction of the living area of the house as the space needs of the family changed. In some cases architects explicitly included secondary units as part of the concept. What served as a family or recreation room in the "multi-purpose" zone of a split-level house was also designed for easy and cheap conversion to a small studio apartment. An accessory unit attached to the side of a ranch style home, where space permitted, served in a less architecturally sophisticated way a similar function and was thought of by both builder and home owner as a flexible adaptation of the single-family house to the highly elastic space demands of the modern American family (see Exhibits 1.11 and 1.12).

Notes

1. A.M. Woodruff, "Conversion of One-Family Houses to Multifamily Use," *Housing Research* No. 7 (1954): 11-20.
2. Ronald Angel and Marta Tienda, "Determinants of Extended Household Structure: Cultural Pattern or Economic Need?" *American Journal of Sociology*, 87 (1982): 1360-82.
3. Grebler, Blank and Winnick, *Ibid.*, 113-22.
4. Bureau of the Census, *1980 Census of Housing, Components of Inventory Change*4, Vol. 4, Appendix B.
5. *Ibid.*
6. Robert V. Wells, "Demographic Change and the Life Cycle of American Families," in Theodore K. Rabb and Robert I. Rothenberg, eds., *The Family in History, Interdisciplinary Essays* (New York: Harper & Row, 1971), 91. See also Paul Glick, "The Future Marital Status and Living Arrangements of the Elderly," *The Gerontologist*, 19 (1979): 301-9.
7. Paul Glick, *American Families* (New York: John Wiley & Sons, 1957), 10-11.
8. Ethel Shanas, "Older People and Their Families, the New Pioneers," *Journal of Marriage and the Family*, 41 (1980): 9-15.
9. Tamara K. Hareven, "The Last Stage: Historical Adulthood and Old Age," *Daedalus*, 105 (Fall 1976):13-27.
10. Earl Morris and Mary W. Winter, *Housing, Family, and Society* (New York: John Wiley & Sons, 1978), 100-103.
11. "Urbanization and the Malleable Households: An Examination of Boarding and Lodging in American Families," in Michael Gordon, ed., *The American Family in Social Historical Perspective*, 2nd Edition (New York: St. Martin's Press, 1978), 51-68.
12. Paul Glick, *American Families*, 80-87.
13. *Ibid.*, 101.
14. U.S. Bureau of the Census, 1980 *Census of Housing, Components of Inventory Change*, Vol. 4, table A-5.
15. Leon F. Bouvier, "America's Baby Boom Generation: The Fateful Bulge," *Population Bulletin*, 35 (1980): 1, 4-5. Louise B. Russell, *The Baby Boom Generation and the Economy* (Washington, D.C.: The Brookings Institution, 1982), 11-14.
16. Neil Foote, Louis Winnick, Janet Abu-Lughod, and Marian Foley, *Housing Choices and Housing Constraints* (New York: Harper, 1962), 212-14.
17. Kate E. Rogers, *The Modern House, U.S.A.* (New York: Harper & Row, 1962), 5-6.
18. "The Case for the Wider Lot," *House and Home*, 2 (1952): 6, 114-16.
19. "The Expandable House," *House and Home*, 1 (1952): 2, 118-22.
20. *House and Home*, 8 (1955): 3, 119.
21. Kate E. Rogers, *Ibid.*, 104-5.
22. "Split Level House is Here to Stay," *House and Home*, 7 (1955): 2, 144-55. "The Split Level Boom," *House and Home*, 9 (1956): 3, 121-50.
23. *Houses for Family Living* (New York: The Woman's Foundation, 1948).
24. Carl Koch, *At Home With Tomorrow* (New York: Rinehart, 1958), 147.
25. "Carl Koch: When Does the Two-Story House Make Sense?" *House and Home*, 5 (1954): 2, 106-17.
26. Koch, *Ibid.*, 1958, 150-51.
27. Carl Koch, *Living for Young Homemakers* (Cambridge, MA: Techbuilt, Inc., 1950).
28. "The Adjustable House," *House and Home*, 2 (1952): 6, 114-16.

2

Supply, Production, and Demand

How common are accessory apartments? How many are in single-family homes? How many in multifamily buildings? What kinds of home owners create them today? Are they really occupied by in-laws and grandparents? These questions cannot be answered with much precision. House conversions have always been difficult to study because so many are created illicitly. The best available source of data on conversions is the *Components of Inventory Change* (CINCH), which has been published as part of the national decennial census since 1960. Although it is a secondary source, the *Components of Inventory Change* contains the best coverage of conversions of all types and includes information about occupancy, utilization, and condition. This chapter will draw heavily upon this source in an effort to estimate the volume of accessory conversions which occurred during the past decade and to characterize the condition, occupancy, use, and ownership of this kind of housing.

Components of Inventory Change

The volume and rate of conversion has always been difficult to measure. Much of it takes place informally, often in violation of local building and zoning regulations, so that no official records are available to document the creation of housing by this means. To estimate the number of conversions that occur in any period one must use either residual analysis or probability sampling techniques. Both methods also require the use of an accounting system to identify the components of change in the total housing inventory.

Net change in the housing stock for any period of time can be expressed as the difference between *gross additions* and *gross losses*.

Gross additions include the following:

1. New construction.
2. Mobile home deliveries.

3. Units produced by conversion of a residential building (few units to more).
4. Units produced by conversions of all or part of a nonresidential structure.
5. Units produced by conversion of buildings used as group quarters (hotels, dormitories, hospitals, and the like, which provide single-room occupancy).
6. Units resulting from houses or mobile homes moved in from elsewhere and placed on vacant sites.
7. Rehabilitated units that were once condemned and awaiting demolition.

Gross losses include the following:

1. Units removed by mergers (from more units to fewer).
2. Units removed by demolition.
3. Units destroyed by fire, flooding, earthquake, and other natural causes.
4. Units removed as the result of conversion to nonresidential use.
5. Units removed as the result of conversion to group quarters.
6. Mobile homes or houses moved away from their current locations to other sites.
7. Units that have been condemned and are awaiting demolition (thus functionally moved from the inventory though still physically in place).

At the local level the number of units added by new construction and mobile home deliveries can be determined with reasonable accuracy from public records; so can demolitions and losses due to natural disasters. The other components of inventory change usually cannot be determined directly but can be estimated as a residual. This is done by taking the known total number of units at the beginning of the period under consideration, subtracting demolitions and losses due to natural causes or fire, and then adding new construction and mobile home deliveries which occurred during the period. The result is then subtracted from the known total stock of units at the end of the period. This procedure yields net additions to the inventory by means other than new construction.

This approach requires accurate measures of the total inventory in the community for the beginning and end of the period. These can be derived from a combination of decennial census counts, postal surveys, and utility company data, and similar sources. Any redefinition of the boundaries of a jurisdiction would also have to be factored in by adding or subtracting as necessary in order to make the equation balance. Existing houses and mobile homes moved from one site to another within the same jurisdiction will cancel each other out; these are not "real" additions. Existing houses or mobile homes which have been moved to or from a site in another jurisdiction will be included in the residual term; if they were recorded as such in public records, they can be netted out.

Total demolitions and losses at the national level are difficult to determine because no national system of public recording exists for them. Consequently, the only accurate way to determine the components of inventory change is by probability sampling across communities in order to derive estimates of each of the components. In this case an ''error'' term would be added to the estimation procedure to make gross additions and losses equal. This term would account for sampling error, response error, measurement error, incomplete coverage, and the like.

The first attempts to estimate components of inventory change were made immediately after the first national Census of Housing in 1940.[1] Statisticians at the U.S. Bureau of Labor Statistics (BLS) estimated individual components by using the findings of the 1940 Census, housing studies conducted during the 1930s by the BLS, the United States Housing Authority and the United States Public Works Administration, and the richly detailed Real Property Survey of 1934. The purpose of this exercise was to determine the accuracy of government estimates of annual housing construction from local reports on completions and starts. This analysis of components of inventory change revealed the impact on the housing sector of the collapse of the construction industry during the Great Depression. Net conversions (conversions less mergers) had accounted for 1,070,000 additions to the housing inventory between 1930 and 1940. Another 416,000 units had been provided by trailers, and about 100,000 were new units converted from nonresidential structures. Altogether, these additions by means other than new construction accounted for 36.7 percent of all ''real'' additions to the housing inventory.

A similar procedure was carried out by the BLS in 1952 to check again for the accuracy of its statistics on housing completions.[2] According to the 1950 Census of Housing the nonfarm housing inventory had increased by nearly 11 million units since 1940, compared with 5.7 million new units recorded by BLS estimates of completions. The reconciliation of these numbers by an analysis of components of inventory change revealed that slightly over 2 million units had been added to the inventory during the decade by net conversions, or 22.5 percent of all ''real'' additions to the stock for that period.

The 1960 Census of Housing involved the first serious attempt to measure the components of inventory change in order to shed light on the changing character and quality of the housing inventory itself rather than merely as a check on government statistical reports of new construction. Multistage probability sampling was used instead of residual techniques.[3] The 1960 *Components of Inventory Change Report* (henceforth referred to as CINCH) represented an advance over these earlier methods of estimation in three ways. First, it gave separate estimates of both mergers and conversions. Ever since the Real Property Survey of 1934, structural alterations that increased or decreased the number of dwelling units in a building had been estimated together, so that only the net change could be known. The 1960 Census also sought to break out various categories of additions and losses. Second, components of inventory change were for the first time estimated and broken out by metropolitan area, regional section, and urban location

EXHIBIT 2.1

Components of Housing Inventory Change, United States, 1890-1980

(dwelling units in thousands)

Period	Change in Year-Round Housing Stock	New Construction	Mobile Home Shipments	Demolitions and Losses	Non-Const. Additions from Other Sources	Conversions in Residential Buildings‡	Non-Const. Additions as a Percent of Total Additions	Conversions as a Percent of Total Additions
1890–1899	2,271	2,941	—	208	—	62–248	—	2.1–7.8
1900–1909	3,736	3,606	—	297	—	81–324	—	2.2–8.2
1910–1919	3,452	3,593	—	414	—	103–412	—	2.8–8.2
1920–1929	7,959	7,004	—	590	—	125–500	—	1.8–6.7
1930–1939	4,014	2,734	—	397	1,586	1,170	36.7	24.8
1940–1949	9,942	7,443	—	1,000	3,442	2,050	31.5	18.3
1950–1959	12,331	14,538	465	4,530	1,714*	1,140	11.0	6.8
1960–1969	11,971	15,177	2,057	6,715	1,136*	765	6.1	4.1
1970–1980	18,350	17,560	3,550	5,495	2,855†	1,580	11.9	6.6

*Includes units reclassified from rural to urban and some sampling error. Estimates for these two decades are from the Components of Inventory Survey. Estimates from earlier decades are from a variety of sources. For a break down of these sources, see L. Grebler, D. Blank, and L. Winnick, *Capital Formation in Residential Real Estate*, National Bureau of Economic Research. (Princeton, N.J.: Princeton University Press, 1954), Appendix A, table A-1, 329.

†"Non-Construction Additions" were estimated by taking the difference between the 1970 and 1980 census counts to total year-round housing units and adjusting it for the 1970 undercount of 2.4 percent. To this sum new construction and mobile home deliveries for the decade were subtracted. The resultant represents total "real" additions to the housing stock by means other than new construction. These are "real" additions as opposed to the estimates reported by the 1980 Components of Inventory Survey by the Bureau of the Census. The latter includes a few houses and many mobile homes moved between sites and is not adjusted for mobile homes in transit from dealers' inventories to sites in 1970 but in place in 1980.

‡Figures for 1890–1949 represent estimated "net conversions." These include gross conversions less mergers. The figures from 1950–1980 include not only residential conversions as defined by the Bureau of the Census, i.e., units created by the conversion of fewer to more, but also units created by the conversion of the nonresidential parts of residential buildings, i.e., detached garages, accessory structures, etc.

Sources: Historical Statistics, From Colonial Times to 1970. Series 192-95. *U.S. Bureau of the Census, Components of Inventory Change, 1960-1980. U.S. Statistical Abstract, 1980-82, Tables: 1339, 1345, 1349. Annual Housing Survey, 1973-1980.*

(central city, suburban, and nonmetropolitan). All units in the sample were surveyed to determine the characteristics of the buildings, the units, and the occupants; these included physical condition, dwelling size, income, tenure, and rent or value. Information for the same characteristics was collected for all the components of change—conversions, mergers, conversions to nonresidential use, demolitions, new construction, and so on. This wealth of data provided for the first time a means of understanding the various ways in which the standing stock adjusts as market factors and housing needs change.

The table in Exhibit 2.1 draws upon these different sources and presents an overview of the contribution of conversions to inventory change in the American housing sector for the ninety-year period from 1890 to 1980. If we ignore the distortions caused by variation in the methods of estimation and the changing definitions of the components, conversions account for between 2 and 8 percent of all additions to the housing inventory prior to 1930. This range estimate comes from Grebler, Blank and Winnick who concluded that the true rate was probably closer to 8 percent.[4] However, their estimates represent net conversions (residential conversions less mergers and less conversions from residential to nonresidential use). Gross conversions would obviously be greater and therefore account for a larger share of all additions to the inventory prior to 1930—probably closer to 9 percent.

The same definitional problem applies to the BLS estimates of conversions for the 1930s and 1940s, but the resulting bias in these figures is probably small.[5] The estimates of conversions for 1950 onward, on the other hand, are gross conversions. They include not only conversions of residential structures (from few to more units) but also conversions to residential use of nonresidential structures such as garages or nonresidential parts of residential buildings such as basements. Because they were derived by probability sampling techniques, these estimates of conversions and additions from other sources include some sampling and response errors. Total additions from other sources for the period 1950-1970 also includes units reclassified from rural to urban as a result of suburbanization, although the Census Bureau does not indicate precisely how many additions are attributable to this source.

Components of Inventory Change in Rental Housing

The proportions of conversions and other additions appear relatively small in the aggregate—only about 9 to 13 percent of the gross additions to the inventory. The vast majority of these conversions however are rental dwellings; since 1950 about 95 percent of all conversions have been rentals. The following table extracted from CINCH reports displays figures for annual average new construction of year-round rental apartments as well as estimates of rental units added to the inventory by means other than new construction. The two have been totaled and the percentage of nonconstruction additions computed (see Exhibit 2.2).

EXHIBIT 2.2
Additions to the Supply of Rental Housing by Type of Addition and Urban Location,
United States, 1950-1980
(dwelling units in thousands)

Period	New Construction	Average Annual Rate	Non-Const. Additions*	Average Annual Rate	Total Additions	Average Annual Rate	Non-Construction as a Percent of Total Additions
Central Cities							
1950–60	1,311	131	600	60	1,911	191	31.4
1960–70	2,261	226	349	35	2,610	261	13.4
1973–80	958	137	628	90	1,586	227	39.7
Suburbs							
1950–60	1,090	109	292	29	1,382	138	21.1
1960–70	2,393	239	173	17	2,566	257	6.7
1973–80	1,354	193	344	49	1,698	243	20.3
Outside SMSAs							
1950–60	1,207	121	482	48	1,689	169	28.5
1960–70	1,093	109	407	41	1,500	150	27.1
1973–80	816	117	393	56	1,209	173	32.5
United States							
1950–60	3,608	361	1,374	137	4,982	498	27.6
1960–70	5,747	575	929	93	6,676	668	13.9
1973–80	3,128	447	1,365	195	4,493	642	30.4

*Non-Construction Additions include both conversions from fewer to more units and conversions from nonresidential uses.
Source: U.S. Bureau of the Census, Census of Housing, Components of Inventory Change, 1960-1980. Annual Housing Survey, 1973-1980.

This table shows that approximately 30 percent of all units added to the rental inventory in the United States between 1973 and 1980 were produced by means other than new construction. While annual average new construction of rental apartments fell from 575,000 units per year in the 1960s to 447,000 units per year in the 1970s, the average annual rate for sources other than new construction rose from 93,000 units per year to close to 195,000. This is even higher than the rate that prevalied during the postwar shortage of the 1950s, when nonconstruction sources provided approximately 27.5 percent of all additions to the rental stock.

In central cities the rate of gross additions to the rental inventory from sources other than new construction has climbed even more dramatically. Whereas only 13 percent of additional rental housing was produced by conversion during the 1960s, between 1973 and 1980 the share of gross rental additions from this source rose to 40 percent. For suburbs the share of rental units produced by conversions rose from 6.7 percent to 20.3 percent. In nonmetropolitan places, where

EXHIBIT 2.3
Additions to the Housing Inventory by Means Other Than New Construction by
Type, United States, 1973-1980
(dwelling units in thousands)

	Number	Percent
Conversions	541	29.86
Nonresidential facilities adjacent to residential buildings*	430	23.73
Nonresidential structures	135	7.45
Group quarters	267	14.74
Rehabilitated structures	147	8.11
Unaccounted for	292	16.11
Total	1,812	100.00

*"Nonresidential facilities" are primarily basements, garages, and accessory structures (sheds, cabins, and the like) which were formerly used for non-residential purposes.

Sources: U.S. Bureau of the Census, 1980 *Census of Housing Components of Inventory Change,* Vol. 4, Part 1, HC80-S1-2. Washington, D.C., June 1983.

the share of additions to the rental supply by means other than new construction has been above 25 percent since World War II, a similar though not so significant increase is discernible.

Estimating Residential Conversions

Unfortunately, the CINCH Reports use a set of classifications for identifying various types of conversions which differs from the one presented in the last chapter and which makes it difficult to distinguish accessory conversions from other types.

CINCH, for example, defines a "residential conversion" as the division of an existing dwelling into two or more units. Under the label "other additions" CINCH includes units created from a variety of sources (see Exhibit 2.3).[6] Roughly half of the units classified as "other additions" (565,000) were conversions from nonresidential uses. Of these, only 135,000 actually involved nonresidential structures such as public schools, warehouses, and manufacturing lofts. The remaining 430,000 were conversions of garages, basements, sheds, or other nonresidential parts of residential buildings. Some were detached garages adjacent to single family homes, but some were also conversions of basements and attached garages in two- to four-unit buildings. Approximately 21.0 percent of "other additions" (267,000 units) were conversions to residential use of group quarters, such as dormitories, hospitals, or residential hotels. Another 23.0 percent (291,900 units) were "residual additions," the precise source of which could not be determined because of nonresponses, missing data, measurement error, and the like.

Exhibit 2.3 does not include houses or mobile homes moved to a vacant site, although the Bureau of the Census normally includes them in their estimates of "other additions." "Mobile homes moved in" represent a significant component of gross additions reported by the CINCH survey: 2,784,000 units between 1973 and 1980. I have eliminated them because they do not represent genuine additions. As indicated in the introduction to this chapter, they are offset by a similar number of houses or mobile homes removed from a site elsewhere. Attempts to estimate "real" gross additions without adjusting for them have produced inflated estimates of the volume of conversions. McGough, for example, failed to factor them out as a separate category of additions. His estimate of units added to the inventory by means other than new construction was consequently 3 million above the true figure.[7]

This table also demonstrates that a substantial number of conversions classified by CINCH as "other additions" in fact involve some type of residential structure. If the units created out of basements, garages, and accessory structures which belong to residential buildings and which are classified as "other additions" are added to "residential conversions" (more from fewer units), then the total number of units created by conversion of the living area or utility area of a residential building between 1973 and 1980 reached 910,000. If we assume that about half of the residual additions also involved conversions of residential structures, then perhaps as many as 1,085,000 or about 59 percent of all units added to the inventory by means other than new construction involved the conversion of an existing residential structure or property.

The Incidence of Accessory Conversions

Unfortunately, CINCH does not distinguish accessory conversions from other types of conversions. These are included under both "residential conversions" (from fewer to more) and "other additions." Conversion of a basement or an attached garage belonging to a single-family house would be considered a "residential conversion," but it would be classified as a "nonresidential conversion" when belonging to a residential building of two units or more. CINCH also treats conversions of detached garages or accessory structures adjacent to single-family properties as conversions from nonresidential use. On the other hand, a cottage or "granny-flat" added to the rear yard of a single-family house would be classified as new construction.[8]

Because of these peculiarities in the Census Bureau's definitions of conversions, it is difficult to derive a precise estimate of the actual volume of accessory apartment conversions in the United States. However, CINCH does contain substantial information about the ownership, occupancy and size, condition, and space utilization characteristics of conversions which allows some reasonable guesses about the incidence of accessory conversions as a component of inven-

EXHIBIT 2.4
Distribution of New, Converted, and Unchanged Dwelling Units by Urban Location, Size and Year Moved In, United States, 1973–1980

	Central City			Suburbs		
	New	Conversion	Same	New	Conversion	Same
Panel A — Occupancy Characteristics						
Percent vacant	10.8	11.1	6.5	9.2	11.5	5.0
Percent owner-occupied	52.3	26.8	50.1	76.3	36.0	70.4
Panel B						
Units in Structure (in percentages)						
Size of Structure						
1 unit	45.2	0.0	51.7	67.5	0.0	74.6
2–4 units	10.8	77.7	20.7	7.3	97.4	10.1
5+ units	41.5	21.9	27.2	18.0	2.6	12.9
mobile home	2.3	0.0	0.4	7.3	0.0	2.4
Total percent	100.0	100.0	100.0	100.0	100.0	100.0
Panel C						
1980 Owner-Occupied Households by Year Moved into Unit, United States (in percentages)						
Year Moved In						
Apr. 1970–1980	100.0	55.4	48.2	100.0	51.7	49.0
1965–Mar. 1970	0.0	10.8	14.4	0.0	5.7	16.0
1960–1964	0.0	9.5	11.4	0.0	16.1	11.4
1950–1959	0.0	6.8	15.2	0.0	16.1	15.2
1949 or earlier	0.0	17.6	10.8	0.0	10.3	8.4
Total percent	100.0	100.0	100.0	100.0	100.0	100.0
Percent moved in before Apr. 1970		44.6	15.8		48.3	51.0
Panel D						
1970 Owner-Occupied Households by Year Moved into Unit, United States (in percentages)						
Year Moved In						
1969 or later	24.6	3.1	8.8	28.3	2.7	8.1
1965–1968	46.0	17.2	18.9	43.7	22.7	19.3
1960–1964	29.4	23.4	16.1	27.9	17.3	16.0
1950–1959	0.0	25.0	31.8	0.0	29.3	36.7
1949 or earlier	0.0	31.3	24.5	0.0	28.0	19.9
Total percent	100.0	100.0	100.0	100.0	100.0	100.0
Percent moved in before 1960		56.3	56.3		57.3	56.6

Source: Panels A and B: 1980 *Census of Housing, Components of Inventory Change*, United States and Regions, Vol. 4.

Source: Panels C and D: 1970 and 1980 *Census of Housing, Components of Inventory Change*, United States and Regions, Vol. 4.

EXHIBIT 2.5

Size of Structure and Occupancy Characteristics by Urban Location and Tenure, Same Units Before and After Conversions, United States, 1973–1980
(units in thousands)

Panel A
Occupancy Characteristics

	Central Cities		Suburbs	
	Before	After	Before	After
Year-round units	137	328	115	270
Vacancy rate	10.2	7.6	7.0	11.5
Percentage owner-occupied	69.5	26.8	76.4	36.0

Panel B
Size of Structure

	Central Cities				Suburbs			
	Before		After		Before		After	
	No.	Percent	No.	Percent	No.	Percent	No.	Percent
Size of Structure								
1 unit	92	67.2	0	0.0	99	86.1	0	0.0
2–4 units	40	29.2	255	77.7	14	12.2	263	97.4
5+ units	5	3.6	72	22.2	2	1.7	7	2.6
mobile homes	0	0.0	0	0.0	0	0.0	0	0.0

Source: 1980 *Census of Housing, Components of Inventory Change,* Vol. 4, Part 1.

tory change. The tables which follow display these data in the form of tabular comparisons between newly built units, units which have undergone conversion, and units that have remained unchanged. This same method of comparison is further broken down by urban location—central city and suburb.

While examining these tables the reader should keep in mind that CINCH estimates are subject to sampling error. The standard error of estimate for small values and small differences between categories can sometimes be quite large. In the analysis that follows the reader should ignore small differences.

Exhibit 2.4 presents general occupancy characteristics for units that were changed by conversion between 1973 and 1980 as well as for new and unchanged dwellings. Although the owner occupancy rate appears lower for converted units, this is deceptive; most units after conversion are reported in the census as two- to four-unit buildings. However, panel A of Exhibit 2.5, which presents similar data for dwellings before and after conversion, shows that 67 percent of the units that underwent conversion in central cities were originally single-family homes,

EXHIBIT 2.5 (continued)
Size of Dwelling by Tenure, Same Units Before and After Conversions,
United States, 1973–1980
(units in thousands)

Panel C
Size of Dwelling in Number of Rooms

	Central Cities				Suburbs			
	Before		After		Before		After	
Number of rooms	No.	Percent	No.	Percent	No.	Percent	No.	Percent
Owner-occupied	79	100.0	72	100.0	82	100.0	86	100.0
3 rooms or less	2	2.5	17	23.6	0	0.0	19	22.1
4 rooms	4	5.1	16	22.2	1	1.2	12	14.0
5 rooms	11	13.9	16	22.2	19	23.2	13	15.1
6 rooms	13	16.5	13	18.1	13	15.9	19	22.1
7 rooms +	49	62.0	10	13.9	48	58.5	23	26.7
Median rooms	6.5+		4.7		6.5+		5.5	
Renter-occupied	46	100.0	198	100.0	25	100.0	153	100.0
1 room	5	10.9	46	23.2	0	0.0	6	3.9
2 rooms	2	4.3	16	8.1	0	0.0	21	13.7
3 rooms	12	26.1	54	27.3	4	16.0	46	30.1
4 rooms	10	21.7	61	30.8	9	36.0	50	32.7
5 rooms	7	15.2	18	9.1	9	36.0	20	13.1
6 rooms	8	17.4	3	1.5	1	4.0	8	5.2
7 rooms +	2	4.3	0	0.0	2	8.0	2	1.3
Median rooms	3.9		3.2		4.6		3.6	

Source: 1980 *Census of Housing, Components of Inventory Change*, Vol. 4, Part 1.

and of these almost three-fourths were owner-occupied. In suburbs 85 percent of the units before conversion were single-family dwellings and 82 percent of them were owner-occupied. After conversion slightly more than half in central cities remained owner-occupied, while almost three-fourths did in suburbs.

Despite high rates of owner occupancy, probably not more than 60 percent of these conversions involved the creation of accessory apartments in single-family houses. Two pieces of evidence support this assertion. First, as panel C of Exhibit 2.4 indicates, half of all owner-occupiers living in buildings with converted units in 1981 had moved into their homes prior to 1970 and one-fourth had moved in prior to 1960. Some fraction of the owners who moved in after 1970 probably also undertook their own conversions. This means that at least half of the owner-occupiers had lived for at least three years in their homes before converting part of them. Panel D of Exhibit 2.4 presents similar figures from the

EXHIBIT 2.6
Estimated Total Accessory Apartment Conversions, United States, 1973–1980
(units in thousands)

CINCH Category	Number	Low Ratio	High Est.	Low Ratio	High Est.
Central Cities					
1-Unit Det. (Other-Renter)	46	0.33	15	0.50	23
2–4 Units (Other-Renter)	78	1.00	78	1.00	78
2–4 Units (Conv.-Renter)	120	0.33	40	0.60	72
5+ Units (Other)	340	0.33	112	0.50	170
Subtotal	584		245		343
As a Percent of Total					
Non-Const. Additions			31		43
Suburbs					
1-Unit Det. (Other-Renter)	85	0.33	28	0.50	43
2–4 Units (Other-Renter)	50	1.00	50	1.00	50
2–4 Units (Conv.-Renter)	145	0.33	48	0.60	87
5+ Units (Other)	41	0.33	14	0.50	21
Subtotal	321		139		201
As a Percent of Total					
Non-Const. Additions			28		40
Outside SMSAs					
1-Unit Det. (Other-Renter)	124	0.33	41	0.50	62
2–4 Units (Other-Renter)	29	1.00	29	1.00	29
2–4 Units (Conv.-Renter)	130	0.33	43	0.60	78
5+ Units (Other)	134	0.33	44	0.50	67
Subtotal	417		157		236
As a Percent of Total					
Non-Const. Additions			19		28
United States					
1-Unit Det. (Other-Renter)	255	0.33	84	0.50	128
2–4 Units (Other-Renter)	157	0.00	157	1.00	157
2–4 Units (Conv.-Renter)	395	0.33	130	0.60	237
5+ Units (Other)	515	0.33	170	0.50	258
Subtotal	1,322		541		780
New Construction			50		80
Unaccounted for			40		80
Grand Total			631		940

Source: See Exhibit 2.5.

1970 CINCH report. Again about 56 percent of the owner-occupants had lived in their houses for at least 10 years before conversion occurred, and almost 30 percent had done so for more than 20 years.

The second piece of evidence concerns the distribution of dwelling units by size (number of rooms) before and after conversion. Exhibit 2.5 presents the distribution of dwellings by tenure and structure size, both before and after conversion. Netting out the increase in the number of units that were added as a result of conversion, it appears that half of all buildings in central cities that were owner-occupied before conversion were still owner-occupied after conversion. For suburbs the figure is about 70 percent.

From these numbers we can infer that probably half of all the units which according to CINCH were "residential conversions" (conversions from fewer to more units) were accessory apartments in single-family houses. Others were added in two- to four-unit structures. How many is unclear, but a conservative estimate might be about 33 percent to as much as 60 percent. This would mean that, at the most, about half of the units added to the inventory by residential conversions between 1973 and 1980, about 250,000 units, were some type of accessory apartment in a one- to four-unit structure. "Other additions" also include accessory conversions: renter-occupied, one-unit detached structures, conversions in two- to four-unit buildings, and some installed in structures with five units or more (see Exhibit 2.6).[9] If one includes a small amount of new construction to account for rear yard additions, and a comparable percentage of those additions that could not be accounted for (about 15 percent), accessory apartments added to the national housing inventory between 1973 and 1980 may have totaled between 600,000 and 950,000. This represents an average of 95,000 to 120,000 units per year. Accessory conversions installed by owner occupants accounted for slightly more than half of this number—probably from 50,000 to 65,000 units per year, or half a million for the entire decade.

Although this is a rough estimate at best, it does provide some idea of the order of magnitude involved. It is considerably smaller than previous estimates. Patrick Hare, citing an interview with Arthur Young of the Bureau of the Census, has claimed that 2.5 million accessory apartments were installed in single-family homes during the 1970s, or about 250,000 units a year.[10] Thomas Thibodeau of The Urban Institute similarly estimated that about 318,000 one-unit structures on average each year were converted into structures with two or more units from 1970 to 1978.[11] Though 50,000 to 65,000 units a year seems small by comparison, it equals about one-fourth of the average annual number of unsubsidized rental housing completions in the United States during the last half of the 1970s.

Comparison of the CINCH reports for 1970 and 1980 using a similar estimating procedure shows that net accessory conversions in single-family homes rose from an annual average of 39,000 units to about 60,000 between the two decades. This suggests that accessory apartment conversions are on the rise, although some of the apparent increase may be the result of changes in CINCH sampling procedures and design between the two censuses. Some impressionistic evidence supports this finding. Two studies of planning politics in Long Island

EXHIBIT 2.7
Conversions and Mergers in the Housing Inventory, Dwelling Unit Characteristics,
United States, 1973-1980
(units in thousands)

	Conversions		Mergers	
	Before	**After**	**Before**	**After**
Year-round units	378	886	873	466
Percent vacant	10.0	15.8	18.8	9.4
Percent				
owner-occupied	69.9	32.2	35.1	71.4
Number of units in structure				
Owner-occupied	237	239	249	299
1 unit	215	0	0	260
2–4 units	19	229	233	29
5+ units	0	7	6	3
mobile homes	3	3	10	7
Renter-occupied	102	503	460	123
1 unit	47	0	0	47
2–4 units	43	424	350	40
5+ units	12	77	102	36
mobile homes	0	2	8	8
Dwelling sizes				
Median number of rooms				
Owner-occupied	6.5+	5.1	4.8	6.5+
Renter-occupied	4.3	3.3	3.3	4.6
Median number of bedrooms				
Owner-occupied	2.7	1.8	1.6	2.7
Renter-occupied	1.5	.7	.8	1.7

Source: 1980 *Census of Housing, Components of Inventory Change,*, Vol. 4, Part 1, Tables A-3, A-5.

and Connecticut suburbs noted the spread of illegal conversions in single-family dwellings during the 1970s. Both studies attributed this phenomenon to local restrictions on apartment development at a time when employment in the suburban sections of the region was growing rapidly. A 1980 survey of local government officials on the subject of accessory apartment conversion activity by the Tri-State Regional Planning Commission in the New York–New Jersey–Connecticut area confirmed these observations.[12]

For the current decade there is little solid information. The National Association of Home Builders has estimated that since 1980 about 300,000 home owners a year have been converting parts of their houses into accessory apartments.[13]

EXHIBIT 2.8
Conversions and Mergers in the Housing Inventory, Household Characteristics, United States, 1973–1980

	Conversions		Mergers	
	Before	**After**	**Before**	**After**
Median household size:				
Owner-occupied	2.8	2.1	2.2	3.1
Renter-occupied	2.3	1.7	1.6	2.7
Percent of households with 1 person:				
Owner-occupied	15.1	25.1	27.4	13.9
Renter-occupied	30.1	44.8	49.4	23.4
Percent of households with children present:				
Owner-occupied	40.3	25.9	31.0	45.3
Renter-occupied	36.9	29.1	27.9	41.1
Percent of households with 2 or more children:				
Owner-occupied	25.2	18.0	16.5	29.1
Renter-occupied	23.3	12.9	13.3	29.0

Source: 1980 Census of Housing, Components of Inventory Change, Vol. 4, Part 1, Tables A-3, A-5.

This figure seems exaggerated. However, even if the number of net accessory conversions in single-family houses has risen to over 120,000 a year, this would equal about half of the average annual new private unsubsidized rental apartments built in the United States between 1980 and 1983.[14]

Conversions and Mergers

Accessory conversions differ from structural ones in one particular way that is not well understood or appreciated: because the primary unit is not subdivided into small apartments, the accessory unit remains subordinate in use to the primary unit and can be easily merged back into it. Mergers require little if any investment in construction or redesign. The only work that need be done is to remove the cooking facilities and replace the furnishings. Merger may involve even less work than this when unrelated occupants of an accessory apartment are replaced by relatives. With a cousin or an aunt living in it the accessory apartment acts as an additional bedroom and becomes functionally part of the primary unit, although it may still have all the physical characteristics of a separate unit, including kitchen facilities.

The ease with which accessory structures and spaces can be converted into

EXHIBIT 2.9
Conversions and Mergers in the Housing Inventory by Year Moved into Dwelling Unit, United States

Panel A
Owner-Occupied Units Converted or Merged, 1973–1980

	Conversion		Merger	
	Before	After	Before	After
Dwelling units (in thousands)	238	239	248	309
Total Percent	100.0	100.0	100.0	100.0
April 1970–1980	18.9	54.8	13.3	62.1
1965 - March 1970	16.0	7.5	19.4	7.8
1960–1964	23.1	14.2	14.9	7.9
1950–1959	19.7	12.6	20.1	9.3
1949 or earlier	22.7	10.9	32.3	12.9
Percent moved into unit 1970 or earlier	81.5	45.2	86.8	37.9

Panel B
Owner-Occupied Units Converted or Merged, 1960–1970

	Conversion		Merger	
	Before	After	Before	After
Dwelling Units (in thousands)	248	196	360	355
Total Percent	100.0	100.0	100.0	100.0
1969 or later	—	2.7	—	3.9
1965–1968	—	22.7	—	23.3
1960–1964	—	17.3	—	21.0
1950–1959	—	29.3	—	25.9
1949 or earlier	—	28.0	—	25.9
Percent moved into unit 1959 or earlier		57.3		51.8

Source: 1980 *Census of Housing, Components of Inventory Change,* Vol. 4, Part 1, Tables A-3, A-5. 1970 *Census of Housing, Components of Inventory Change,* Vol. 3, Part 1, Tables 2, 5.

separate residential units and merged back into the building means that accessory apartments move in and out of the stock quite frequently. This probably occurs when the property changes ownership; but it can also occur in the absence of turnover because of the changing needs and preferences of whoever owns or occupies the primary unit.

The CINCH surveys provide substantial evidence that many converted units eventually are merged back into primary units. Exhibits 2.7 to 2.9 compare units before and after conversion in terms of size of structure, size of unit, types of occupants, and so on. For each characteristic the same before-and-after comparison is presented for mergers. Exhibit 2.7, for example, shows that the vast majority of conversions from few to more residential units involve the transformation of one-family structures into two-family ones, while mergers turn two-family dwellings back into one-family dwellings.

The same pattern of changes can be observed in dwelling-unit sizes. The median number of rooms for owner-occupied dwellings falls from above 6.5 to 5.1 when conversion occurs, and it rises from 4.8 to above 6.5 in the case of mergers. The difference in the medians before and after is about 1.5 rooms. This difference suggests that a substantial number of the conversions are accessory apartments rather than structural conversions of single-family houses into duplexes. Otherwise the average rooms gained and lost would be higher, probably on the order of 2.5 to 3 rooms. Also, rooms lost during conversion in many of the largest houses were probably guest rooms, offices, or basements.[15]

The comparison of bedrooms gained or lost from merger and conversion supports this interpretation. The median number of bedrooms falls by about 1.0 in the case of conversions and rises by slightly more than 1.0 for mergers (see Exhibit 2.7). Typically, many accessory apartments probably were once extra bedrooms, some of which were room additions while others were bedrooms converted from attics, basements, or garages.[16]

The panels on household composition in Exhibit 2.8 underscore this point—increases and decreases in household size account for much of the change in number of rooms that occurs in conversions and mergers. Conversions result in a main dwelling that is more suitable for occupancy by a small household, either a single person or a couple without children; mergers work the other way and create units appropriate for larger households, especially families with children.

That conversions and mergers are performed by owner-occupants on their own homes is clear from Exhibit 2.9. This table indicates how long owners lived in their units before and after conversion or merger occurred. As noted earlier, half of all owners living in units converted after 1973 had been living in them prior to 1970. What is also surprising is that approximately 38 percent of all the owners living in units that had been created by mergers since 1973 had also moved into their houses prior to 1970. These owners represent 47 percent of all the owners who prior to 1970 lived in unmerged units that were merged after 1973. For the 1960s the proportion is even higher: approximately 52 percent of all owners living in units that had been merged during the 1960s had moved into them in 1959 or before; this represents slightly over 60 percent of all the owners who had been living in unmerged units prior to 1960 that were eventually merged later in the decade. These high percentages provide solid evidence that accessory apartments do in fact move in and out of the stock quite frequently, as a result of the changing needs and preferences of their owners.

EXHIBIT 2.10
Estimated Annual Losses from the Housing Inventory, United States,
October 1973 to October 1980
(units in thousands)

		Permanent		Retrievable	
	Total	Number	Percent	Number	Percent
1973–1974	1,211	n.a.	n.a.	n.a.	n.a.
1974–1975	1,581	587	37.1	994	62.9
1975–1976	1,322	469	35.5	853	64.5
1976–1977	1,456	604	41.5	852	58.5
1977–1978	1,335	526	39.4	809	60.6
1978–1979	1,390	468	33.7	922	66.3
1979–1980	1,213	485	40.0	728	60.0

Source: Annual Housing Surveys, 1973–1980; also national data from other surveys conducted by the United States Department of Commerce, Bureau of the Census and the United States Department of Housing and Urban Development, Office of Policy Development and Research.

This notion of accessory apartments as a "swing" supply of units that moves in and out of the inventory has received confirmation from studies of inventory removals by the United States Department of Housing and Urban Development and the Bureau of the Census. Estimates of actual losses made each year during the 1970s in the *Annual Housing Survey* (AHS) were larger than average annual losses derived from comparison of the housing inventory over longer spans of time. The reason for this is that only some losses are "permanent," whereas others are "retrievable." Permanent losses include units destroyed or demolished because of natural disaster, fire, or code enforcement, as well as units moved from their original sites. Retrievable losses include some units that have been damaged by fire or natural disaster and have consequently become uninhabitable but can be rehabilitated. These represent only a small fraction of the total, however. The great bulk of retrievable losses are of two types: mobile homes that are moved to alternative sites and units that are removed as a result of residential mergers and conversions to nonresidential use. Permanent losses are counted only once in both the long-term comparison and the annual estimates. Retrievable losses, on the other hand, are units that can move in and out of the stock several times. As a result they may be counted more than once in the annual AHS estimates, but they are counted only once in the long-term comparison if they are out of the inventory at the end of the period. Based on an analysis of losses in the AHS, the Bureau of the Census has estimated that up to two-thirds of all losses in any one year may be retrievable (see Exhibit 2.10).

The estimates of conversions and mergers obtained from CINCH represent a long-term comparison that yields net estimates and therefore includes only permanent losses and permanent conversions. The CINCH figures consequently underestimate the gross amount of conversion and merger activity that actually occurs because CINCH does not include units that have been converted and merged back during the period, or likewise, merged and converted back into accessory apartments again.[17] From CINCH it was estimated earlier that about 45,000 to 60,000 accessory apartments annually were created in owner-occupied homes between 1973 and 1980; that represents a net figure. If units lost through merger represent the same share of retrievable losses as they do of permanent losses, or about 7.8 percent, then, given an annual average of 859,000 retrievable losses during the late 1970s, one would expect that as many as 65,000 accessory conversions per year in single-family houses moved out of the stock through merger and back into it by reconversion. Conversions of detached structures adjacent to single-family houses to and from nonresidential use would probably increase this by another 10,000 to 15,000 units per year. Thus the annual average gross volume of accessory apartment conversions produced during the past decade was probably on the order of 100,000 units per year, with between 50,000 and 60,000 representing "permanent" net additions to the inventory.

That such a large proportion of accessory apartment conversions are not permanent indicates that many of them are nonstructural conversions of multi-use rooms. As mentioned above, the act of conversion or merger may involve little more than the installation or removal of a stove, the replacement of some fixtures, the parting of a room, or the locking or opening of a door.

Occupancy and Physical Condition

Although CINCH contains information on space utilization and the physical condition of converted dwellings, the reader should remember that CINCH identifies only units converted during the decade between the decennial census. It would be a mistake to draw inferences from CINCH about the stock of converted dwellings as a whole, because incomes, tastes, and standards and consequently the quality of conversions have varied from era to era. Nevertheless, this rich source of data provides some important insights that may apply to all housing created by residential conversion.

Exhibit 2.11 indicates what kinds of home owners live in houses that underwent conversion during the 1970s. In general, they are smaller than average households. About two-thirds contain either one or two persons; for home owners overall, only half do. Owner-occupants of houses with converted units are also more likely to be persons living alone; fewer are married couples than is true of home owners in general. Slightly more than 75 percent do not have children under 18 years present compared to about 60 percent for owners of unchanged dwellings.

Home owners with converted units are older than buyers of new homes. About 26 percent are middle-aged (between 45 and 64 years old), and another 23 percent are 65 years or older. Although a similar proportion of buyers of new homes are middle-aged, only about 5 percent of them are over 65. Household heads

EXHIBIT 2.11
**Owner-Occupied Households by Urban Location, Household Type and Component
of Inventory Change, United States, 1973–1980**

	Central City			Suburbs		
	New	Conversion	Same	New	Conversion	Same
Percent male head with wife present	75.7	59.7	66.3	82.4	65.1	74.8
Percent other male head	12.1	16.7	10.2	8.5	11.6	8.2
Percent female head	13.2	23.6	23.6	9.1	23.3	17.1
Percent households heads age 65+	5.8	26.4	22.5	5.4	23.3	21.4
Percent household heads age 45+	31.4	59.4	62.8	30.1	59.4	62.8
Percent households with no children	42.5	77.8	64.9	40.9	76.7	58.6
Percent one-person households	13.5	31.9	18.4	8.5	20.9	13.5

Source: 1980 *Census of Housing, Components of Inventory Change,* Vol. 4, Part 1.

whose homes contain converted units are the same age as those home owners who occupy dwellings that remained unchanged during the period. The high proportion of home owners over the age of 45 who are living in converted units confirms our earlier assertion that changes in space needs over the life cycle account for much of the incidence of accessory apartment conversions.[18] Compared to owners of unchanged buildings or new homes, owners whose houses were changed by conversion were more often either male or female heads of household with no spouse present. About 77 percent of the female heads of household in central cities and 85 percent of them in suburbs who were owners of homes with conversions were above the age of 44.

Exhibit 2.12 presents a similar breakdown for renters living in units created by conversion. Their household composition is similar to that of renters in general. Slightly greater proportions are single-person households and households without children, particularly in the suburbs. Relatively small proportions are senior citizens. This is consistent with the findings of local studies which show that most renters living in accessory apartment conversions are young singles or couples. Some of these studies indicate that many senior citizens living in accessory apartments are home owners who moved into them after conversion and then rented out the main part of the dwelling.[19]

As noted in earlier tables, most households living in single-family dwellings that have been converted contain either one or two persons. Exhibit 2.13 confirms this point. This table compares the median household size of owners and renters in new dwellings, converted dwellings, and units that have remained un-

EXHIBIT 2.12
Renter-Occupied Households by Urban Location, Household Composition and
Component of Inventory Change, United States, 1973–1980

	Central City			Suburbs		
	New	Conversion	Same	New	Conversion	Same
Percent male head with						
wife present	37.4	32.5	31.0	41.6	34.0	41.5
Percent other male head	27.6	29.5	24.4	22.5	36.6	21.3
Percent female head	35.0	38.0	44.7	35.9	29.4	37.2
Percent households with head						
age 65+	12.2	18.0	17.8	12.9	11.1	14.7
Percent of households						
with no children	42.7	72.7	68.9	70.3	74.5	63.6
Percent one-person						
households	39.3	42.4	38.6	32.7	43.1	31.6

Source: 1980 *Census of Housing, Components of Inventory Change*, Vol. 4, Part 1.

changed over the past three decades. During the 1950s households occupying newly built and older unchanged units were much larger than those in converted dwellings. Since then the average size of all households has declined, and the difference in size between those occupying converted dwellings and those occupying units in the rest of the inventory has narrowed. This convergence in household sizes appears to be more pronounced among renters than home owners.

As for condition and quality, the differences between converted units and unchanged units is much greater in central cities than in suburbs. In the cities converted dwellings of both owners and renters were much older than the central city stock as whole. In suburbs owner-occupied houses that had undergone conversion were newer—27.9 percent were built before 1939 as compared to 22.1 percent for unchanged dwellings. Renter-occupied units created by conversion also appeared to be in somewhat newer structures (see Exhibit 2.14).

In terms of dwelling size, about 28 percent of all renter-occupied conversions in central cities contained no separate bedroom, compared to only 3.6 percent in suburbs. Suburban rental conversions were larger by comparison, as median dwelling size indicates. Many of the rental units created by conversion in central cities were studio apartments, whereas in the suburbs they were one-bedroom apartments.

As compared to units in suburban houses which were unchanged or converted, relatively greater percentages of rental units created by conversion in the central cities were substandard. More of them had no separate kitchen facilities or bathrooms; more of them had substandard heating and lacked some or all plumbing.

EXHIBIT 2.13
Median Household Size by Tenure and Component of Inventory Change,
United States, 1950–1980

	New Construction	Other Additions	Conversions	Unchanged Dwellings	Range (High-Low)
Owner-occupied dwellings					
1950–1960	3.7	2.4	2.2	2.8	1.5
1960–1970	3.6	2.3	2.3	2.7	1.3
1973–1980	3.1	2.3	2.1	2.5	1.0
Percent change 1950–1980	−16.2	−4.2	−4.5	−10.7	
Renter-occupied dwellings					
1950–1960	3.9	2.5	2.1	2.7	0.8
1960–1970	2.2	1.7	1.5	2.4	0.7
1973–1980	1.9	1.7	1.7	2.0	0.2
Percent change 1950–1980	−51.3	−32.0	−19.0	−25.9	

Source: U.S. Census of Housing, Components of Inventory Change, 1960, 1970, 1980.

Owner units in central cities also had some of these same defects; 7 percent had no kitchen facilities or shared them with another household, and 16.7 percent had substandard heating. The lower quality of the central city conversions is also evident from the high percentage that were located on streets containing abandoned or boarded-up buildings: 15.8 percent of the conversions were on such streets, as compared to only 8.5 percent of unchanged units.

Suburban conversions, on the other hand, were comparable in quality and physical condition to unchanged houses. Proportionally fewer rental units created by conversions had substandard heating than did rental apartments in unchanged structures. High percentages of conversions, however, had no garage or carport located on the property: 61.6 percent of all recently converted dwellings had no parking facilities available, compared to only 20.9 percent for existing units.

Fewer of today's conversions are substandard than those created in the past, particularly during the 1930s and 1940s, when conversions comprised a major share of gross additions to the housing inventory. Lipstein's 1949 study of conversions in Chesapeake Bay cities during World War II, for example, showed that 70 percent lacked private bathrooms and half had neither permanent nor temporary cooking facilities.[20] A.M. Woodruff's 1951 survey of accessory conversions in Pittsburgh and Milwaukee found somewhat better conditions: 29 percent of the Pittsburgh conversions lacked private bathrooms, whereas only 11 percent of those in Milwaukee did. In both cities, however, close to a third lacked permanent kitchen facilities.[21]

EXHIBIT 2.14

Condition, Quality, and Size of New, Unchanged, and Converted Dwellings by Urban Location, Tenure and Component of Inventory Change, United States, 1973–1980

	Central City			Suburbs		
	New	Conversion	Same	New	Conversion	Same
Percent built 1939 or before						
Owners	0.0	73.6	38.8	0.0	27.9	22.1
Renters	0.0	62.1	48.1	0.0	35.6	28.4
Median number of rooms						
Owners	6.0	4.7	5.8	6.2	5.4	6.0
Renters	3.6	3.2	3.8	4.0	3.6	4.1
Percent without separate bedrooms						
Owners	0.6	0.0	0.2	0.2	6.0	0.2
Renters	3.6	27.9	7.0	1.0	3.6	2.9
Percent lacking some or all plumbing						
Owners	0.2	2.8	0.7	0.4	0.0	0.9
Renters	0.2	7.5	1.8	0.4	2.0	1.8
Percent with shared or no bathrooms						
Owners	0.1	2.8	0.6	0.5	0.0	1.0
Renters	0.6	7.1	2.5	1.0	3.3	2.5
Percent with shared or no kitchen facilities						
Owners	0.4	6.9	0.3	0.3	2.3	0.1
Renters	0.0	8.6	2.4	0.6	3.3	2.1
Percent without modern heating*						
Owners	1.2	16.7	7.9	2.3	10.5	7.0
Renters	0.1	18.7	13.6	2.7	4.6	12.2
Percent without garage or carport	37.3	69.2	44.7	18.4	61.6	20.9
Percent with abandoned or boarded-up buildings on same street	2.2	15.5	8.5	0.8	2.1	2.5

*Includes dwelling units with room heaters (with and without flue), fireplaces, stoves, portable room heaters, or no heating equipment.

Source: 1980 *Census of Housing, Components of Inventory Change*, Vol. 4, Part 1.

EXHIBIT 2.15

Rents and Incomes of Households in New, Converted, and Unchanged Dwellings by Urban Location, Tenure, and Component of Inventory Change, United States, 1973–1980

	Central City			Suburbs		
	New	**Conversion**	**Same**	**New**	**Conversion**	**Same**
Median income						
Owners	$28,100	$13,500	$18,800	$28,500	$17,300	$22,700
Renters	$14,100	$ 7,700	$ 9,500	$14,800	$13,500	$12,200
Median gross rent	$ 301	$ 227	$ 230	$ 333	$ 256	$ 276
Percent of households paying no cash rent	1.5	3.5	2.4	3.1	7.8	4.7
Percent of households paying 25 percent or more of income on rent	48.8	73.3	55.1	54.3	41.7	43.5
Percent of households paying 35 percent or more of income on rent	22.3	55.0	36.0	31.7	20.1	21.6

Source: 1980 *Census of Housing, Components of Inventory Change*, Vol. 4, Part 1.

Rents and Incomes

Exhibit 2.15 compares incomes and rents between converted and unconverted housing. As one might expect, owners and renters in buildings that have been converted have lower incomes than those in unchanged or new buildings. Suburban renters living in converted units are an exception. They have a higher median income that their suburban counterparts who live in unchanged units. Median rent for converted units is lower than the rent for new units, as one might expect. Whereas in central cities there is almost no difference between the median rents for converted and unchanged dwellings, in the suburbs, on the other hand, median rents for converted rentals are about 8 percent lower than for apartments in unchanged buildings.

It is difficult to draw any solid inference from this analysis, because the observed differences between medians may be the result of regional composition effects.[22] But a number of things seem clear from this analysis. First, rents of converted units are in general lower than rents of unconverted units. These lower rents might reflect the relatively smaller size of these units, the lack of off-street parking space, and perhaps also lower quality because of greater age. This would be true in central cities, where a substantial fraction of converted rental units are also substandard. Some part of the difference in median rents may also reflect the discounts associated with illegal conversions. This may explain, for example, why rents of suburban conversions do not reflect the effective demand of their renter occupants, who appear to have higher incomes than renters living in unchanged units. In the case of accessory conversions in suburban single-family homes, these lower rents for conversions may also reflect the practices of small owner-occupant landlords who customarily charge below market in order to keep tenants whom they consider to be good neighbors. Lower rents may also reflect a discount for services that tenants provide owners in some cases, such as gardening or babysitting. In addition, some accessory apartments are occupied by relatives of the owner-occupants who live in the primary unit. They pay a very low rent or no rent at all. This seems to occur most commonly in the suburbs, where 7.8 percent of all renters pay no cash rent for their units.

Conclusion

Since 1973 as many as 100,000 home owners a year have been converting parts of their houses into accessory apartments. Many of these were eventually merged back with their primary units. Impressionistic evidence suggests that the annual number of accessory conversions has increased in many parts of the country during the past decade and is continuing to rise in the 1980s. The National Association of Home Builders, for example, has estimated that since 1980 about 300,000 home owners a year have been converting parts of their homes into accessory apartments. Given the estimates presented in this chapter this figure is probably too high. However, even if the gross number of accessory conversions in single-family houses has risen only to 130,000 per year, this would still represent close to half of the new private unsubsidized rental apartments built each year in the United States between 1980 and 1983.

The types of home owners most likely to create accessory apartments are one-person households, childless couples, and unmarried adults. High proportions of those who install accessory apartments in their homes are either middle-aged or retired home owners. This suggests that many conversions represent adaptations of single-family dwellings to changing space needs of families over the life cycle. For one- and two-person households, both young and old, who out of habit or preference own large single-family houses, conversion appears to be a way to adapt these family-size houses to their more modest space needs and incomes.

Few accessory conversions appear to be "mother-in-law" apartments in the literal sense of the term. Very few are occupied by persons over 65. Renters living in them are not different from the renter population as a whole. A slightly greater proportion in accessory conversions do live rent-free than is true of renters generally; some of them may be occupying accessory units intended by their owners to provide separate accommodations for friends or relatives. Finally, although many conversions in central cities are in poor condition, suburban conversions appear to be of average quality, and surprisingly few are substandard.

Notes

1. M.H. Naigles, "Housing and the Increase in Population," Serial No. 1421, U.S. Department of Labor (Washington, D.C.: United States G.P.O., 1942).
2. Leo C. Grebler, David M. Blank and Louis Winnick, *Capital Formation in Residential Real Estate, Trends and Prospects*, National Bureau of Economic Research (Princeton, NJ: Princeton University Press, 1956), Appendix D., 373.
3. U.S. Bureau of the Census, 1960 *Census of Housing, Components of Inventory*, Vol. 4, Appendix A. Primary sampling units (PSU)—a county, a group of counties, or a Standard Metropolitan Statistical Area (SMSA) were classified into 357 strata based on population size. From each stratum, one PSU each was selected. Then entire sample consisted of 701 counties and independent cities with coverage in each of the 50 states and the District of Columbia. Within each sample PSU, a sample of housing units was selected from two sources: units enumerated in the 1950 Census in order to determine the disposition of the 1950 inventory, and a sample of units enumerated in the 1960 Census that had been built or added to the housing inventory since 1950.
4. Grebler, Blank and Winnick, *ibid.*, 276.
5. According to impressionistic accounts from the 1930s, widespread business failures produced high vacancy rates along commercial strips. Many vacant storefronts were converted to residential use. Few residential buildings were converted to commercial use during the Depression. In addition, a declining birth rate and falling incomes reduced household sizes and consequently the demand for large dwellings. This meant fewer mergers. The researches of Benjamin Lipstein of the BLS after World War II in Baltimore City and County and the Norfolk-Portsmouth Metropolitan Area showed that mergers and conversions to nonresidential use even during the 1940s when both birth rates and incomes were on the rise accounted for less than a 10 percent difference between gross and net conversions as estimated by the Real Property Survey. Benjamin Lipstein, "How Important are Conversions in the Current Housing Scene," *Housing Research*, 3 (1950): 1-14.
6. All additions other than new construction are divided into "residential conversions" (conversions from fewer to more units) and "other additions." The former includes both structural and nonstructural conversions. "Other additions" includes a little bit of everything: conversions to residential use of nonresidential structures and group quarters, and accessory structures (basements, detached garages, sheds, etc.) adjacent to residential structures. Lumped into this category also are mobile homes or houses moved into a locality and placed on a formerly vacant site. "Other additions" also includes a small number of dilapidated dwellings intended for demolition that were rehabilitated and additions that could not be accounted for. See 1980 *Census of Housing, Components of Inventory Change*, Vol. 4, Appendix B.
7. Duane McGough, "Additions to the Housing Supply by Means Other Than New Construction" (Washington, D.C.: U.S. Department of Housing and Urban Development, Office of Policy Development and Research, 1982). Unpublished report.
8. Telephone interview with Stuart Kaufman, Housing Division, United States Bureau of the Census, August 10, 1983.
9. Interview with Stuart Kaufmann, Housing Division, U.S. Bureau of the Census, July 15, 1983.
10. Patrick Hare, with Susan Conner and Dwight Merrian, *Accessory Apartments: Using Surplus Space in Single Family Houses*, Planning Advisory Service Report No. 365 (Chicago, IL: American Planning Association, 1982), 2.
11. Thomas Thibodeau, "Estimating Dwelling Conversions During the 1970s" (Washington D.C.: The Urban Institute, 1981). Unpublished paper. These estimates, including those of McGough's cited earlier, were based on a residual analysis of additions and losses estimated from the Annual Housing Survey for 1973 to 1980. The residual represents the number of housing units added to the stock that remained after factoring out new construction, mobile home deliveries, and removals from the estimated net change in the inventory from 1973 to 1980. These residual addi-

tions contain conversions, but they also include sampling, response, and other errors, as well as a large number of existing mobile homes that were moved onto new sites.

The research of Weicher, Yap, and Jones demonstrates how poor a measure of conversion activity is the Annual Housing Survey residual additions. These researchers attempted to model the conversion submarket as part of an effort to forecast metropolitan housing demand for the 1980s and 1990s. The model used SMSAs as the unit of analysis. Only two variables in the conversion model were statistically significant. One of them—the rate of growth of nonhusband-wife households—had a negative rather than a positive sign. This seems implausible unless one considers that AHS residual additions contain large numbers of mobile homes moved into vacant sites. The other—median household income—had a negative sign as expected. John C. Weicher, Lorene Yap, and Mary S. Jones, *Metropolitan Housing Needs for the 1980s* (Washington, D.C.. The Urban Institute, 1982), 42-45.

12. Mark Gottdiener, *Planned Sprawl, Private and Public Interest in Suburbia* (Beverly Hills, CA: Sage Publications, 1977), 36-37. Sam Hall Kaplan, *The Dream Deferred: People Politics and Planning in Suburbia* (New York: Seabury Press, 1976), 212. Findings of the Tri-Regional Planning Commission are summarized in an article by Phyllis Ann Santry, "Legalizing Single Family Conversions," *Planning 1981: Proceedings of the National Planning Conference* (Washington, D.C.: American Planning Association, 1982), 167-78.

13. Press Release, Washington, D.C., November 12, 1983.

14. U.S. Department of Commerce, "Market Absorption of Apartments," *Current Housing Reports*, Third Quarter 1982 (H-130-82-Q3), Second Quarter 1984 (H-130-84-Q?).

15. The CINCH surveys utilize the standard Bureau of Census definition of a room: " . . . whole rooms used for living purposes, such as living rooms, dining rooms, bedrooms, kitchens, finished attics or finished basement rooms, recreation rooms, permanently enclosed porches that are suitable for year-round use, and . . . lodger's rooms." Also included are rooms "used for offices by a person living in the unit." United States Bureau of the Census, 1980 *Census of Housing, Components of Inventory Change*, Vol. 4, Part 1, Appendix B, 6.

16. The census also employs a broad definition of bedrooms, which includes guest rooms or other rooms used mainly, though infrequently, for purposes of sleeping. "The number of bedrooms in a housing unit is the count of rooms used mainly for sleeping, even if also used for other purposes. Rooms reserved for sleeping, such as guest rooms, even though used infrequently, are counted as bedrooms." United States Bureau of the Census, 1980 *Census of Housing, Components of Inventory Change*, Vol. 4, Part 1, Appendix B, 7.

17. United States Bureau of the Census, 1980 *Census of Housing, Components of Inventory Change*, Vol. 4, Appendix B, 4.

18. See also Patrick Hare, "Accessory Apartments: A New Housing Option for the Elderly Homeowner" (Washington, D.C.: Center for the Study of Retirement and Aging of the Catholic University of America, 1982). Unpublished. See also, Metropolitan Washington Council of Governments, *Accessory Apartments: A Local Housing Alternative*, Housing Technical Report No. 1981-4, 1981, 13.

19. A survey of registered accessory apartments in San Anselmo found that only 1 percent of occupants were 62 years or older. A Lincoln, Massachusetts survey found that 85 percent of the occupants of accessory apartments were between 21 and 40 years old. Patrick Hare's survey (supra note 18) also found a very low incidence of seniors among renters of accessory apartments. See also the following surveys: Lisa Burglin, "Survey of Registered Second Units" (San Anselmo, CA: San Anselmo County Planning Department, 1982). Town of Lincoln, Massachusetts, "Survey of Illegal Units," 1978. Unpublished.

20. Benjamin Lipstein, "How Important are Conversions in the Current Housing Scene," *Housing Research*, 3 (1950): 1-14.

21. A.M. Woodruff, "Conversion of One-Family Houses to Multifamily Use," *Housing Research*, 7 (1954): 11-19.

22. Some of the differences between observed difference between median rents and incomes may be the result of regional composition effects when conversions are concentrated in one or two locations. The 1980 CINCH report does not provide estimates of components of inventory change for individual metropolitan areas. The 1960 and 1970 reports did so but only for 14 SMSAs. If this information were available for a sufficient number of SMSAs one could model median conversion rents and isolate effects that are due solely to local market effects of those localities that have higher conversion rates than others.

3

Space Standards and Social Change

Accessory apartment conversions in single-family homes have received public attention because many local government officials and public-interest organizations see them as a cheap and simple way for the public sector to respond to the tremendous demand that is now pressing on the housing market.[1] Household formations are at an all-time high, largely because members of the postwar "baby-boom" birth cohort are now passing through that stage of the life cycle when adults normally establish households. Although net household formation is expected to level off during the 1980s it will remain above one million per year for most of the decade.

The interest in accessory apartments and other types of conversions also reflects a fundamental change in the nature of housing problems in our society. Over the past forty years we have reduced substandard housing in the country to a negligible amount. In 1940 half of all dwellings in the United States lacked some or all plumbing and about 10 percent were severely overcrowded (more than 1.5 persons per room). By 1980 less than 1 percent of all occupied housing units were overcrowded and only 2.4 percent were deficient in plumbing. At the same time per capita space consumption as measured by the number of rooms per person rose from 1.45 to 1950 to 2.06 in 1980—an increase of 42.7 percent. More than half of all American households occupy housing today at a rate in excess of two rooms or more per person.

Although Americans now enjoy a very high standard of housing, our ability to pay for it has deteriorated because the cost of land, construction, and mortgage financing have increased faster than household incomes. Many persons who enter the market to purchase a home or rent an apartment today must pay a substantially greater portion of their income to achieve the same standard of housing that consumers in previous decades could obtain with a much smaller relative expenditure. For most people today the "affordability" crisis in housing does not mean that they cannot obtain a "decent home"; it means that they cannot afford the standard of housing consumption to which they aspire and which recent generations widely enjoyed. And in many respects this standard of aspiration is still geared to the space needs of the bigger families of an earlier era.

It will take at least a decade for these relatively greater housing expense burdens to affect consumption standards in the owner-occupied sector, because many home owners are still able to pay for their housing with low-interest, fixed-payment, pre-inflation mortgages. In rental housing the change will occur more rapidly. It is true that rents have lagged far behind the rate of inflation during the past ten years; but this situation will not last much longer. Both rents and renters' incomes have also lagged behind construction costs, which have risen faster than the rate of inflation. As net household formation continues to press upon scarce supply in the existing inventory, rents are bound to catch up with development costs. Renters are also more mobile, and as apartments turn over, landlords have the opportunity to raise the rent on their units to market levels.

Anthony Downs has projected a shortfall in rental housing production during the 1980s of 1.38 million units.[2] He projects an annual demand for 612,000 additional units throughout the decade. That would be enough units to meet not only a projected average annual net increase in renter households of 425,000, but also 165,000 units a year for replacement and 22,000 units a year for vacancies. Downs has forecast however that annual production of rental housing will likely average no more than about 475,000 units. This is slightly more than the annual net increase in renter households expected for the decade and allows no replacement of units lost by demolition and conversion to other uses. The resulting shortfall will probably force real rents to rise. The short-run effect will be a tight market for rental apartments and the long-run effect a greater rent burden.

Part of the solution to the affordability problem may lie in finding ways to produce dwellings that are smaller and cheaper but nevertheless satisfying places in which to live. One of the main arguments of this book is that we may be able to accomplish this, and also meet a substantial segment of our housing needs for at least the next decade, by making more intensive use of existing residential and nonresidential structures. Higher relative land and financing costs will place a premium on making better use of the existing housing inventory. To some extent, we began such a reorientation in national housing policy during the 1970s, when the federal government abandoned slum clearance programs and authorized more spending on housing rehabilitation and conservation efforts both in older cities and in suburbs. In practice, this policy has been limited to efforts at improving maintenance in the older portions of the stock and upgrading vacant and abandoned units that might otherwise be demolished. In the future, however, both local and national housing policy should place more emphasis on conversion and adaptive reuse. The flight of industry from the central cities and the decline of the school-age population has left many sections of the country with schools, warehouses, and old factories that are eminently suitable for residential reuse. We also have a good deal of existing housing with surplus space that can be recy-

EXHIBIT 3.1
Size of New Homes, United States, 1950–1980
Panel A
Percentage Distribution of New Homes by Number of Bedrooms

Year	2 Bedrooms or Less	3 Bedrooms	4 Bedrooms or More	Total
1956	21.0	71.0	8.0	100.0
1966	13.0	63.0	24.0	100.0
1971	13.0	62.0	25.0	100.0
1973–80	17.5	59.0	23.5	100.0
1970–73*	30.1	53.4	16.5	100.0
1973–80*	22.5	57.0	20.5	100.0

*Includes mobile homes.

Panel B
New Homes By Number of Rooms, 1950–1980

Number of Rooms	1950–1960 (1,000s)	Percent	1960–1970 (1,000s)	Percent	1973–1980 (1,000s)	Percent
1–2	171.4	1.67	108.0	1.03	106.3	0.85
3–4	2,210.4	21.59	1,825.0	17.42	1,710.1	13.61
5–6	6,658.8	65.03	5,464.0	52.16	6,293.5	50.07
7+	1,199.3	11.71	3,079.0	29.39	4,458.0	35.47
Total	10,239.9	100.0	10,476.0	100.0	12,568.0	100.0

Sources: Abraham Goldblatt, "Profile of New One-Family Homes," *Construction Review*. 19:2 (February 1973), 4-8. United States Department of Housing and Urban Development, *Housing Surveys, Part 1: Occupants of New Housing Units*. Washington, D.C.: United States Government Printing Office, 1969, 1–64. United States Bureau of the Census and United States Department of Housing and Urban Development, *Annual Housing Survey*, 1973. United States Bureau of the Census, 1980 *Census of Housing, Components of Inventory Change*, Vol. 4, Part 1.

cled in a similar fashion. By "surplus space" I mean space that is in excess of the occupants' actual needs, when measured by the most generous standards of space consumption.

There are several reasons for this phenomenon. One is the large size of the average American home. Since 1960, 80 percent of all new homes built in the United States contained three bedrooms or more and about 25 percent had four bedrooms or more. During the 1970s this trend abated slightly, as the share of new construction represented by smaller homes increased in response to the entry of large numbers of first-time home buyers into the new home market (see Exhibit 3.1). If size is measured in terms of rooms per house instead of bedrooms per house, the increase in average space consumption among home owners appears even greater. During the 1960s, houses of seven rooms or more accounted for about 29 percent of all new homes; between 1973 and 1980, 35 percent had seven rooms or more. In addition, during the 1960s and 1970s, home owners

EXHIBIT 3.2
Owner-Occupied Dwellings by
Number of Rooms, 1950, 1980

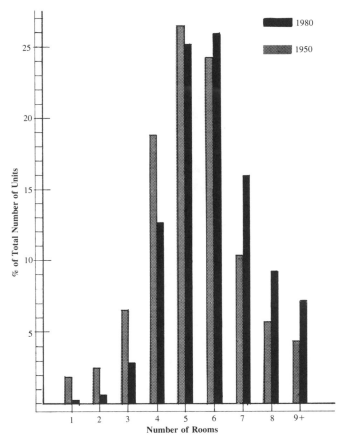

Source: Winnich & Shilling, *American Housing and Its Use*, New York: Columbia University Press, 1957, Appendix A, 140; and 1980 *Census of Housing, Components of Inventory Change*, vol. 4.

added another 1.1 million units to the inventory of houses with seven rooms or more by expanding 5- and 6-room dwellings.

Thus, as a result of upgrading and new construction, the median size of the stock of owner-occupied residences rose considerably during the past three decades. The number of houses with seven rooms or more increased almost twice as fast as the stock of owner-occupied housing in general. Whereas only 20.3 percent of all owner-occupied dwellings had seven rooms or more in 1950, by 1980, 32.5 percent did (see Exhibit 3.2).

At the same time large houses were being built, the fertility rate began dropping, family-size preferences were reduced, and average household size fell. The result has been a widespread increase in the average number of rooms per person and a sharp increase in the proportion of American home owners who occupy houses containing surplus space. By itself, this achievement would constitute economic progress rather than a social problem. People will ordinarily consume as much space as they can afford, and nobody would argue that there is anything inherently wrong with two people living in a 3000 square-foot house. It is however a problem in one sense; it is not the best utilization of that space when many other persons are having great difficulty obtaining adequate shelter. This surplus space also presents an opportunity to address the housing needs of these other persons if ways could be found to recycle some of it into additional dwellings.

Population Structure and Housing Demand

The growing prevalence of smaller households and fewer children per household reflects the emergence of a new type of family and population structure. By the term *population structure* I refer to the actual social divison of the population into separate households, that is, its state or degree of differentiation with respect to sizes and types of households. *Population structure* is not a demographic concept, and should not be confused with *population composition*, which refers to the distribution of the population according to its age, sex, and marital status characteristics.

The division of the population into households is the product of social beliefs about groupings of people who ought or ought not to share the same roof and the customs based on these beliefs. The housing commodity in this sense is not simply shelter or a pure service flow as economists like to conceive of it; it also represents a means by which people establish private households and achieve *separateness* from others. Hence, the demand for housing is not just a demand for shelter, but also a demand for privacy and thereby for separate dwelling units. The definition of the housing commodity as a service flow is a conceptual device that provides a way to distinguish analytically between the investment and consumption aspects of housing and to specify the relationship between the quality of housing and its price. If housing services (space for sleeping, food preparation, and relaxation) were consumed as pure flows, as many models suggest, then we could satisfy the demand for housing by building dormitories rather than single family homes, or apartments. In such a world, the rich would live in luxurious dormitories while the poor would crowd together in barracks.

The differentiation of population structure can be measured in several ways: (1) by the average propensity for adults to form households—the headship rate, (2) by the low degree of complexity or jointness of household composition—the number of adults per household, and (3) by the distribution of households by type—i.e., family, non-family, and primary individual households. The headship rate (the proportion of adults who are household heads) is the inverse of the indicator of household complexity (the average number of adults per household). Household complexity or jointness refers to the propensity of adults to live to-

EXHIBIT 3.3
Average Household Size,
United States, 1970-1980

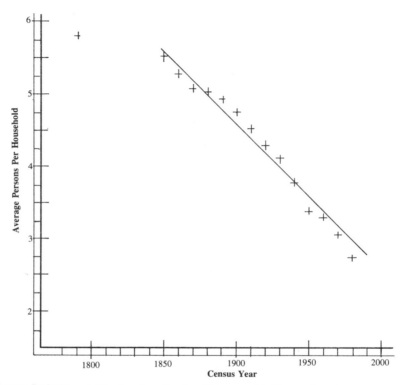

Source: Rudy Seward, *The American Family, A Demographic History*, Beverly Hills, CA: Sage Publications; and U.S. Bureau of the Census, *Census of Population*, 1950-1980.

gether. Complex households are thought of primarily as "extended families." This can take many forms: two or more related married couples living together, unmarried relatives or unmarried adult children residing with a married couple, or an unmarried household head living with brothers, sisters, or other relatives. The notion also extends to households that contain servants, boarders, or lodgers who may be unrelated to the household head.

Population structure becomes more differentiated when the average number of adults per household declines, headship rates rise, and average household size falls. Generally this process of change involves the splitting up of complex households, or "undoubling," as it is sometimes called. This can occur in numerous ways. The most common form of undoubling is the departure of grown children from the home of their parents in order to establish their own households. A second form of differentiation occurs when adults split off from households headed by other adults to form separate households. In the past this usually

EXHIBIT 3.4
Distribution of Households by Size, United States, 1790–1980
(percentages)

Year	Household Sizes					Average Household Size
	1	2	3	4	5+	
1790*	3.7	7.8	11.7	13.8	62.9	5.8
1900	5.1	15.0	17.6	16.9	45.5	4.8
1950	9.3	28.1	22.6	17.8	20.0	3.4
1960	13.1	27.8	18.9	17.7	22.6	3.3
1970	17.6	29.6	17.3	15.8	21.1	3.1
1980	22.7	31.4	17.5	15.7	12.8	2.8
Change						
1900–1950	4.2	13.1	5.0	0.9	−25.5	
1950–1980	13.4	3.3	−5.1	−2.1	−7.2	

*Includes "free" population only.

Source: Conrad and Irene Taeuber, *People of the United States in the Twentieth Century: A Census Monograph*. Washington D.C.: U.S. Government Printing Office, 1971. U.S. Bureau of the Census, *Current Population Reports*, Series P-20, No. 371 and earlier reports.

involved the splitting off of a relative or non-kin who had been living with a married couple; more recently, undoubling has occurred as the result of the breaking up of nuclear families through divorce. In either case, the average number of children per household will fall as more adults live apart from children.

Let us examine this relationship between population structure and household size more closely before we turn to the implications of housing demand and consumption.

The Historic Decline in Average Household Size

The most important trend affecting the way we use housing today in the United States is the long-term decline in average household size. Although average household size has been declining steadily since 1850, it fell almost twice as fast during the twentieth century than it did in the nineteenth century. Between 1950 and 1980, the persons per household ratio declined by an average of 8.4 percent per decade, compared to 6.8 percent between 1900 and 1950, and 3.1 percent between 1850 and 1900. During the 1970s the ratio declined 11.6 percent. This was the largest percentage drop in average household size for any decade in American history since population statistics have been kept.[3]

The Rise of the Empty Nester

The reasons for this decline in average household size are quite complex. Exhibit 3.4, which compares the distribution of household sizes over time, sug-

EXHIBIT 3.5

Median Age of Once-Married (Never Divorced) Mothers at Selected Stages of the Family Life Cycle and Estimated Number of Years Between Selected Events for Women Born 1880–1959, by Decade of Birth

	Year of Birth							
	1880 to 1889	1890 to 1899	1900 to 1909	1910 to 1919	1920 to 1929	1930 to 1939*	1940 to 1949*	1950 to 1959*
Age at:								
First marriage	21.4	21.2	21.2	21.8	21.2	20.4	20.3	21.2
Birth of 1st child	23.0	22.9	23.4	24.1	23.4	22.0	21.8	22.7
Birth of last child	31.9	32.0	31.2	32.1	31.5	29.3	25.7	23.9
End of childrearing	—	—	49.2	50.1	49.5	47.3	43.7	41.9
Marriage of last child	55.4	54.8	53.0	53.2	53.2	53.6	52.7	52.3
Death of spouse	57.0	59.6	62.3	63.7	64.4	65.1	65.2	65.7
Average no. of children								
per woman	3.3	3.0	2.8	2.9	3.1	3.2	2.3	1.5
Difference between events (in years):								
A. Marriage and birth								
of 1st child	1.6	1.7	2.2	2.3	2.2	1.6	1.5	1.5
B. Marriage and birth								
of last child	10.5	10.8	10.0	10.3	10.3	8.9	5.4	2.7
C. Birth of 1st child								
and birth of last	8.9	9.1	7.8	8.0	8.1	7.3	3.9	1.2
D. Birth of 1st child and								
end of childrearing	—	—	25.8	26.0	26.1	25.3	21.9	19.2
E. Marriage of last child								
and death of spouse	1.6	4.8	9.3	10.5	11.2	11.5	12.5	13.4
Total married								
years without								
children at home (A + E)	3.2	6.5	11.5	12.8	13.4	13.1	14.0	14.9
Percent of married years without								
children at home	8.9	16.9	27.9	30.6	31.0	29.3	31.2	33.5

*Estimates for the cohorts from the 1930s to the 1950s are based on partial marriage and fertility experience. The timing of the later phases of the life cycle for these groups was extrapolated from life expectancy and marriage statistics.

Sources: Paul Glick and Robert Parke, Jr., "New Approaches in Studying the Life Cycle of the Family," *Demography*, 2 (1965): 187–202, table 1. Paul Glick, "Updating the Life Cycle of the Family," *Journal of Marriage and the Family*, 39 (February 1977): 5–13, table 1. Arthur J. Norton, "The Influence of Divorce on Traditional Life Cycle Measures," *Journal of Marriage and the Family*, 42 (February 1980): 63–69, table 1.

gests that two different processes have been at work. First, from 1900 to 1950, the decline in average household size was primarily caused by a decline in the number of households with five persons or more. Married couples were having fewer children than their counterparts in earlier generations: between 1920 and 1940, the total fertility rate dropped from 3,248 children born per 1,000 women to 2,235 per 1,000—a decline of slightly more than 31 percent.[4] (The total fertil-

EXHIBIT 3.6
Changes in Mean Family Size, Mean Members Less Than 18 Years, and Mean Members 18 Years and Older, United States, 1948–1978

	Change in Mean Family Size	Change in Mean Members Less than 18	Change in Mean Members over 18
1948–1978			
Married couple	−.26	−.18	−.08
Female head	−.10	+.41	−.51
Other male head	−.48	+.08	−.56
1948–1958			
Married couple	+.06	+.17	−.11
Female head	−.02	+.20	−.22
Other male head	−.14	+.13	−.27
1958–1968			
Married couple	.00	.00	.00
Female head	+.18	+.31	−.13
Other male head	−.10	+.08	−.18
1968–1978			
Married couple	−.32	−.35	+.03
Female head	−.26	−.10	−.16
Other male head	−.24	−.13	−.11

Source: Judith Trea, "Postwar Trends in Family Size." *Demography,* 18 (1981): 326.

ity rate is the number of children that 1000 women would have in their lifetime on average, assuming they bear children at each age at the rate prevailing in the specified year.)

Second, there was a rapid growth of households with two persons because married couples were living together longer after their children were grown. In the 19th century married couples survived together on the average less than a year after the last child had left home. By 1920 increased life-expectancy led to the appearance of the "empty nester" phenomenon as we know it today: couples could expect to spend about twelve years together between the departure of their last born and the death of one spouse.[5] Since then life expectancy has continued to increase, and the time between the birth of the first and the last child has declined from eight to two years, as births have been spaced closer together and the average number of children born per woman has fallen (see Exhibit 3.5). Couples entering marriage during the years since the 1950s could expect to spend an average of almost fifteen years, or slightly more than a third of their married life, alone together without any children in the home.

These trends during the first half of the twentieth century led to an increase in the ratio of adults to children in American households and accelerated the aging of the population. Between 1920 and 1950 the median age of the United States population rose from 25.3 to 30.2 years, and the proportion of adults over 55 years of age rose from 10.8 percent to 17.0 percent of the population. Moreover, Louis Winnick and Ned Shilling have shown that five-sixths of the total fall in average household size between 1900 and 1950 was attributed to population aging; the remaining one-sixth was accounted for by increases in age-specific headship rates.[6]

The Rise of the One-Person Household

The decline in average household size after 1950 has altogether different causes. From Exhibit 3.4 we can see that falling household size reflects an increase in both the number and proportion of one-person households in the population. The growth of these households has occurred as more young unmarried persons between 20 and 29 years of age, more never-married persons over 30 years, as well as more adults who have been divorced, separated, or widowed have been able to live by themselves apart from families and relatives.[7] With the exception of elderly widows, divorced and unattached persons prior to 1950 represented a relatively small part of the population, and few of them ever established households of their own. Most lived with parents or other relatives, or as boarders with non-kin.[8] Many who had no kin lived in temporary quarters and boarding houses.[9] The YMCA and YWCA hotels developed by early twentieth-century social reformers were an attempt to provide standard quality housing for this sector of the population, which for various reasons was not being served by the market.[10] Since the 1950s unmarried or previously married adults have split off from families headed by a married couple or other relative and established their own households. During the 1970s children who grew up and left the homes of their parents became an additional source of one-person households.

This process is illustrated in Exhibit 3.6, which divides total changes in average household size into changes in the average number of adults per household and the average number of children eighteen years or under per household by type of family, for ten-year intervals from 1948 to 1978.

From 1948 to 1958, the average size of married-couple and female-headed households changed little. Although the average number of children per household increased, a substantial amount of undoubling took place, and this lowered the average number of adults per married-couple family. At the same time that the "baby boom" increased family size, the splitting off of single adults from families worked in the other direction. The net effect was a slight increase in average family size for married couples. For female-headed and male-headed families with no spouse present, the splitting off of adult members was even more substantial and their average size declined also. Between 1958 and 1968, the size of married-couple families—which had already been pared down by undoubling—remained stable, and the other family types continued to lose adult members. The undoubling of male-headed families with no spouse present continued at a fairly high rate.

After 1968 a major shift in patterns occurred. While female- and male-headed households with no spouse present continued to lose adult members, the mean number of children declined for all family types. This reflected the coming of age of the postwar baby-boom cohort. For married couples, the change was especially dramatic—they became, on the average, about one-third of a person smaller because of a drop in the mean number of children. The small increase in the mean number of adults per husband-wife family probably occurred because some children remained living with their parents into their early twenties.

The fall in average household size accelerated after 1968 because of a sharp drop in female fertility and an increased rate of undoubling among adults owing to rising divorce rates.[11] Divorce and marital separation alone accounted for 28 percent of the increase in non-family households during the 1970s.[12] Approximately one out of ten married persons now become divorced every year. Glick and Norton have estimated that 38 percent of all first marriages now end in divorce and 40 percent of all marriages since the 1960s will eventually end in divorce.[13] One scholar has estimated that close to half of all marriages involving couples born since 1940 will end in divorce.[14]

Attenuation of the Nuclear Family

Decreasing average household size and increasing headship rates have been widely attributed to economic affluence; many studies have demonstrated that headship rates increase when real income does.[15] However, although these studies attribute the rising headship rates of unmarried persons to tremendous gains in real income since 1950, they fail to explain why headship rates in the United States changed very little among the unmarried before 1950. In fact, doubling-up among couples and singles actually increased during the decades before 1950, even though real per capita disposable income rose steadily throughout most of the first half of the twentieth century. Those who lived alone rarely did so by choice. The majority of them were women, mostly poor widows, often with no family nearby or with children living great distances away.[16]

Some evidence suggests that the underlying relationship between income and the propensity of individuals to establish separate households probably takes the form of an S-shaped curve.[17] This means that there is an income threshold for single persons above which it becomes relatively easy to establish a household, but below which doing so is prohibitive. Theoretically speaking, this income threshold must be enough so that the individual can afford to make rent payments, pay the cost of utilities, and meet the overhead and labor costs associated with maintaining a separate household. Overhead costs include the cost of domestic capital: furniture, dishware, kitchen equipment, appliances, and the like.[18]

The tremendous increase in real per capita income that began in 1950 and continued throughout the entire postwar era enabled a large number of people to pass that income-cost threshold point at which living alone is economically feasible.[19]

EXHIBIT 3.7
Distribution of Households by Household Types, United States, 1940–1983
(in percentages)

Household Types	Year								
	1940	1950	1955	1960	1965	1970	1975	1980	1983
Families	90.1	89.2	87.2	85.0	83.3	81.2	78.1	73.7	73.2
Married couples	76.0	78.2	75.7	74.3	72.6	70.5	66.0	60.8	59.5
Male head	4.3	2.7	2.8	2.3	2.0	1.9	2.1	2.1	2.4
Female head	9.8	8.3	8.7	8.4	8.7	8.7	10.0	10.8	11.3
Non-families	9.9	10.8	12.8	15.0	16.7	20.0	21.9	27.3	26.8
Male head	4.6	3.8	4.3	5.1	5.7	6.9	8.3	11.5	11.3
Female head	5.3	7.0	8.9	9.8	11.0	13.0	13.6	15.8	15.5
Total	100.0	100.0	100.0	100.0	100.0	100.0	100.0	100.0	100.0
Percent living alone	7.7	9.1	10.9	13.1	15.0	17.1	19.6	22.7	22.9
Unrelated individuals per household	.166	.101	.078	.061	.048	.048	.050	.064	.066
Unrelated individuals other than head per non-family household	1.683	.937	.610	.405	.285	.240	.228	.236	.247

Source: U.S. Bureau of the Census, *Current Population Reports: Households, Families, Marital Status, and Living Arrangements.* Series P-20, No. 382, July 1983.

This in turn accelerated a fundamental change in the pattern of residential living arrangements—what Beresford and Rivlin have called a "basic shift in tastes . . . after which people tend to use their rising incomes to purchase additional privacy."[20]

Rising headship rates since 1950 reflect a fundamental change in social values and in the structure of the family as an institution. I call this change *the attenuation of the nuclear family system.* To become "attenuated" means to become "weakened" or "lessened" in substance. This term does not imply the destruction or disappearance of the nuclear family (a married couple with children), but rather signifies a basic fact about American society today: namely that *more people* spend *greater parts of their lives* residing by themselves or in other arrangements outside of "traditional" nuclear families than was true for generations in the past. More people live physically apart from their families, although family and kin continue to be important in their lives, particularly during times of personal crisis.[21] The attenuation process has three defining characteristics:

1. Lower female fertility and an increased rate of participation by women in the labor force, in the aggregate as well as over the life cycle.
2. Increased age segregation expressed in the divergence of lifestyle between generations and the weakening of family and kinship ties across generations.
3. A strong tendency toward marital instability, which has caused the family experience for many individuals to become less continuous over the life cycle.

No moral judgment is being made here about whether this change is for the better or the worse.

As our population structure becomes more diverse, and other household types become more numerous, the nuclear family will no longer be the dominant form of householding in our society that it once was. Since 1950 married-couple families have declined from 78.2 percent of all households to 60.8 percent in 1980 (see Exhibit 3.7). By contrast, "non-families" have risen from 10.8 percent of all households to 27.3 percent. Most "non-families" consist of persons who live alone, or "primary individuals": since 1950 they increased from 10.9 percent to 22.7 percent of all households. As this table shows, the preference for living alone has affected large numbers of individuals who, prior to 1950, lived in shared housing arrangements. The number of these "secondary individuals" per household declined from .166 in 1940 to .048 in 1970; from 1970 onwards the ratio has risen slightly, as has the number per non-family household, which also fell after 1940.[22]

The attenuation of the family system also means that we are now much less a nation of families and households with children. While 41.5 percent of all households were married couples with children in 1960, only 31.4 percent were by 1975.[23] This downward trend in families and households with children will probably not be reversed during the 1980s, even though the number of married

EXHIBIT 3.8
Median Rooms and Rooms
Per Person by Size of Household,
Renters and Owners, United States, 1970

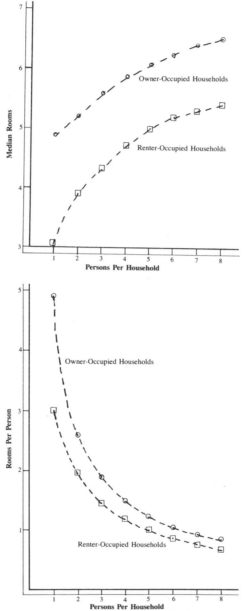

Source: U.S. Bureau of the Census, *1970 Census of Housing, Space Utilization of the Inventory,*
vol. 2.

couples with children is expected to increase as the baby-boom generation enters its peak childbearing years. George Masnick and Jo Bane of the Harvard–M.I.T. Joint Center for Urban Studies, for example, have projected that during the 1980s the number of married couples with children will increase on net by about 3.47 million.[24] The growth in other types of households at the same time should continue to outpace that of married couples. Masnick and Bane project that by 1990 married couples will represent about 55 percent of all households, and those with children under 15 slightly more than a quarter of all households.[25]

The Implications for Housing Consumption and Demand

These changes in family structure and householding arrangements have had two important impacts on housing demand. First, the attenuation of the nuclear family system has shifted the composition of market demand away from married couples toward non-family and one-person households. Second, increased headship rates have caused an increase in the aggregate demand for housing services and capital stock, not only in terms of a demand for more separate dwelling units but also in terms of greater per capita consumption of housing services and stock. Per capita space consumption will invariably rise as average household size falls, even when the total housing stock does not increase. This occurs because average dwelling size tends to fall more slowly than average household size.

The graph in Exhibit 3.8 shows how the median dwelling size (number of rooms per dwelling) and per capita space consumption (rooms per person) behave as household size increases or falls. Because it is difficult to obtain data on the square footage of living area in occupied dwelling units, housing analysts have resorted to measuring space consumption by the number of rooms per person; its inverse, the persons-per-room ratio (PPRR), is an indicator of the intensity of occupancy. This graph shows that, as household size declines, so does the number of rooms per dwelling; however, the number of rooms falls more slowly so that the number of rooms per person increases at an accelerating rate. The acceleration in rooms per person is also much greater for home owners than for renters.

This non-linear relationship between household size and space utilization was first analyzed systematically by Louis Winnick in his 1957 study, *American Housing and Its Use*.[26] Winnick found that the relationship held true not only cross-sectionally, but also as the average household size of the population changes over time. Winnick attributed the relationship to three factors: (1) the need on the part of large households to devote more of their budgets to food and clothing and to less housing; (2) the more efficient utilization by large households of ''overhead'' rooms (dining areas, circulation areas, living rooms, bathrooms, utility rooms, and the like); and (3) the greater ''inertia and immobility'' of home owners.

EXHIBIT 3.9
Minimum Space Required for Basic Household Activities
by Number of Persons in Household

Panel A:
Area per Person
(in square feet)

	Number of Persons					
Household Activity	**1**	**2**	**3**	**4**	**5**	**6**
Total area per person	380.0	382.5	329.7	289.8	284.0	258.3
Sleeping & dressing	74.0	74.0	74.0	74.0	74.0	74.0
Personal hygiene	35.0	17.5	11.7	8.8	14.0	11.7
Food preparation	8.0	38.0	32.3	24.3	23.6	19.7
Food service & dining	53.0	35.0	30.3	26.3	23.8	24.3
Recreation	125.0	82.0	73.7	71.5	71.4	63.8
Entertaining	17.0	8.5	11.3	8.5	10.2	8.5
Housekeeping	48.0	45.5	36.7	31.8	29.2	24.8
Care of infant or ill	0	62.0	41.3	31.0	24.8	20.7
Circulation	20.0	10.0	11.7	8.8	9.0	7.5
Operation of utilities	0	10.0	6.7	5.0	4.0	3.3

Panel B:
Percentage Distribution of Space

	Number of Persons					
Household Activity	**1**	**2**	**3**	**4**	**5**	**6**
Total	100.0	100.0	100.0	100.0	100.0	100.0
Sleeping & dressing	19.5	19.3	22.4	25.5	26.1	28.6
Personal hygiene	9.2	4.6	3.5	3.0	4.9	4.5
Food preparation	2.1	9.9	9.8	8.4	8.3	7.6
Food service & dining	13.9	9.2	9.2	9.1	8.4	9.4
Recreation	32.9	21.4	22.3	24.7	25.1	24.7
Entertaining	4.5	2.2	3.4	2.9	3.6	3.3
Housekeeping	12.6	11.9	11.1	11.0	10.3	9.6
Care of infant or ill	0	16.2	12.5	10.7	8.7	8.0
Circulation	5.3	2.6	3.5	3.0	3.2	2.9
Operation of utilities	0	2.6	2.0	1.7	1.4	1.3

Source: American Public Health Association. *Planning the Home for Occupancy.* Chicago, IL: Public Administration Service, 1950, p. 15.

Family Budgets, Family Size, and Space Consumption

A number of famous budget studies have confirmed Winnick's hypothesis about the effects of this first factor on residential space utilization.[27] Money income does not rise proportionately with household size because additional family members, particularly children, make little, if any, contribution to family income. As a result, as family size increases, expenses for clothing and food increase faster than income; this has been demonstrated by studies of equivalence scales.[28] Because less of their income must be devoted to expenses for children, smaller households will be able to spend more on housing and therefore consume more space per person than larger families.[29]

This assertion, however, is subject to an important qualification. In housing consumption decisions, people make tradeoffs between different housing attributes. Growing families with fixed incomes can maintain their space standards by trading off other aspects of the housing commodity, such as physical condition, amenities, or location, for additional space. This may mean moving to a dwelling of similar size or to one located in a less desirable neighborhood. By the same token, as family size declines, smaller households may prefer to spend their additional income on higher quality housing rather than on a larger dwelling. Kain and Quigley's study of the St. Louis housing market has provided econometric evidence that consumers do in fact behave this way.[30]

Overhead Space as a Factor

More intensive use of overhead space by large households also explains why per capita space consumption will rise as average household size falls.[31] This effect is the product of the fact that a large amount of space in homes is overhead space, which increases little as one moves from smaller to larger dwellings. Evidence of this can be found in studies by the American Public Health Association (APHA) on space standards during the late 1940s. Findings from these studies were incorporated into the Federal Housing Administration's Minimum Property Standards for one- and two-family dwellings.[32] The APHA standards are displayed in two panels in Exhibit 3.9. The first shows how the area per person devoted to each household activity (in square feet) changes as family size increases; the second panel does the same in terms of the percentage of total area devoted to each activity.

These tables show that area per person increases for almost all activities as household size declines. The only exceptions are "sleeping and dressing" and perhaps "personal hygiene," where the increase in space for four to five persons is due mainly to the addition of a second bathroom. In terms of the percentage of space devoted to each activity, the only activities besides sleeping and hygiene that register any increase as the number of household members increases are recreation and the entertaining of guests; however, the response elasticities are quite low. Thus as households increase in size, the greatest demand for extra space is exerted for bedrooms and for social activity, whereas the hard core of the dwelling unit meets the additional demand through more efficient utilization and by relatively small expansion.

This technological relationship between household size and dwelling size suggests two reasons why per capita expenditure for housing should also increase as household size falls. First, smaller households necessarily consume more square footage of housing per person because of the relatively inelastic amount of overhead space in the average dwelling. Second, the overhead capital of a dwelling includes the utility core, the per-square foot cost of which exceeds that of the bedrooms and other parts of a house that are more elastic with respect to household size.

As the population structure become more differentiated, then, the demand for housing should also increase, even if no change occurs in the size or the age composition of the population. This effect will be expressed in the market not only in the form of an increased demand for separate dwellings but also in an increased aggregate demand for housing services and capital stock, and consequently in a higher price per unit of service. These two effects combined imply a higher ratio of per capita housing expenditure to per capita income as average household size declines—unless, of course, more efficient dwelling design and construction methods can be developed.

For example, if 70 percent of the population consists of 4-person families (married couples with two children) living in six-room houses, these households will consume less housing per capita than if 70 percent of the same population were singles and couples living in two-room and three-room apartments. The houses themselves will be larger in the first case, but there will be many fewer dwellings. Although the units will be smaller in the second case, the much higher ratio of rooms per person will mean that in the aggregate this population of smaller households may require about 15 to 20 percent more total rooms than the population composed mainly of four-person families.

Surplus Space

As average household size declines, the observed number of rooms per person may also increase because of "underutilization." Per capita consumption will increase in this case because people will be living in dwellings that have surplus space. There are several reasons why this occurs. First, residential space norms may change slowly and continue to reflect the space preferences that existed when households were larger. Second, market conditions or institutional arrangements may continue to permit the consumption of more space than required on the basis of household size alone and normal domestic uses.

An "underutilized" house is generally taken to mean a house designed for occupancy by more persons than currently live in it. It would be more precise to define underutilization as the occupancy of a dwelling in which there is an excess of living space—that is, more living area within and around a house than is required for normal domestic activities, and more than is required by the space consumption standards to which a household is accustomed given its income, occupation, family size, marital status, and lifestyle.

This extended definition is more difficult to use for measurement purposes, but there are good theoretical reasons for adopting it. Unlike the case of food consumption, where both nutritional science and physiology provide some kind of objective basis for determining when a person eats too much, in the case of housing it is difficult to determine what is "too much." We have a better idea about what is "too little." Indeed, the literature on space standards focuses solely on this problem of crowding and "overutilization," and on what by contrast constitutes a "minimum" standard of provision.

It is much more difficult, on the other hand, to decide when a house is "undercrowded." Some types of space, for example, are held in reserve for guests and relatives—a function that is ignored in specifications of minimum space standards. Middle-class families commonly maintain an extra bedroom, or "guest room" for visitors. The "formal" dining room is similarly used in middle-class homes only when relatives or guests are visiting, while everyday meals for family members are usually served in the kitchen or a "breakfast nook." Likewise, the den or family room may be for private family use and the formal "living room" reserved for entertaining company.

Part of the difficulty in specifying "normal" space standards arises from the fact that housing is a capital good which provides more than just shelter. People use housing for productive activities that require additional space beyond what is necessary for eating, sleeping, and personal care. Residential dwellings are used for the practice of all kinds of crafts, trades, arts, and professional occupations. Extra bedrooms are used not only for infrequent visitors but also as sewing rooms, hobby rooms, and offices for secondary occupations. Carpentry, furniture making and refinishing, music, painting, weaving, sewing, pottery-making, jewelry-making and all types of home repair are carried on in houses, the aggregate economic value of which the output of these types of "home production" is by no means trivial, as some recent studies on non-market contributions to national income have demonstrated.[33]

From this perspective, a house with surplus space would be one which has rooms originally intended for specific activities that are no longer performed by the occupants, such as child-rearing or entertaining. These rooms may, of course, be put to other uses, as guest rooms, offices, or workshops. In the strict sense, then, a house with underutilized space would have space that serves no domestic, productive, or reserve function for the household that occupies it. In practice, however, it is difficult to distinguish those houses which contain spaces that have these functions from those with space that is surplus. Census data tell us something about the number of rooms but little about actual use. Bedrooms may be an exception; but even here, it is wrong to assume that bedrooms are used only as sleeping rooms.

By employing the term "underutilization," I intend no judgment about whether people "overconsume" or "waste" space or are dissatisfied with the size of their homes. Persons who do have surplus space, as it has been defined here, probably feel satisfied with their homes and would not think of them as being underutilized. People underutilize space because it is rational for them to do so. They will generally consume as much housing and space as they can afford. The couple, for example, who bought an eight-room house 20 years ago with a $20,000, 6-percent mortgage and are still living in it today have the good

EXHIBIT 3.10
Actual and Expected Space Consumption
Over the Family Life Cycle for a
Typical Home Owner

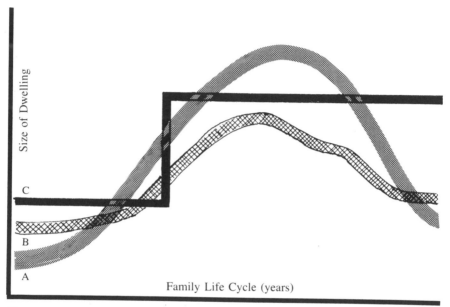

Notes:
A = Expected space consumption as a function of household income
B = Expected space consumption as a function of household size
C = Actual space consumption.

fortune of being able to pay off their 1960 mortgage in 1980 dollars. Their ample home is in part a product of their hard work and earnings, but they are also the beneficiaries of special social institutions and a unique historical set of circumstances.

Factors Influencing Space Standards in Owner-Occupied Housing

To a considerable extent, surplus space exists in American homes because of a disequilibrium between space consumption, income, and family size which is structured into the family life cycle. As household size rises and falls during the life cycle, dwelling size does not adjust smoothly along with it. The typical pattern is illustrated in Exhibit 3.10.

The vertical axis represents per capita consumption of housing services as measured by the size of the dwelling, that is, by number of square feet, number of rooms, or number of bedrooms. The horizontal axis represents the length of the average family life cycle in years. Line A represents the adjustment process

EXHIBIT 3.11
Percentage Distribution of Non-Farm Families by Rooms
Per Person and Age of Head, United States, 1955

Rooms per Person	All Families	Age of Head					
		Under 25	25–34	35–44	45–54	55–64	65 and Over
Less than 0.5	1	1	2	1	0	0	0
0.5–1.0	12	16	19	17	10	2	1
Overcrowded	13	17	21	18	10	2	1
1.0–1.5	31	46	40	39	28	17	14
1.5–2.0	17	13	20	19	17	17	9
2.0–2.5	14	11	10	13	17	18	19
Normal	62	70	70	71	62	52	42
2.5–3.5	16	7	8	8	20	30	27
Over 3.5	9	5	1	3	7	15	29
Undercrowded	25	12	9	11	27	45	56

Source: "Housing Arrangements of Consumers," in *Survey of Consumer Finances.* Federal Reserve Board, August 1955, supplementary table 5, p. 10. Reprinted in N. Foote, M. Foley, J. Abu-Lughod, and L. Winnick, *Housing Choices and Housing Constraints.* New York: McGraw-Hill, 1960, Table 23, p. 220.

of consumption to demand that would occur given the life cycle pattern of income of the average middle-class family. Line B represents the optimal pattern of consumption that would occur if housing services adjusted smoothly to changes in the demand for space over the life cycle. Line C represents the way the majority of home owners actually do adjust their space consumption; it does not follow the "hump" pattern of space demand, but appears as an upward shifting line. Toward the late stages of the life cycle, space consumption tends to exceed the demand for space based on household size and income by a fairly wide margin.

Home owners tend to invest in large houses toward the end of the long child-rearing phase of the family life cycle. Children are born during the early years of the family life cycle when income is low, and so growing families are usually pressed for space. Family size and space needs tend to be out of balance until middle age, when child-rearing ends and income and accumulated equity, which are at an all-time high, permit for the first time the consumption of more space than is needed. Abu-Lughod and Foley, in their 1962 study of space needs of the American family, noted this phenomenon and underscored its importance in understanding the variation of housing demand across the life cycle.

It is in the later years, just preceding the final departure of the children from home that the house assumes its greatest value as an extension of the family: a symbol of economic achievement and social standing. A larger home in a more select neighborhood now becomes an urgent goal. . . . Only five to ten years after the second house has been bought, the children marry or leave the family home for jobs within the city. After more than twenty years of adjusting to minimum quarters, and a short interim of space balance, the family is now suddenly "undercrowded." . . . During the period when space was most necessary, it was often unobtainable; once it has been achieved, it soon becomes unnecessary.[34]

Abu-Lughod and Foley also presented evidence on space utilization over the family life cycle. Their data, taken from the 1955 Survey of Consumer Finances, showed that the proportion of home owners who consumed more than 2.5 rooms per person ranged from 10 to 12 percent for household heads between ages 25 and 44, but then rose sharply for each age group above 45, until it reached 56 percent for household heads 65 years or older (see Exhibit 3.11).

Winnick attributed this propensity of home owners to underutilize space to their greater "inertia and immobility" as compared to renters.[35] This greater disinclination of home owners to move as they age and their household size decreases may reflect a strong attachment to the neighborhood environment and a "sense of integration" with it. Immobility may also stem from substantial satisfaction with other aspects of one's housing situation that presumably offset the inconvenience or cost of holding extra space.[36]

Home owners are also less inclined to reduce the amount of space they occupy when family size falls because of the much higher transaction costs they must absorb when moving as compared to renters. Brokers fees, escrow fees, closing costs, and title search and insurance costs usually amount to as much as 15 to 20 percent of annual housing expenses; for renters, transaction costs are usually between 8 to 12 percent.[37] Because of these higher transaction costs home buyers have a longer planning horizon than do renters and move with the intention of remaining in place much longer.[38] Research on intraurban residential mobility has also shown that "undercrowding" generates relatively little incentive for home owners to move, whereas "overcrowding," by contrast, is often generally the source of major dissatisfaction with one's current housing and a prime reason for moving.[39]

Aside from transaction costs, moving may also involve large adjustment costs in current housing expenses. Home owners who stay put for long periods of time enjoy housing costs that are fixed at lower historic levels because of the widespread use of the fixed-payment, fully-amortizing mortgage. The higher the rate of inflation over any period of time, the greater will be the gap between historic and current costs of ownership based on market rates, and consequently the greater will be the adjustment cost of moving.[40] In addition, once the mortgage is paid off, effective occupancy costs will be limited to only hazard insurance, utilities, maintenance, and property taxes. Institutional arrangements that reduce property taxes for home owners by means of "circuit-breakers" or permanently fix assessed values at some lower historic level (as did California's Proposition 13) will also decrease the occupancy cost of home ownership and further encourage immobility.[41]

At the same time, home owners do not pay income taxes on the imputed net rent from their homes. The difference between the current rental value of the home and the nominal costs to own and operate the building would be taxable income if the owner were not occupying the unit. This is a form of implicit income which is not taken in the form of cash but rather through direct consumption of housing services. For owners who bought homes long ago at much lower prices and with fixed-payment mortgages, the imputed net rent can be substantial. The failure by state and federal government to tax this form of income also encourages owner-occupants to continue living in large dwellings even when they do not need the extra space for child-rearing or business purposes.

Space Consumption and the Income Tax

So far we have considered how mortgage instruments and income tax laws influence the propensity of home owners to move or to remain living in houses designed for large families after the child-launching stage of the life cycle. A related issue concerns the influence of income tax laws on how much space home buyers purchase. Does the income tax treatment of home ownership induce home buyers to purchase more housing than they require given their current and expected household size?

Home owners benefit in two ways from the tax laws. First, they can deduct annual payments, mortgage interest, and property taxes. Second, they can also defer capital gains tax upon sale of their current home and reinvestment of the net proceeds in another residence. The latter provides a much greater incentive for people to own houses with surplus space than is generally realized.

Prior to 1954 any home owner who moved to another owner-occupied dwelling incurred a capital gains tax liability. Since the 1954 revision of the United States federal tax code, all capital gains on the sale of any primary residence can be deferred indefinitely so long as they are reinvested in another owner-occupied dwelling.[42] This change provided an inducement for home owners to move up to larger houses and was probably responsible in part for the emergence of the market for "trade-up" homes during the 1960s.[43] Capital gains tax deferral, however, provided no incentive to "trade-down" and thereby discouraged aging home owners from reducing their space consumption when their children had moved away. One could sell the house and move to a rental apartment, but this meant the end of capital gains deferral and a large tax liability. The 1978 and 1980 revisions of the United States tax code for the first time gave home owners 55 years and older an exemption of up to $125,000 of realized capital gains from selling a home which was their primary residence. This reform encourages home owners over 55 to "trade-down" to smaller, cheaper accommodations upon retirement without incurring a large tax liability against their accumulated equity.[44]

A number of studies done in the last decade indicate that capital gains tax deferral accounts for some of the difference in per capita space consumption between older, married couples and other types of home owners. These studies have shown that home owners over 45 years of age who bought homes after their children were no longer living with them tended to make little if any downward adjustment in their space consumption, even though their households had become smaller. Doling in England found no drop in the gross dwelling size, and McCarthy in the United States found some decline in gross size but substantial increases in both rooms per capita and square feet per capita.[45] MacLeod and Ellis in Australia have reported similar findings. Their analysis of a sample of home purchases showed that buyers over 45 who were moving into their second or third homes (after their children had left home) tended to move to houses that allowed them to maintain a standard of space consumption comparable to that of owners of the same age group who had not moved. After controlling for income, the authors found that wealth in the form of equity accounted for a substantial proportion of the differences in per capita space consumption between younger and older home buyers. They concluded that high per capita space consumption by home owners 45 years and older was attributable not only to lower historic costs associated with long tenures, but also to the large equities accumulated over time and to capital gains tax deferral. Hence, home owners who have held or owned houses for long periods can substitute accumulated equity for long tenures to achieve roughly the same level of housing consumption in terms of both space and quality even when they do move and buy another house.[46]

Insofar as it lowers the real marginal cost of housing, the deductibility of mortgage interest and property taxes on state and federal income tax returns may also encourage people to increase space consumption, particularly during periods of high inflation. The inducement rises with income because the value of housing-related income-tax deductions is greater for people in higher marginal tax brackets. The value of capital gains tax deferral is similarly more valuable for people in higher marginal tax brackets than for those in lower ones.

Based on this analysis, Douglas Diamond has estimated that while the *average* real after-tax cost of ownership fell 37.5 percent between 1970 and 1979, the *marginal* real after-tax cost fell by 46.7 percent.[47] Diamond contends that the tax benefits from home ownership interacted with inflation during this period to give home buyers in the highest tax brackets a strong incentive to purchase more housing in terms of space or quality than they would have if the rate of inflation had been lower. This occurred in part because the expected annual rate of appreciation on homes during these years exceeded both mortgage interest rates and returns on alternative investments. Hence households at or above the 50 percent combined state and federal marginal tax bracket could expect to gain a better return from buying an additional room when purchasing a house than from investing in stocks, bonds, or savings accounts. Diamond contends that this drop in the real after-tax marginal cost of ownership accounts for the 47 percent increase in the number of new homes with more than 1,600 square feet of living area constructed between 1970 and 1978. This analysis is supported by surveys of new home buyers in California conducted by Grebler and Mittlebach between 1975 and 1977; these surveys found that tax and investment considerations were important motivations cited by those respondents (18 percent of the sample) who reported purchasing more extra rooms than they required on the basis of household size alone.[48]

The only study of the differential effects of income tax treatment of home ownership on housing costs at different stages of the life cycle indicates that tax subsidies give young home owners a greater incentive than older ones to increase their space consumption.[49] Using data on mortgage payments by age of household from the 1972–73 Consumer Expenditure Survey, Nonna Noto showed that the mortgage payments of middle-aged home owners tend to be just as high as those of younger owners, but with a smaller fraction going for interest. The average yearly interest payment per home owner was highest for household heads between 25 and 34 years old ($1,181) and declined with age, dropping to $744 for household heads between 45 and 54 years old and to $492 for those 65 and over. A good part of this difference is explained by the fact that younger households have higher loan-value-ratio mortgages with longer maturities. Middle-aged owners with older mortgages make more of their payment for principle and less for interest.[50] On the other hand, the marginal tax bracket is on average not much higher for older households than for younger ones. The result is that the average tax reduction per home owner filing an itemized return was $222 for a head 25 to 34 years old and only $119 for one 45 to 54, a difference of 87 percent.

There is little direct evidence, however, on the magnitude of the joint effect of inflation and income tax subsidies on space consumption by young, first-time buyers. Most of the studies of the effects of the income tax treatment of home ownership on housing, like Diamond's and Noto's, are based on aggregated data and simulation models.[51] Follain is one of the few researchers, however, who has used household sample data from HUD's Annual Housing Survey to examine this question. He found that the joint impact of inflation and income tax subsidies induces only those home owners in the highest marginal brackets to consume more housing than they "need."[52] Boehm and McKenzie using the Panel Study of Income Dynamics from the University of Michigan also found that expectations of higher than normal appreciation leads home buyers to purchase more housing than they would otherwise, and that this tendency is greater for buyers in the highest marginal income tax brackets.[53]

Lowry, Hillestad, and Sarma have shown that per capita space consumption by young first-time buyers from 1970 to 1980 increased more than for older owners, and that a combination of inflationary expectations and the income tax treatment of home ownership account for this difference.[54] Their study is interesting because it uses data from California, where house prices in the 1970s not only increased faster than inflation but also faster than anywhere else in the nation. On the one hand, their findings show that young owners were spending comparatively more for their housing than households with older heads. Monthly cash outlays for owner-occupied housing had increased at an annual rate of 14 percent between 1970 and 1980 for household heads under 35 years old, at 12 percent for heads between 35 and 64, and at 7 percent for those 65 and over. However, a housing consumption index derived by hedonic price modeling revealed that real per capita housing consumption between 1970 and 1980 had increased by 46 percent for heads 35 years and under, by 30 percent for heads between 35 and 64, and by only 17 percent for household heads 65 years and over.

Part of this increase in consumption took the form of more rooms per person, which rose by 25.2 percent for owners 35 years and younger as compared to only 16.5 percent for owners between 35 and 64 years old. The authors point out that young, first-time buyers were not acquiring larger houses than their counterparts in previous decades; they were buying houses of similar size, but their average household size was 20 percent lower.[55]

Exclusive Single-Family Zoning

Another institutional factor that encourages ownership of houses with surplus space is zoning regulation. Zoning attempts to restrict the density of both structures and population. The unit of density in most zoning ordinances is the "dwelling unit," not "person space" (population per acre). Because zoning creates density districts based on this measure, it results in different building types in different zones—one-family houses in one district, two-family houses in another district, and so on. Residential population density is rarely controlled directly, unless a zoning law sets some limitation on the number of bedrooms per lot area or restricts the number of occupants per unit or lot.

This approach works only if the relationship between population and buildings is stable and predictable; that is, for example, if all or most single-family dwellings contain four persons. If building density is to act as a control on population density, then average household size cannot change over time and its cross-sectional variance should be small if not negligible. If average household size falls and household composition becomes more diverse as a neighborhood ages, the effort to maintain the higher historic standard would force many households to underutilize. Exclusive single-family zoning has probably always encouraged a certain amount of underutilization because of the divergence between house size and family size during the later stages of the life cycle. Today, however, families are smaller and the decline in average household size has pushed effective population densities below the historic density standards that zoning restrictions have established.

Zoning in suburbs also tends to favor large lots with large houses on them, and this also encourages more ownership of houses with surplus space. This practice has been supported by the belief that large lots will create the greatest future value for the developer, the property owner, and the community. Large lots are thought to assure "quality development" because large and therefore more expensive lots will receive more valuable improvements. Economically, it makes no sense to build a small house on a large lot when a four- or five-bedroom house will yield the developer a greater profit. Large houses on large lots have consequently become the standard in most suburban communities.[56] This may have been rational policy when family sizes were on the increase and society as a whole was growing more affluent. Today, however, with the number of children per household declining and the middle-income standard of living under stress, the market for large homes has thinned considerably and development standards are being pared down.

An Empirical Analysis of the Incidence of Surplus Space in Single Family Housing

So far we have discussed a number of factors that explain why people own houses with surplus space. It is important to untangle the effects of these different causes and to determine the relative importance of each, especially the effects of life cycle stage and zoning. This may help reveal where the real opportunities may be for public intervention to encourage better utilization of some of these houses.

The Northern California Community Survey

To do this we will look at some data on space utilization from a random sample of 1100 households in Northern California. This data set was originally constructed by urban sociologist Claude Fischer as part of an investigation of social networks.[57] The sample was designed to represent the household population of the northern half of Northern California; this includes San Francisco and all counties within 200 miles north and east of the city.[58] Despite the small sample size, the data set lends itself well to analyzing space consumption patterns among home owners and renters. Each record contains information not only about household composition and the size and type of dwelling unit but also about neighborhood characteristics of the block on which the dwelling is located. This block data includes the predominant type of land-use (residential, commercial, or mixed use), net dwelling density (units per net residential acre and average number of units per lot), and type of zoning district (single-family, two-family, and so forth).

Exhibit 3.12 provides a breakdown of the sample by type of household. The distribution of household types is fairly representative of the nine-county Bay Area, except that the sample contains fewer households with children and under-

EXHIBIT 3.12
Household Composition of Sample in the Northern California
Community Study by Tenure

	Sample Total Households	1980 Census*	Sample Owner Households
Married couples	54.98	52.40	70.49
with children	23.28	26.16	30.29
without children	25.67	26.24	31.46
with other adults	6.03	—	8.74
Unmarried adults	14.37	11.81	12.43
Single parents	5.84	8.50	3.88
Persons living alone	24.81	26.80	13.20
Total	100.00	100.00	100.00
Number of cases	1044	—	515
Percent of households with children	29.12	35.15	34.17

*These percentages reflect the social characteristics of households in the nine-county San Francisco Bay Area (which includes the San Francisco–Oakland, Vallejo–Santa Rosa and San Jose SMSAs) and therefore are not strictly comparable with the figures for the much larger territory covered by the Northern California Community Study. Differences in percentages are also attributable to sampling variability.

Sources: Claude Fisher, *Northern California Community Study*, 1977. United States Bureau of the Census, 1980 *Census of Housing and Population*, STF-1.

samples blacks. Because the sample covered more than the 9 counties of the Bay Area, it also included rural areas.

Definitional Problems in Measuring Surplus Space

Measuring surplus space is difficult because one must first determine at what threshold or level of space consumption "normal" occupancy verges on underutilization. This in turn requires that one specify space norms consistent with the actual consumption behavior of households of different sizes and types. Space consumption itself is also difficult to measure precisely. Because accurate measurements of the square footage of existing dwellings are rarely obtainable by survey, dwelling size is usually expressed in terms of the number of rooms per dwelling. As noted earlier, the fundamental problem with using rooms per capita as a measure of space consumption is that it assumes that all rooms are alike in size and function and that all persons use space in identical ways, regardless of their life-styles, ethnicity, household composition, and occupation. Because reported room counts include only "habitable" rooms, various kinds of space that go underutilized are often excluded from the census and other surveys. Such

EXHIBIT 3.13
Space Standards and Thresholds for Measuring Underutilization by Household Size

Number of Persons in Household	Overcrowding Threshold	Normal Occupancy	Underutilization Thresholds	
			Number of Rooms	Rooms per Persons
	Number of Rooms			
A. American Public Health Association				
1	+1	1–2	3+	3.0+
2	+2	2–4	5+	2.5+
3	+3	3–5	6+	2.0+
4	+4	4–6	7+	1.8+
5	+5	5–7	8+	1.6+
6	+6	5–8	9+	1.5+
B. Niebanck				
1	1	2–3	4+	4.0+
2	1	2–4	5+	2.5+
3	1–3	4	5+	1.7+
4	1–4	4–5	6+	1.5+
5	1–4	5–7	8+	1.6+
6+	5	6+	*	*
C. Baer				
1	—	—	4+	4.0+
2	—	—	5+	2.5+
3	—	—	6+	2.0+
4	—	—	8+	2.0+
D. "Extra bedroom" standard				
1	—	—	5+	5.0+
2	—	—	6+	3.0+
3	—	—	8+	2.7+
4	—	—	9+	2.3+
5	—	—	11+	2.2+

*Indeterminate

Sources: American Public Health Association, *Planning the Home for Occupancy.* Chicago: Public Administration Service, 1950, p. 15. Paul Niebanch, *Rent Control and the Rental Housing Market: New York City, 1968.* New York Housing and Development Administration, 1970, 131. William C. Baer, "Empty Housing Space: An Overlooked Resource," *Policy Studies Journal.* 8:2 (1979), 220-227.

spaces include unfinished basements and attics, accessory structures, garages, and undeveloped yard space within the permitted building envelope. Despite all its disadvantages, the Bureau of the Census has continued to use number of rooms as a measure of dwelling size.

The few attempts to measure underutilization that can be found in the housing

EXHIBIT 3.14
**Owner-Occupied Dwellings With and Without Surplus Space by Household
Composition, Northern California, 1977**

Type of Household	Without Surplus Space		With Surplus Space		Households with Surplus Space as a Percentage of Household Type
	Number	Percent	Number	Percent	
Adult alone	42	10.6	23	23.5	35.4
One adult with children	18	4.5	1	1.0	5.3
Married couple without children	105	26.5	53	54.1	33.5
Married couple with children	141	35.6	7	7.1	4.7
Related adults only	35	8.8	8	8.2	18.6
Married couple plus other adult	39	9.8	5	5.1	11.4
Other adults	16	4.0	1	1.0	5.9
Total	396	100.0	97	100.0	19.7

Source: *Northern California Community Study,* 1977.

literature use a "theoretical" space standard expressed in rooms per person. I call them "theoretical" because they are not derived from empirical studies. Instead, a judgmental standard is used that presumes a constant overhead requirement plus a bedroom multiplier. Normal occupancy is derived by allocating a specific number of rooms as overhead space and then adding one sleeping room for each additional household member. The multiplier itself can vary depending on whether the household is headed by a married couple or a single adult. The amount of overhead space can also be varied to account for separate dining and living rooms.

Several examples of these space standards are presented in Exhibit 3.13. Developed during the 1940s, the APHA standard was based on the famous study of space utilization described earlier. Except for one-person households, its underutilization threshold is not very different from that in the standards developed by Niebanck and Baer, which are of more recent vintage. Niebanck's threshold for underutilization is somewhat lower than Baer's; it was developed as part of a study of the effects of rent control in New York City and therefore reflects space standards that are more typical for renters in that city.

The major drawback of these theoretical standards is that they are "shelter" standards. They do not allow for productive activities in the home or for the common practice of maintaining "reserve" space—extra rooms for guests or visitors. Young couples anticipating the birth of children in the future tend to purchase homes with extra bedrooms. "Empty nesters" keep their houses with more bedrooms than they need so their children who live out of town can visit. This practice has become widespread in the United States because of the high degree of mobility among young adults, who increasingly live at great distances from their parents.[59] Morris's work on space norms suggests that reserve space has become a normal part of the space standards of middle-class American home owners.[60] Grebler and Mittlebach also found a high incidence of "extra bedrooms" among buyers of new homes in California during the 1970s. Approximately 65 percent of all buyers reported that their new home included an "extra bedroom." As for the use of this extra room, respondents specified a study or office (59.3 percent), guest room (24.2 percent), sewing room (10.1 percent), and space for recreational activities (9.9 percent) in that order.[61]

Although the amount of reserve space each household possesses cannot be easily distinguished from surplus space, adopting a very generous space standard may be a way to get around this problem. I have formulated a theoretical space standard based on the findings of Morris's research (see panel D of Exhibit 3.13). This standard assigns two rooms for overhead space for each household and one bedroom for each person in the household. Each household is also allowed "one extra" room as reserve space. This is a very generous standard for any household of two persons or more that includes a married couple because the bedroom multiplier in effect adds an extra overhead room. These "requirements" establish the threshold levels for each household size.

Empirical Results

When this "extra bedroom" standard was applied to the data from the Northern California Community Survey, the result showed that approximately 19.7 percent of all owner-occupiers in the sample had surplus space in their homes. Exhibit 3.14 compares owner-occupied households which have surplus space with those which do not. The presence or absence of children is clearly a major factor. Over half of the households with surplus space are married couples with no children. Almost one-fourth are adults living alone; half of these are widows, and the rest are divorced or single.

A multiple regression analysis was also performed on the sample in order to more carefully analyze the relative incidence of underutilization among households of different composition and life-cycle status. The Ordinary Least Squares method of estimation was used.[62] The dependent variable was a dummy which can be interpreted as the conditional probability that a household was underutilizing space based on our "extra bedroom" standard. Independent variables as predictors included: the density standard of the zoning district; life-cycle stage defined as a composite of age, marital status, and presence of children; and household income. Households were stratified into sixteen life-cycle stages and six use-and-density zoning categories. Except for household income, all the other variables were entered as dummies. The first regression does not include income as a variable; it was entered in a second run.

EXHIBIT 3.15

Linear Probability Regression Model of Space Underutilization in Owner-Occupied Single-Family Dwellings, Northern California, 1977

	Coefficient	T-Statistic	Coefficient	T-Statistic
Household composition				
Not married, under 30	−0.072	−0.392	−0.121	−0.521
Not married, 30–55	0.078	0.603	0.032	0.236
Not married, over 55	0.428	2.414†	0.456	2.396†
Married, under 30, no children present	0.142	2.013*	0.089	1.320
Married, 30–55, no children present	0.112	0.962	0.094	0.382
Married, over 55, no children present	0.287	2.292*	0.238	2.116*
Married, under 30, children present	−0.094	−0.660	−0.118	−0.822
Married, 30–55, children present	−0.190	−2.215*	−0.254	−2.333*
Married, over 55, children present	−0.181	−2.055*	−0.220	−2.188*
Divorced, 30–55, no children present	0.151	1.320	0.117	1.594
Divorced, over 55 no children	−0.005	−0.035	0.007	0.040
Divorced, 30–55 children present	−0.145	−1.062	−0.157	1.153
Divorced, over 55 children present	−0.052	−0.552	−0.081	−0.679
Widowed under 55	0.052	0.293	0.009	0.042
Widowed over 55	0.202	2.048*	0.131	1.699
Zoning Districts				
Single-family, <4 units/acre	0.141	2.243*	0.110	2.142*
Single-family, >4 units/acre	0.241	2.445*	0.177	2.203*
Townhouse-duplex low-density	−0.088	−1.498	−0.050	−0.811
Multi-family, low-density	−0.047	−0.410	−0.038	−0.336
Multi-family, high-density	−0.020	−0.532	−0.019	−0.329
Income (in $1,000s)	—	—	0.004	2.947†
Constant	0.121	1.521	0.105	1.179
R–squared	0.188		0.195	
Adjusted R–squared	0.137		0.151	
Number of Cases	402		395	
F–test	3.869		4.091	
Significance	0.001		0.001	

Notes:

*Significant at the .05 level.

†Significant at the .01 level.

The results of the regression analysis are presented in Exhibit 3.15. The constant term in this equation represents a reference household headed by a divorced person 30 years of age or younger living with no children in an owner-occupied dwelling in a trailer park or nonresidential zone. The regression coefficients represent the marginal probability relative to the reference category that a household with the characteristic listed will be underutilizing the dwelling it occupies. For example, the coefficient for a married couple above age 55 with no children present means that, after controlling for household income and characteristics of the zoning district, this type of household is 28 7 percent more likely to underutilize the dwelling it occupies than the reference household.

All the coefficients for households without children present were positive, but only those for married couples under 30 and over 55 were statistically significant. As expected, householders above age 55 without children present have the highest marginal probabilities of underutilizing space, even after controlling for income and zoning district. They were twice as likely to underutilize as any household head under 55. This finding is important because it confirms our earlier hypotheses and indicates that life-cycle stage does in fact have an influence on space consumption independent of other factors. The coefficient for widows over 55 is also statistically significant and relatively large, but it falls in both significance and magnitude after income is entered into the equation. This suggests that widows who live in homes which contain surplus space are able to do so because their incomes and/or savings permit it. The coefficient for married couples under 30 with no children present is just barely significant at the .05 level. It also drops in magnitude and significance after income is entered into the equation. This result supports the hypothesis discussed earlier—that young households in the highest marginal income tax brackets have a greater propensity to underutilize than households of the same age and size with lower incomes.

The most striking results of this analysis are the zoning district coefficients. Both the variables indicating location in an exclusive single-family zoning district are statistically significant. Even after controlling for household composition and income, single-family houses in exclusive single-family districts are more likely to contain surplus space than single-family houses located in other types of zoning districts. Out of a total of 429 single-family houses in the sample, only 365 (85.1 percent) were located in single-family zones. This was true also for underutilized single-family houses: 85.4 percent of these were located in single-family zones.

These results are attributable to the relatively greater size of single-family homes in single-family zones. A t–test showed that the mean size of owner-occupied single-family homes located in a single-family zone was approximately 0.8 rooms larger than those located in other types of residential districts. The difference was statistically significant at the .05 level. Hence any household living in an exclusive single-family district is more likely to underutilize because its home is probably going to be larger than that of a household of the same size located outside a single-family zone.

likely to underutilize because the home is probably going to be larger than that occupied by a household of the same size outside of a single-family zone.

The slightly larger coefficient of the moderate-density, single-family zone dummy does not contradict this inference. Moderate single-family densities are primarily found in older suburbs located in the inner rings around central cities. These suburbs have relatively high concentrations of middle-aged and elderly home owners. Owner-occupied dwellings in these locations accounted for 35 percent of all underutilized dwellings in the entire sample. This echoes the finding of Dowell Myers, that older suburbs tend to have more elderly and middle-aged home owners than newer ones. When first developed, suburbs fill up with young families. Although some eventually move to other locations, a substantial number remain and age along with their housing. Hence in neighborhoods and communities that are predominantly owner-occupied, the older the average age of the housing stock, the higher will be the proportion of middle-aged and elderly household heads. Moreover, the closer a community is to being completely built up, with a consequently lower rate of new construction, the more marked will be this concentration of aging home owners.[63] Although the lots are smaller in these districts than in newer, outlying suburbs, many of the houses have been expanded by room additions and are comparable in size to houses in zones with larger lots.[64]

Houses With Surplus Space in the National Inventory

How much underutilized housing do we have in the United States today, and how great has been the increase in the rate of underutilization over the past thirty years?

The United States Bureau of the Census publishes data on space utilization as part of the decennial census of housing which can be used to estimate the number of dwellings in the nation that contain surplus space. This information is published in the form of cross-tabulations of the number of rooms per dwelling unit by the number of persons per dwelling unit. To derive estimates from this data, a procedure was employed similar to the one used in the preceding analysis. However the thresholds were allowed to vary so that upper-range and lower-range estimates could be obtained. The lowest threshold, for example, includes all households with more than two rooms per person. Higher thresholds, which allow a more generous allocation of reserve space to each household, can be set at 2.5, 3.0 and 3.5 rooms per person.

These alternative measures are displayed in Exhibit 3.16. The number in each cell of the table indicates the smallest dwelling (in rooms per unit) that a household of any given size would have to occupy at the maximum space standard threshold indicated at the top of each column for that household to be classified as underutilizing. Thus, at a maximum space standard threshold of two rooms per person, two persons living in a house with five rooms or more would be clas-

EXHIBIT 3.16
Underutilization Threshold as a Function of Space Standards

	Space Standards (rooms per person)			
	2.0	2.5	3.0	3.5
Number of Persons per Household	(rooms per unit)			
1	4+	5+	6+	6+
2	5+	6+	7+	8+
3	7+	8+	10+	12+
4	9+	11+	13+	15+

sified as living in a dwelling with surplus space; but at a maximum space standard threshold of 2.5 rooms per person, they would not be so classified. In general, the higher the threshold, the more likely it is that the dwelling would contain surplus space rather than space reserved for special uses. Also, the higher the threshold point, the more likely that any household occupying a dwelling with surplus space will be a person living alone, because persons living alone generally consume a very high rate of overhead rooms per person.

Exhibit 3.17 presents estimates of the number of households living in dwellings with surplus space for 1950, 1970, and 1980. In the first panel these estimates are presented in terms of tenure-specific percentages; in the second panel they are expressed in terms of millions of dwelling units. Thus according to panel A, when the maximum space standard threshold is set at two rooms per person, 28.42 percent of all home owners can be classified as living in houses with surplus space in 1950 and 46.98 percent of them were so classified in 1980. By contrast, at a maximum space standard threshold of three rooms per person, only 7.06 percent of all home owners were underutilizing in 1950 and 14.48 percent were doing so in 1980. Panel B expresses these percentages in terms of millions of dwelling units. Thus at a standard of three rooms per person, approximately 1,398,000 owner-occupied residences contained surplus space in 1950, whereas 7,500,000 did in 1980.

These estimates are revealing. In 1980, 30 percent of all home owners (approximately 15,518,000 households) were living in dwellings large enough so that they were consuming space at a rate exceeding 2.5 rooms per person. This includes all individuals living alone in houses with five rooms or more, all couples living in houses with six rooms or more, and families of three persons living in dwellings with eight rooms or more. As panel A of Exhibit 3.18 reveals, about 33 percent of this group were persons living alone; 55.6 percent were two-person households; and three-person households made up the remaining 11 percent. If underutilized rental dwellings are included, the total number climbs to

EXHIBIT 3.17
Estimates of Underutilized Housing at Varying Space Standards by Tenure of Occupied Dwelling Units, United States, 1950, 1970, 1980

Panel A — Percentages

Underutilized dwellings	1950	1970	1980
2.0 rooms per person, as a percent of:			
Owner-occupied	28.42	37.84	46.98
Renter-occupied	10.33	17.77	24.95
Total	19.97	30.30	39.14
2.5 rooms per person, as a percent of:			
Owner-occupied	16.21	21.99	29.96
Renter-occupied	4.04	6.31	9.03
Total	10.52	16.17	22.52
3.0 rooms per person, as a percent of:			
Owner-occupied	7.06	9.81	14.48
Renter-occupied	1.31	2.05	2.80
Total	4.37	6.93	10.33
3.5 rooms per person, as a percent of:			
Owner-occupied	4.25	6.05	8.58
Renter-occupied	0.81	1.44	2.14
Total	2.64	4.34	6.29

Panel B — Number of Occupied Dwellings (in millions)

	1950	1970	1980
2.0 rooms per person:			
Owner-occupied	5.628	15.093	24.333
Renter-occupied	1.791	4.187	7.134
Total	7.419	19.280	31.468
2.5 rooms per person:			
Owner-occupied	3.210	8.771	15.518
Renter-occupied	.701	1.487	2.582
Total	3.911	10.258	18.100
3.0 rooms per person:			
Owner-occupied	1.398	3.913	7.500
Renter-occupied	.227	.483	.801
Total	1.625	4.396	8.301
3.5 rooms per person:			
Owner-occupied	.842	2.413	4.444
Renter-occupied	.140	.412	.612
Total	.982	2.825	5.056

Sources: Louis Winnick and Ned Shilling, *American Housing and Its Use*. Table A-1, 104. United States Bureau of the Census, 1970 *Census of Housing, Space Utilization of the Inventory*, Vol. 3. United States Bureau of the Census, 1980 *Census of Population and Housing*, STF 2c, Table 19.

18 million dwellings, or approximately 22.5 percent of all occupied dwellings in the country. Even at a more generous maximum space standard threshold of three rooms per person, 7.5 million units, or one-seventh of all owner-occupied dwellings in the United States can be classified as containing surplus space. These units would include dwellings in which one person occupied six rooms or more and in which two persons occupy seven rooms or more. Including an additional 800,000 rental units brings the total number of dwellings with surplus space to about 8.3 million units, or 10.3 percent of the entire inventory.

When these estimates are broken out by household size, the proportion occupied by only one person appears to have increased over time (see Panel B of Exhibit 3.18). The share of underutilized dwellings owned and occupied by one person living alone rose from 28.9 percent in 1950 to 37.9 percent in 1980, whereas the share of two-person households (primarily married couples) dropped from 64.6 percent to 55.2 percent over the same period. This is consistent with the relative increase during the last thirty years in the proportion of all home owners who were persons living alone, which rose from 7.21 percent to 15.3 percent.

It is a mistake to assume that all houses which contain surplus space remain that way permanently. Many do, but some do not. Tables from CINCH not displayed here show that only 60 percent of all units with 2.5 rooms per person in 1973 were still occupied at that high a ratio by 1980.[65] Much of the change was accounted for by turnover. This is an important finding, because it suggests that insofar as accessory conversions permit merger in the future, they represent an ideal way to adapt the single-family inventory to a more highly differentiated population structure with more diverse household composition.

Conclusion

Our single-family housing inventory contains a large number of very spacious dwellings. Social and economic change has pared down average household size of home owners so that many of these houses, although built for families with two or more children, now contain surplus space. There is nothing inherently bad about people having surplus space in their homes. On the contrary, it presents us with a great opportunity to meet some of our housing needs by encouraging the recycling of some of that space.

By my estimate, at least 10 million and perhaps as many as 18 million single-family homes in the United States contain surplus space and have the potential for some form of conversion. Clearly, not all of these houses can be adapted. In some cases, the design and layout are inappropriate; in others, the owners lack the desire or the resources to undertake the work required. But if only 15 percent of these dwellings were to have an accessory conversion during the next ten years, the average annual production of rental apartments would be increased by at least 150,000 units, or by more than 25 percent. This would be enough to

EXHIBIT 3.18

Panel A
Underutilized Dwellings by Household Sizes and Tenure

Space Standard Threshold

Number of Persons	@ 2.0 Rooms per Person		@ 2.5 Rooms per Person		@ 3.0 Rooms per Person		@ 3.5 Rooms per Person	
	Number	Percent	Number	Percent	Number	Percent	Number	Percent
Owner-occupied								
1	7,090,687	29.1	5,143,208	33.1	2,812,449	37.5	2,812,449	63.3
2	13,570,196	55.8	8,628,988	55.6	4,143,571	55.2	1,574,557	35.4
3	3,345,934	13.8	1,672,967	10.8	543,844	7.3	56,974	1.3
4	326,306	1.3	72,513	0.5	0	0.0	0	0.0
Total	24,333,123	100.0	15,517,675	100.0	7,499,864	100.0	4,443,980	100.0
Renter-occupied								
1	4,100,541	57.5	1,509,823	58.5	488,977	61.1	488,977	79.9
2	2,705,099	37.9	986,532	38.2	297,389	37.1	122,959	20.1
3	311,687	4.4	82,926	3.2	14,298	1.8	0.	0.0
4	14,298	0.2	2,860	0.1	0	0.0	0.	0.0
Total	7,134,484	100.0	2,582,140	100.0	800,664	100.0	611,936	100.0

Panel B
Change in Number and Percentage of Underutilized Dwellings by Household Size @ Maximum Space Standard Threshold of 3.0 Rooms Per Person: 1950–1980

Number of Persons	Owners				Renters			
	1950		1980		1950		1980	
	Number	Percent	Number	Percent	Number	Percent	Number	Percent
1	403,961	28.9	2,812,449	37.5	202,878	57.9	488,977	61.1
2	902,971	64.6	4,143,571	55.2	135,252	38.6	297,389	37.1
3+	91,089	6.5	543,844	7.3	12,138	3.5	14,298	1.8
Total	1,398,021	100.0	7,499,864	100.0	350,268	100.0	803,664	100.0

Source: See Exhibit 3.17.

eliminate the production shortfall that Anthony Downs has predicted for the decade.[66]

How could this be done? The findings of the research presented in this chapter point toward one approach. First, most houses with surplus space are owned by elderly adults living alone or middle-aged couples with no children present at home. Findings from the CINCH reports that were discussed above in Chapter Two indicate that this sector of the population has been responsible for a substantial amount of accessory conversion.

However, the potential for conversion does not lie with the current occupants of large houses with surplus space, although much of the planning literature on accessory apartments presumes that it does.[67] Some of these middle-aged and retired owners may want to convert parts of their houses into accessory apartments, but the vast majority probably do not. Because of the institutional factors discussed in this chapter, they enjoy a standard of space consumption that they are not likely to give up unless forced to do so by deteriorating finances. On the other hand, many young adults, who represent the largest share of the home-buying market, are not so fortunate. These latter face a considerably higher real cost of ownership over both the short run and the long run. For this reason, I suspect that the greatest potential for accessory apartment conversion lies with young couples, individuals, and single parents. Many can afford to own homes only by incurring extraordinarily high housing expenses. The incentive to install accessory apartments is thus much stronger for them than it is for middle-aged empty nesters. Young home buyers today also have smaller families than those of the 1950s and 1960s, and they are more likely to be willing to adjust their space standards in order to secure the benefits of home ownership over the longer term.

When older couples and widows move away or die, their houses turn over and in the process are transferred to younger families and individuals. This is the time when accessory apartments can be created in these houses. It is also the time when the public sector has the opportunity to become involved. Public policy can encourage these younger home buyers to make more conversions by providing them with various kinds of assistance. In the process, the public sector can also create a regulatory handle for controlling the quality and location of the accessory apartments that will be produced in the community.

Notes

1. For a discussion of the costs of accessory apartment conversions see Martin Gellen, "A House in Every Garage: The Economics of Secondary Units," Working Paper, Center for Real Estate and Urban Economics, Institute of Business and Economic Research (Berkeley, CA: University of California, 1982). Bert Verrips, *Second Units: An Emerging Housing Resource*, People for Open Space Housing/Greenbelt Program, Technical Report #2-E (San Francisco, CA: People for Open Space, 1983), 21-39. For the best "do it yourself" book on conversions, see Herb Hughes, *More Living Space: Interior Conversions for Attics, Basements, Bathrooms, Storage, Second Story Additions* (Passaic, NJ: Creative Homeowner Press, 1980).
2. Anthony Downs, *Rental Housing in the 1980s* (Washington, D.C.: The Brookings Institution, 1982), 121–26.

3. Note that prior to 1900 average household size exceeds average family size; after 1940, average family size is greater. The most likely explanation for why household size is greater than family size prior to 1900 is the presence of boarders. Boarders were quite common in American families up until even the second quarter of the twentieth century. For a discussion of this change in household arrangements, see John Modell and Tamara K. Hareven, "Urbanization and the Malleable Households: an Examination of Boarding and Lodging in American Families," in Michael Gordon, ed., *The American Family in Social-Historical Perspective* (New York: St. Martin's Press, 1976), 51–68.

4. A total fertility rate of 2,110 per 1,000 women represents the "replacement level" fertility for the total population under current mortality conditions and assuming zero net migration. The total fertility rate declined between the two World Wars but never dropped below replacement level. After 1960 it declined once more and by the late 1970s dropped below replacement level. See, Arnold Coale and Melvin Zelnick, *New Estimates and Fertility and Population in the United States* (Princeton, NJ: Princeton University Press, 1963) 22–23. See also United States Bureau of the Census, *Current Population Reports*, Series P-23, No. 36.

5. *American Housing and Its Use, The Demand for Shelter Space* New York: Russell & Russell, 1957), 80-84.

6. Paul Glick and Robert Parke, Jr., "New Approaches in Studying the Life Cycle of the Family," *Demography*, 2 (1965): 187–202. For a discussion by a family historian, see Robert V. Wells, "Demographic Change and the Life Cycle of American Families," in Theodore K. Rabb and Robert I. Rothberg, eds., *The Family in History: Interdisciplinary Essays* (New York: Harper & Row, 1971), 85–94. Paul Glick and Arthur J. Norton, "Marrying, Divorcing and Living Together in the U.S. Today," *Population Bulletin*, 32 (1979).

7. George Masnick and Jo Bane, *The Nation's Families: 1960–1990* (Boston, MA: Auburn House, 1980), table 2.10.

8. Paul Glick, *American Families* (New York: John Wiley & Sons, 1957), 160–62. See also John Modell, Frank F. Furstenberg, Jr. and Theodore Hershberg, "Social Change and Transitions to Adulthood in Historical Perspective," in Michael Gordon, ed., *The American Family in Social-Historical Perspective* (New York: St. Martin's Press, 1958), 192–219.

9. Arnold M. Rose, "Living Arrangements of Unattached Persons," *American Sociological Review*, 12 (1947): 429–35.

10. Arnold M. Rose, "Interest in the Living Arrangements of the Urban Unattached," *American Journal of Sociology*, 51 (1948): 483–93.

11. Robert T. Michael. "The Rise in Divorce Rates, 1960–1974: Age-Specific Components," *Demography*, 15 (1978): 177–82. This study demonstrates that the rise in the divorce rate since 1960 has been less a product of changes in the age structure of the population and more the result of increases in age-specific divorce rates. Using data from fifteen states, Michael found that changing age composition of the population accounted for only about 40 percent of the rise in divorce rates; 60 percent of the increase was explained by higher age-specific divorce rates, particularly for women in their twenties. Michael's study also provides some limited but suggestive evidence that this higher risk of divorce may be a factor which, by increasing general marital instability, has also depressed female fertility.

12. Masnick and Bane, *ibid.*, 25–29.

13. Paul Glick and Eliot Norton, "Marrying, Divorce and Living Together in the United States," *Population Bulletin*, 32 (October 1977).

14. Samuel H. Preston, "Estimating the Proportion of American Marriages That End in Divorce," *Sociological Methods and Research*, 3 (1975): 435–60.

15. Geoffrey Carliner, "Determinants of Household Headship." *Journal of Marriage and the Family*, 37 (February 1975), 28–38. Simon Kuznets, "Size and Age Structure of Family Households: Exploratory Comparisons," *Population and Development Review*, 4 (1978): 187–223. James Sweet, "Living Arrangements of Separated, Widowed and Divorced Mothers," *Demography*, 9 (1972): 142–58. Robert T. Michael, Victor R. Fuchs, and Sharon R. Scott, "Changes in the Propensity to Live Alone: 1950–1976," *Demography*, 17 (1980): 39–56. John F. Ermisch, "An Economic Theory of Household Formation," *Scottish Journal of Political Economy*, 28 (1981): 1–19. Anil Markandya, "Headship Rates and the Household Formation Process in Great Britain" (Berkeley, CA: University of California, Center for Real Estate and Urban Economics, Working Paper 82-50, 1982). Lawrence B. Smith, Kenneth T. Rosen, Anil Markandya, and

Pierre-Antoine Ullmo, "The Demand for Housing, Household Headship Rates, and Household Formation: An International Analysis" (Berkeley, CA: University of California, Center For Real Estate and Urban Economics, Working Paper 82–55, 1982).

16. Winnick and Shilling, *ibid.*, 87.

17. Robert T. Michael, Victor R. Fuchs, and Sharon R. Scott, *ibid.*

18. Paul Glick and Eliot Norton, "Marrying, Divorce and Living Together in the United States," *Population Bulletin*, 32 (October 1977). In addition, individuals living alone must also bear the opportunity cost of time involved in homemaking and housekeeping. This opportunity cost was much higher in the past than it is today, because the average work day was longer and household production was less capital intensive. Insofar as one or more women ordinarily were responsible for most household production in a family, unmarried persons probably found it more economic to dwell with a family, even if as a boarder. An indication of how great was the opportunity cost of household labor is demonstrated indirectly by the fact that most unattached individuals who could not live with families chose to live instead in hotels or boarding houses where these domestic services were supplied as part of the rental agreement. The large cash outlays needed to acquire household overhead capital may also explain why primary individuals also preferred to rent furnished apartments.

19. The change in consumer behavior that occurred was considerably more dynamic than our discussion indicates. As the number of persons with the income necessary to establish separate households increased, markets responded in a way that encouraged more of them to set up separate households. While more individuals gained the income to live alone, the introduction of services and housing to meet the needs of this segment of the population have simultaneously increased the opportunity for living alone. An expanding market for these goods and services made possible economies of scale as well as technological and product innovations that in turn helped to lower the full economic cost of living alone, thus reinforcing the initial income effect itself. One need only enter the average supermarket anywhere in the United States today and glance at the immense variety of prepared and pre-cooked foods as well as other household goods to appreciate the vast scale on which American enterprise caters to the needs of single adults, divorced parents, and childless working couples.

20. John Beresford and Alice Rivlin, "Privacy, Poverty, and Old Age," *Demography*, 3 (1977): 247.

21. The nuclear family is more a state of mind than a particular set of householding arrangements. What distinguishes the nuclear family from other family forms is that its members feel they have more in common with each other than they do with anyone else in the community around them and consider the family to be a precious emotional unit that must be protected from intrusion by the outside world by isolation in a private domestic setting. In this sense, single-parent households can be considered nuclear families even though no spouse is present. In this book, however, I have used the term "nuclear family" to refer to one particular household type: a married couple with children. Married couples without children are not nuclear families in the pure sense, but nuclear "dyads." In terms of the nuclear family as an institution, the dyad is a "transitional" stage with which the "family cycle" is supposed to begin and end. The increasing popularity of childless marriage represents a substantial departure from the traditional nuclear family.

22. Francis Kobrin, "The Fall in Household Size and the Rise of the Primary Individual in the United States," in Michael Gordon, ed., *ibid.*, 1976, 69–81.

23. United States Bureau of the Census, *Current Population Reports*. "Households, Families, Marital Status and Living Arrangements," March 1983 (Advanced Report) Series P-20, no. 382, 1983.

24. Masnick and Bane, *ibid.*, table 2.14, 45-50.

25. Richard A. Easterlin, *Birth and Fortune, The Impact of Number of Personal Welfare* (New York: Basic Books). Richard Easterlin is one of the few demographers who has predicted that age-specific marriage and fertility rates will rise during the 1980s and generate another baby boom in the 1990s. An outcome of this sort would reverse to some extent the changes in population structure (falling average household size and rising headship rates) that have occurred over the past twenty years. For a critique and refutation of his predictions, see Sar A. Levitan and Richard S. Belous, *What's Happening to the American Family?* (Baltimore, MD: Johns Hopkins University Press, 1981): 46–49.

26. Winnick, *ibid.*, 12–40.

27. J. Prais and H.H. Houthhakker, *The Analysis of Family Budgets* (Cambridge, U.K.: Cambridge University Press, 1955). John Muellbauer, "Testing the Barten Model of Household Composition Effects and the Cost of Children," *Economic Journal*, 87 (September 1977): 460–87.

28. Edward P. Lazear and Robert T. Michael, "Family Size and the Distribution of Real Per Capita Income," *American Economic Review*, 70 (March 1980): 91–107.

29. Some evidence indicates that this is not a hard and fast principle of consumer behavior. Although non-housing consumption absorbs larger proportions of household income as family size increases, expenditures for housing do tend to increase also. Some recent econometric analysis of the Annual Housing Survey has shown that for any given level of income, expenditures increase as household size increases up to about five persons; beyond that point however, expenditures on housing will decline as other household spending priorities predominate. See Judith D. Feins and Terry Saunders Lane, *How Much for Housing? New Perspectives on Affordability and Risk* (Cambridge, MA: Abt Books, 1981), 14. Kain and Quigley in their St. Louis study found that for home owners expenditures on housing increased with family size; only for renters did they decrease with family size. See John F. Kain and John M. Quigley, *Housing Markets and Racial Discrimination: A Microeconomic Analysis* (New York: National Bureau of Economic Research, 1975), 180–83.

30. *Ibid.*, 217–29. Kain and Quigley's analysis also showed that there are important interactions between payments for size and other housing attributes, especially physical condition and proximity to the workplace. This suggests that while some trade-offs between space and other housing attributes are possible for growing families, the "jointness" of size, quality and access may limit the degree to which these types of adjustments will be feasible.

31. Leo Grebler, David Blank and Louis Winnick, *Capital Formation in Residential Real Estate, Trends and Prospects*, National Bureau of Economic Research (New York: Columbia University Press, 1956), 276–77.

32. *Planning the Home for Occupancy* (Chicago, IL: Public Administration Service, 1950), 15. These space standards took account of both health requirements and space required for furniture and equipment of average dimensions. The standards were more concerned with household functions than with privacy and were independent of any subdivisions into rooms. Nor was household composition taken into consideration. Despite these limitations, the data reflect a level of development of domestic technology that is not very different from our own. The modern house of 1950 contained most of the mechanical systems that make up the utility core of the average new home today as well as many of the appliances (washing machine, gas ovens, refrigerators, vacuum cleaners) that are also commonly found in contemporary households.

33. Robert Eisner, Emily R. Simons, Paul J. Pieper, and Steven Bender, "Total Incomes in the United States, 1946–1976," *Review of Income and Wealth*, 28 (June 1982): 133–74.

34. Neil Foote, Janet Abu-Lughod, Marian M. Foley and Louis Winnick, eds., *Housing Choices and Constraints* (New York: McGraw-Hill, 1962), 111–13.

35. Winnick and Shilling, *ibid.*, 26.

36. Peter A. Morrison, "Duration of Residence and Prospective Migration: The Evaluation of a Stochastic Model," *Demography*, 4 (1967): 553–61. Anthony Speare, Jr., "Residential Satisfaction as an Intervening Variable in Residential Mobility," *Demography*, 11 (1974): 173–88.

37. John P. Shelton, "The Cost of Renting Versus Owning A Home," *Land Economics*, 44 (1968): 49–72. See also John B. Lansing and Eva Mueller, *Residential Location and Urban Mobility* (Ann Arbor, MI: Institute for Social Research), 11–12.

38. Daniel R. Fredland, *Residential Mobility and Home Purchase: A Longitudinal Perspective on the Family Life Cycle and the Housing Market* (Lexington, MA: Lexington Books, 1974), 21–22, 100–101. See also Eric A. Hanushek and John M. Quigley, "An Explicit Model of Intraurban Mobility," *Land Economics*, 54 (1978): 411–29.

39. Alden Speare, Jr., Sidney Goldstein, and William H. Frey, *Residential Mobility, Migration and Metropolitan Change* (Cambridge, MA: Ballinger, 1975), 150–54.

40. One can easily simulate the effects of a fixed payment mortgage in lowering real housing costs for home owners who remain in place by assuming that the rental value of housing rises at the same rate as inflation and by comparing the relative cost of owning over renting. Before-tax occupancy cost for the house would be about a third of the market rent of a dwelling of similar size and about two-thirds of the rental cost of a dwelling half the size. If the mortgage is not paid off, and the general price level has risen since the mortgage was originated, the real cost of the

monthly payment for the home owner will be less than the market rent for a similar dwelling depending on the average rate of inflation during that time. For example, the real cost of the monthly payment will have declined by a third if the rate of inflation averaged 2 percent for twenty years of a thirty-year fixed payment mortgage, and by 6? percent if the rate of inflation averaged 5 percent during that time. At a 2 percent inflation rate, the before-tax occupancy cost of the home will be 89 percent of the rental cost of a dwelling half the size; at 5 percent inflation, staying in the home will cost 20 percent of the rental expense for a dwelling half the size. For simulations that show these effects as well what happens with adjustable rate mortgages see the studies in Franco Modigliani and Donald R. Lessard, eds., *New Mortgage Designs for an Inflationary Environment* (Washington, D.C.: Federal Reserve Bank of Boston, 1975), 13–74.

41. Henry Tomassen, *ibid.*, "Circuit Breaking and Life Cycle 'Lock-In,'" *National Tax Journal*, 31 (1978): 59–65.

42. Henry J. Aaron, *Shelter and Subsidies: Who Benefits from Federal Housing Policies* (Washington, D.C.: Brookings Institution), 68–73. See also, David Laidler, "Income Tax Incentives for Owner-Occupied Housing," in Arnold C. Harberger and Martin J. Bailey, eds., *The Taxation of Income from Capital* (Washington, D.C.: Brookings Institution, 1969).

43. Emil Sunley, "Tax Advantages of Homeownership Versus Renting: A Cause of Suburban Migration?" in *Annual Conference on Taxation* (Columbus, OH: NTA-TIA, 1971), 377–92.

44. See *Prentice-Hall Federal Tax Course, 1984* (Englewood Cliffs, NJ: Prentice-Hall, 1983), 1518–19.

45. John Doling, "The Family Life Cycle and Housing Choices," *Urban Studies*, 13 (1976): 55–58. Kevin F. McCarthy, "The Household Life Cycle and Housing Choices," *Papers of the Regional Science Association*, 37 (1976): 55–80.

46. P.B. McLeod and J.R. Ellis, "Housing Consumption over the Family Life Cycle: An Empirical Analysis," *Urban Studies*, 19 (1982): 177–83.

47. Douglas Diamond, "Taxes, Inflation, Speculation and the Cost of Homeownership," *Journal of the American Real Estate and Urban Economics Association*, 8 (1980): 281–98. The real after-tax cost of ownership is derived from the nominal before-tax cost by *subtracting* expected annual appreciation and reduced income taxes as a result of the deductibility of mortgage interest and property taxes, and by adding an amount equal to the foregone interest on the downpayment.

48. Leo Grebler and Frank G. Mittlebach, *The Inflation of House Prices* (Lexington, MA: D.C. Heath, 1979), 76–78. For some indirect evidence on the influence of expected capital gains on the purchase of large homes, see David Dale-Johnson and G. Michael Phillips, "Housing Attributes Associated with Capital Gain," *Journal of the American Real Estate and Urban Economics Association*, 12 (Summer 1984): 162–75.

49. Nonna Noto, "Difference in Mortgage Behavior by Age of Household: Implications for the Mortgage Interest Deduction in a Period of Demographic Change," Unpublished paper presented at the American Real Estate and Urban Economics Association Annual Midyear Conference, May 28, 1980.

50. Home buyers over the age of 40 tend to borrow at much shorter maturities in order to ensure that the debt is paid off before retirement. For the same reasons, maturities and loan-to-value ratios also tend to be lower for home owners over forty who refinance. Rarely will the loan-to-value ratio exceed 75 percent: maturities are typically twenty years or less.

51. Frank DeLeeuw and Larry Ozane, "Housing," in Henry J. Aaron and Joseph A. Pechman, eds., *How Taxes Affect Economic Behavior* (Washington, D.C.: Brookings Institution, 1981), 283–326. Patric H. Hendershott, "Real User Costs and the Demand for Single Family Housing," *Brookings Papers on Economic Activity*, 2 (1980): 401–52. Harvey Rosen and Kenneth Rosen, "Federal Taxes and Homeownership: Evidence from Time Series," *Journal of Political Economy*, (1980), 59–75.

52. James R. Follain, Jr., "Does Inflation Affect Real Behavior: The Case of Housing," *The Southern Economic Journal*, 48 (1980): 570–82.

53. Thomas P. Boehm and Joseph A. McKenzie, "Inflation, Taxes, and the Demand for Housing," *Journal of the American Real Estate and Urban Economics Association*, 10 (Spring 1982): 25–38.

54. Ira S. Lowry, Carol E. Hillestad, and Syam Sarma, *California's Housing Adequacy, Availability and Affordability* (Santa Monica, CA: RAND Corporation, 1983).

55. *Ibid.*, 84–89.

56. Oliver P. Williams, Harold Herman, Charles S. Liebman and Thomas R. Dye, *Suburban Difference and Metropolitan Policies, A Philadelphia Story* (Philadelphia, PA: University of Pennsylvania Press, 1965), 187–210.

57. Claude S. Fischer, *To Dwell Among Friends, Personal Networks in Town and City* (Chicago, IL: University of Chicago Press).

58. Fischer, *ibid.*, Appendix A, 267–84. The sample was drawn by randomly selecting households on census blocks or neighborhood units as appropriate from within larger sampling units: namely, *census tracts* in cities over 10,000 people in the San Francisco–Oakland and Sacramento SMSAs and *municipalities* for nonmetropolitan towns under 10,000 in population. Ten of these sampling units were selected from each of the five following strata: (1) *major central cities*—San Francisco, Oakland, and Sacramento; (2) *inner suburbs*—tracts outside the center cities of Oakland and San Francisco but within fifteen miles of San Francisco and ten miles of Oakland; (3) *outer suburbs*—all other tracts in both the San Francisco–Oakland and Sacramento SMSAs; (4) *small cities*—all other cities and towns in the region; and (5) *small towns and unincorporated places*—primarily rural areas. Weighting procedures were used to adjust the data for the sampling process. Each case was weighted by the reciprocal of the probability of the selection of its housing unit to reflect the distribution of households as a whole throughout the region.

59. John L. Goodman, "Urban Residential Mobility: Places, People and Policy," (Washington, D.C.: Urban Institute, 1978).

60. Earl W. Morris and Mary Winter, "A Theory of Family Housing Adjustment," *Journal of Marriage and the Family*, 37 (1975): 309–20. Earl W. Morris and Mary Winter, *Housing, Family and Society* (New York: John Wiley and Sons, 1978), chap. 3.

61. Leo Grebler and Frank G. Mittlebach, *The Inflation of House Prices, Its Extent, Causes and Consequences* (Lexington, MA: D.C. Heath, 1978) Table H-20.

62. The estimation method used was Ordinary Least Squares (OLS), which produces inefficient estimates. The coefficients are unbiased, but they do not have the minimum variance property among the class of unbiased linear estimators. OLS thus produces estimates with larger variances than can be obtained with Weighted Least Squares (WLS). However, WLS suffers from the problem that the error distribution is not normal and classical statistical tests cannot be used. See Robert S. Pindyck and Daniel L. Rubinfeld, *Economic Models and Economic Forecasts* (New York: McGraw-Hill, 1976), 240–41.

63. Dowell Myers, "Aging of Population and Housing, A New Perspective on Planning for More Balanced Metropolitan Growth," *Growth and Change*, 9 (July 1978): 8–13.

64. See discussion of this phenomenon below in Chapter Five. This phenomenon has been documented by a number of research studies. See David Popenoe, *The Suburban Environment: Sweden and the United States* (Chicago: IL: University of Chicago Press), 118.

65. 1980 *Census of Housing Components of Inventory Change*, United States & Regions, Vol. 4, table 5A.

66. See note 1 *supra*.

67. Katherine P. Warner, "Neighborhoods as Housing Environments for Maturing People," in Urban Land Institute, *Housing for a Maturing Population* (Washington, D.C.: Urban Land Institute, 1983), 112–35; see also Laszlo Papp, in Urban Land Institute, *ibid.*, 232–43.

4

The Problem of Exclusive
Single-Family Zoning

Accessory apartments create two types of problems. The first type concerns physical impacts: increased parking and traffic, and alterations in the appearance of buildings that are seen as disrupting the architectural harmony of a neighborhood. The second type concerns social and cultural conflict. The accessory apartment represents a deviation from the traditional image of housing, family, and neighborhood. It symbolizes a change in the way the single-family house is used, a change that clashes with the traditional meanings attached to the categories of residential zoning.

Residential zoning is locally legislated regulation for land use and building form. It is an instrument by which a community can control its social and economic composition. It is a kind of rationing and categorizing device that puts people in their places. Zoning gives a community control over the direction of change and development and also over the definition of the place of its members in society. It protects old-timers from newcomers, thereby giving continuity to the character of a community.

American zoning is based on an implicit value judgment about the ordering of land development. Central to this ordering is the separation of single-family housing from apartments, which provides the theoretical basis for much residential zoning as it is practiced today. Constance Perin has described this ordering as a hierarchy that parallels the ladder of life.

> The hierarchy of land uses is at the same time the ladder of life: one climbs the ladder as the "natural progression" through the stages of the life cycle—from renting an apartment or townhouse, duplex, or attached row house, to owning, as still another step, any one of those along the way to the ultimate rung, that of owning a single-family detached house. . . . A sacred quality endows both the family and its "home," sacred in the sense of being set apart from the mundane and having a distinctive aura. . . . In the hierarchy of land uses all those below the apex partake less of this sacred quality, but when one follows those "natural and orderly processes of

progress," then one can achieve the ideal family existence, fulfilling both the American Dream and the American Creed. Any other residential dwelling . . . is a "compromise" with those ideals.[1]

Today the traditional ordering of land uses, as reflected in the categories of residential zoning, is under great stress. The structure of the family and the economics of housing are changing, and new forms of tenure and householding have been emerging. People's beliefs about what housing and family should be, by contrast, have remained relatively fixed; accessory apartments challenge these beliefs.

Although today accessory apartments are seen by many as a way to improve housing opportunities, they were once considered a reliable indicator of blight. They were found only in marginal single-family neighborhoods that showed signs of deterioration and decline. This perception is difficult to alter, despite the presence of conversions in many stable and well-maintained neighborhoods. (Even in the most exclusive communities, the customary maid's quarters may now serve as an accessory apartment.) But even if its association with blight could be removed, the accessory apartment would still be feared, for it makes multifamily use of a single-family house—a practice that violates the sanctity many people attribute to the single-family house and neighborhood.

These fears and perceptions cannot be accepted at face value, but must be evaluated in relation to the "rational basis" of exclusive single-family zoning. What public purpose is in fact served by preventing individual home owners from creating accessory apartments in response to changing life-styles and economic needs? Zoning regulation, both individual provisions as well as the entire zoning ordinance, must have a "substantial" relation to the health, safety, morals, comforts, convenience, and general welfare of the community. This "rational basis" test is not simply a legal requirement; it is also an acknowledgement that zoning is to a large degree an instrument of social policy and must therefore serve legitimate social ends.

This chapter endeavors to explain the obvious as well as the more subtle reasons why American zoning has been so strongly attached to the concept of the exclusive single-family district. It examines the rationales developed to justify the exclusion of building types other than one-unit dwellings from single-family zones. The final sections argue that this practice of exclusion is on the verge of changing because the legitimacy of its underlying rationale is open to question. Some of the environmental problems associated with accessory apartments, particularly parking and visual impacts, will be discussed in Chapter Five.

The Purposes of Zoning

Comprehensive zoning ordinances divide communities into districts, each with its own set of controls on type of use, intensity of use, and building bulk and height. Use regulations separate residential, commercial, and industrial activities as well as subclasses of each of these. Intensity regulations limit the amount of an activity that can occur in any given unit of land area; they are aimed at limiting population density and controlling the load on available facilities including streets, water, sewerage, police, and other basic city services. Finally, bulk controls regulate light, air, and open space in the interest of enhancing human comfort, health, and enjoyment. Typical bulk controls include setback requirements, yard and court regulations, and height and lot coverage controls.

Historically, districting served as a device for mediating the cultural and economic conflicts produced by urban growth and decentralization during the early twentieth century. Urban decentralization was not a smooth process. From the 1890s up to the 1920s, many suburbs underwent what Herbert Gans has called "definitional struggles" to determine whether middle-class or working-class culture would prevail along the transit corridors. Zoning was one response to these conflicts. To the residents of old established suburbs, the electric trolley and the five-cent fare introduced in the 1890s served as a magnet that attracted the multiple dwellings and the saloons of the working class. Fears of newcomers and property deterioration led to a series of attempts to halt these incursions with laws prohibiting saloons and wood-frame tenement buildings.[2]

During the 1920s the struggles intensified. Encouraged by outlying railroad beltlines and the availability of electric power, telephone exchanges, and cheap land, thousands of manufacturers sought to build factories at the metropolitan periphery. Up until this time, suburban growth had been primarily a process of residential decentralization. In the 1920s retail stores began moving out of the central business district, locating at new commercial subcenters around suburban transit intersections.[3] Along with the businesses and factories came duplexes and townhouses and modern apartment buildings, which made suburban residence possible not only for working-class families but for many others who because of their life-styles did not prefer or need a single-family dwelling. This spectacular growth at the metropolitan fringe, when combined with the practice of unregulated land use, led to enormous land speculation, piece-meal development, incomplete provision of services and facilities, and the depreciation of many old, established residential areas that had consisted exclusively of single-family homes.

Zoning was seldom seen or used as a tool for changing the essential character and structure of American cities. It was rather a means of stabilizing the single-family neighborhoods of burgeoning suburbs from "harmful intrusions."[4] Its popular appeal and mass political support were based largely on the conviction that it would protect home owners of all classes from the most unscrupulous and speculative use of individual parcels of land.[5] Thus zoning did not alter the basic pattern of expansion in the American metropolitan system. On the contrary, zoning turned this pattern into a set of norms for the spatial ordering of urban communities.

This ordering was both hierarchical and cumulative. Under traditional zoning, a community was divided into five districts—single-family, two-family, multiple-family, business and industrial. These use-categories were ranked in terms of need for protection and degree of exclusiveness, with single-family districts being the highest and industrial the lowest. The ordering of uses was also cumulative. All uses permitted in a higher district were also permitted in a lower district; but lower uses were excluded from higher-use districts. Industrial zones, in which all uses were allowed, were often designated as "unclassified zones."[6] Over time city planning agencies used different densities within these broader use-categories as the basis for creating more specialized districts, and the number of categories eventually increased.

The cumulative system of districting reflected the historical inheritance of the "stage theory of neighborhood evolution." According to this theory, which land economists had derived from observing the history of American cities, all urban residential neighborhoods began as homogeneous districts of single-family housing or cottages, became increasingly heterogeneous with age as multiple dwellings appeared, and eventually were transformed into predominantly industrial or commercial areas as cities expanded geographically and their populations grew.

Zoning did not protect the single-family home so much as the exclusive single-family neighborhood; single-family housing in multiple-residence and nonresidential districts received no special protection whatsoever.[7] Single-family neighborhoods were thought to deserve this protection because they were the most vulnerable and unstable parts of growing cities. Single-family housing was the least productive of rental income of all private land-uses, and was therefore the least able to compete in an unregulated land market when the demand by higher-density and higher rent-paying uses increased. According to the stage theory of growth, the replacement of single-family neighborhoods by higher-density, higher rent-paying uses was a natural law of urban development. The acceptance of this "theory" by land investors made single-family neighborhoods the most susceptible to speculative abuses, social disruption, depreciation, deterioration, and eventual blight.

At the same time, city planners, the courts, and public officials saw single-family residential areas as worthy of special protection because of the vital socialization functions of family life and neighborhood. Protection could be provided by excluding all other competing uses on a permanent basis, so that ownership and use of housing in single-family neighborhoods would be subject to little risk or uncertainty. Restrictive covenants among private home owners had been developed for this purpose and were accepted as legitimate devices by the courts, but covenants were difficult to enforce because they required unanimous participation by all property owners in a particular area. Violation of a covenant could only be enforced by civil court action, a very costly process subject to all the uncertainties and delays of litigation.

The Principle of Exclusive Districts

The novel feature of zoning, in contrast to building codes, has been the establishment by government of different districts for different kinds of buildings. The separation of uses into districts was not new; this had been accomplished on a piecemeal basis by private covenants which the courts had long been in the business of enforcing.[8] What was new was that government took over this power from the private market and the courts.[9]

The idea that government could create districts which established different regulations for different areas, however, appeared to be a discriminatory and arbitrary violation of private property rights. Edward M. Bassett, the lawyer from Flatbush who authored the nation's first comprehensive zoning law, points out that it was important for the success of early zoning laws to counteract this impression by demonstrating that the transfer of such a power to government was dictated by overriding matters of public health, safety and welfare.[10] In addition, because of the constitutional requirement of "equal protection," districts themselves had to be uniform with respect to the specific regulations established for each one.[11]

During the early evolution of zoning, height and bulk districts brought little or no criticism from the courts because of their immediate and apparent relationship to public health and safety.[12] Not only was the risk of fire greater in high buildings, but fire-fighting technology to deal with these types of hazards had not yet been developed. The health and safety associated with traffic congestion were also deemed by the courts to be a valid reason for height and bulk controls insofar as they prevented overloading of the capacity of the streets.[13]

Use-districts proved to be more problematic. The separation of industrial activities from residential uses had been upheld numerous times by the courts as a form of nuisance control.[14] The exclusion of commercial activities from residential areas, however, could not be easily justified by the common law of nuisances. Evidence had to be shown that a store or office building in a residential area increased the risk of fire, street traffic, and disease. This was never easy to demonstrate. Efforts to do so resorted to flimsy evidence of health disorders caused by mixing of uses which bordered on folklore more than science. For example, in a famous Washington, D.C. trial, expert testimony was presented by a physician who had worked in the Panama Canal Zone. He had studied house flies and concluded that their short lives were spent primarily near the spot of their origin. They spread disease, not by transmitting it from infected meat or vegetables, but by coming in contact with sick persons first and then lighting on meat and vegetables in stores, thereby infecting the food supply which went out to the neighborhood.[15]

If it was difficult to justify the exclusion of businesses from residential areas, it was virtually impossible to make a case that municipalities were in some way protecting public health and safety by setting up residential districts from which apartments would be excluded. Nuisance control could not provide a rational basis for this extension of the police power.[16] In order to create protection in American law for single-family housing as a building type, the zoning movement convinced the courts to accept an expanded conception of the public welfare which encompassed issues of social policy including the protection of family life, the encouragement of home ownership, and the maintenance of a stable local tax base. Once the courts had legitimized this broader conception of the public welfare and this extension of the regulatory authority of local government, municipalities began to define a set of residential norms based on the family life cycle and to separate out residential districts not by density so much as a building-type and life-style.

Rationales for Exclusive Single-Family Zoning

At the time he wrote New York City's 1916 zoning law, Bassett believed that the police power could not be used to protect single-family neighborhoods by excluding multiple-unit housing from them.

> When Greater New York was zoned there was no segregation of residence districts according to the number of families in a dwelling. It was feared that courts would not uphold districting on that basis because of the difficulty of showing that the number of families, apart from space requirements per family, was substantially related to the health and safety of the community. For instance, a two-family house on a lot twice as large as the lot for a one-family house might seem to be equally safe and healthful. Accordingly control of the number of families was left to area-district regulations. But the demand throughout the country for the segregtion of detached, one-family houses from multi-family houses was so great, and the proof so clear that there were health and safety considerations that justified such a separation that courts gradually recognized as valid the gradations of residence districts according to number of families per unit building. This means that a two-family-house district or a multi-family-district is based on a use regulation and not on an area [bulk] or density-of-population regulation.[17]

Bassett's distinction between "use" and "area" controls as a basis for regulating density has had profound implications for the evolution of American cities. Density controls were intended to eliminate the "congestion" caused by the "overloading" of land. The aim was to prevent a deterioration in the health, safety, and welfare of persons living in a specific locality because of the sheer concentration of buildings or the intensity of activities. Although state enabling laws give municipalities the power to regulate density of population, zoning laws have rarely done so directly. The earliest attempts to do so encountered such complex problems of measurement and enforcement that most communities found it easier and cheaper to regulate population density indirectly by controlling the number of dwellings per acre with the implicit assumption that each dwelling would be occupied by a "family."[18] Because residential districting was based on this measure of density rather than persons per acre, the density standards in traditional zoning led to limitations on the residential building types expressed as use-controls, i e , one-family houses in one zone, two-family houses in another zone, and so on. Bulk and lot coverage controls were added to reflect local preferences regarding open space, views, and natural amenities.[19]

Bassett recognized that this approach was not a genuinely effective means of controlling population density.

> Although the segretion of dwellings according to the number of families is recognized by the courts as lawful, yet this segregation does not necessarily have any relation to density of population. Some multi-family houses are smaller than some one-family houses. The number of families does not measure the size of the building, and therefore does not necessarily measure the density of population.[20]

Restricting building types is a crude and largely ineffective control on population density, because population density depends only partly on building size and the degree of multiple occupancy. Population density also depends on the utilization rate of dwellings, which in turn depends on income, household size, lifestyle preferences and other factors.

Residential districting by building type will provide effective control on population density only as long as two conditions hold. First, household size must remain constant as the number of units per dwelling increases. If it declines, then one will frequently find multi-unit structures with a population density similar or lower than that of single-family houses—for example, a single-family house occupied by six persons and a three-unit structure on the same size lot with an average of 1.5 persons per unit. This example is not so farfetched as it might at first seem. Until the 1960s, when restrictive family definitions became popular, municipalities rarely set any limitation on the size of households that might occupy a dwelling in a single-family district. Instead "family" in exclusive single-family zoning was defined as an *unlimited* number of individuals residing as a "single housekeeping unit," a definition which has been expanded to include extended families, groups of nuns, etc.[21] Thus, as long as the intensity of occupancy can vary inversely with the degree of multiple occupancy, restricting the number of dwelling units per lot by itself will not be an effective means for regulating population density, except in the most extreme cases, such as a one-unit building as compared to a ten-unit building.

The second condition is that multiple-unit buildings cannot be placed on lots larger than those allowed for single-family houses. Quite often this condition is now met in low-rise town-houses and condominiums. Some of these developments contain multiple-unit buildings with population densities similar or even lower than those of older single-family house districts in the same community.

If the objective of density restrictions was simply to provide sufficient natural light and air, whether for public health or private pleasure, residential districting solely by height, bulk, and lot coverage controls would have been sufficient. These controls, in combination with the redesign of the shape of lots to accommodate small multi-unit structures, would have prevented the introduction of bulky apartment buildings into low-density residential districts, which was the object of so much controversy in early twentieth-century suburbs.[22] Indeed, some city planners argued that such regulations on apartment buildings and two-family structures were simpler and less legally complicated than use-districts based on building types; they would have allowed various kinds of multi-family buildings to be mixed with single-family houses in the same zone.[23]

Even the state courts were quick to recognize that the single-family district itself had little to do with regulating population density. A New York state court, for example, ruled that "the resolution of [the] City Planning Commission restricting the use of property in a specified area to single-family dwellings did *not* constitute a 'regulation of the density of population,' though it might tend indirectly to have such effect." In this case, a single-family district in New York City, called a G-district, was upheld as involving not a density but a use regulation. In addition, the court said that there was nothing to prevent a single-family house from containing more people than a multiple dwelling.[24]

A 1948 case from Massachusetts offers an even more striking illustration of how zoning by building type may have little or nothing to do with the controlling population density or even building density. The owner of a lot in an R-1 zone of a suburban town wanted to build a two-family, ranch-style house with two separate entrances and no interior communication between the units. One of the units would be occupied by the owner and his wife and the other by their in-laws. The lot was large enough to permit two normal single-family detached houses. Both population density (persons per acre) and building density (dwellings per acre) would have been the same as with two separate conforming dwellings, and the open space on the lot with the two-family structure would have actually been greater. The board of appeals granted a variance for the building, subject to a requirement that the owner must always occupy one of the units. The variance was challenged by a neighbor. The court held that the lot was perfectly well adapted to two conventional detached single-family houses with side yards between, and that therefore the variance was not justified.[25]

Zoning and Family Life-styles

If exclusive single-family zoning does not control population density, what precisely is its function? The purpose of the single-family district as a use-control is to promote and protect a family life-style and to encourage home ownership. Single-family housing represents an arrangement of indoor and outdoor space especially suited for private family living. The promotion of exclusive single-family home districts through zoning is intended to create a "favorable" environment for this style of living and to encourage families with children to own their own homes.

During the early 20th century, environmental social theories and social psychology were extremely influential in providing the rationale for exclusive single-family districts. Early childhood was thought to be a period during which the moral, emotional, and physical health of adults were determined. Because of their decisive influence on later life, the personal interactions and psychological associations experienced by the child had to be carefully controlled. A good home life became the means for instilling love, spirituality, and altruism—values that were essential for the survival of society and the family itself but which, according to the sociology of the time, were being eroded by the competitive, morally fragmented, impersonal, and highly stratified world of the urban-industrial order.[26]

The exclusive single-family zoning district was explicitly intended to foster a purified environment which protected children from interaction with the wider world of adult life, and which required the full-time presence of women to care for and nurture them. Hence to the middle classes in the 1920s, an exclusive single-family neighborhood meant not just a low-density living environment, but a home in a neighborhood with other families who were pursuing this same lifestyle and would reinforce their efforts to instill proper values and behavior in their children.

From this perspective, apartment living was viewed as objectionable not only because of the lack of play space for children but also because it encouraged a lifestyle in which women were not home-bound and in which children were exposed to single men and women of different social backgrounds and cultural values. Social workers and housing reformers alike believed that exposure to the lifestyles of the unattached had a detrimental effect on the moral development of young children, especially girls. It was this fear of exposure to strangers in and around the home environment that similarly inspired the tirades of housing reformers against "lodging."[27] Environmentalist and social psychological theories, combined with a pervasive middle-class fear of a breakdown of family morale under modern urban conditions, thus led to a surgical approach: isolate the family from all persons and experiences that threaten its cohesion, integrity, and socializing influence.

Throughout the 1920s the state courts followed this line of reasoning in upholding the power of municipalities to create residential districts that excluded apartments.[28] The courts declared that the protection and promotion of family life was in the greater public interest because of its important role in the socialization of children, which would influence the values and moral behavior of future generations. The most famous and probably the most elaborate articulation of this view can be found in the 1925 California State Supreme Court decision on the constitutionality of zoning in *Miller v. Board of Public Works of the City of Los Angeles:*

> We think it may be safely and sensibly said that justification for residential zoning may, in the last analysis, be rested upon the protection of the civic and social value of the American home. The establishment of such districts is for the general welfare because it tends to promote and perpetuate the American home. It is axiomatiç that the welfare, and indeed the very existence, of a nation depends upon the character and caliber of its citizenry. The character and quality of manhood and womanhood are in a large measure the result of home environment. The home and its intrinsic influences are the very foundation of good citizenship, and any factor contributing to the establishment of homes and the fostering of home life doubtless tends to the enhancement, not only of community life, but of the life of the nation as a whole.[29]

Alfred Bettman in his *amici curiae* brief before the United States Supreme Court in *Euclid v. Ambler Realty* (1926) made a similar argument but underscored the deterministic relationship between environment and moral character as the factor warranting special protection of residential neighborhoods.

> The essential object of promoting what might be called orderliness in the layout of cities is not the satisfaction of taste or aesthetic desires, but rather the promotion of those beneficial effects upon health and morals which come from living in orderly and decent surroundings. . . . The man who seeks to place the home for his children in an orderly neighborhood, with some open space and light and fresh air and quiet, is not motivated so much by considerations of taste or beauty as by the assumption that his children are likely to grow mentally, physically, and morally more healthful in such a neighborhood than in a disorderly, noisy, slovenly, blighted, and slumlike neighborhood. . . . The researches of physicians and public health students have demonstrated the importance of our physical environment as a factor in our physical health, mental sanity, and moral strength. . . . The individual can control the conditions inside his house; but except in the case of the rarely wealthy individual who can afford to buy large open spaces owned and controlled by himself, it is the community and the community alone which can furnish the necessary environmental protection.[30]

The Promotion of Home Ownership

The exclusive single-family district (R-1) was not simply a low density residential zone but one in which the use of land was restricted to a specific type of building. As a use-district, R-1 was an area in which each lot was permitted to have only one dwelling unit to be used exclusively as a residence by one family. The purpose of this restriction was to ensure that every building in a single-family district was not only *occupied* but also *owned* by a single household.

Although protecting the residences of the rich might have been one motivation behind traditional residential zoning laws, the theoreticians of early city planning in the United States wanted to make owner-occupancy the primary and dominant housing tenure for all classes.[31] City planners and housing reformers agreed that mass home ownership was a convenient solution to the problem of promoting good citizenship in a modern urban-industrial order, where government was becoming increasingly bureaucratic and impersonal and community ties increasingly tenuous. Because of their personal financial investment, home owners would have an enduring stake in the creation and maintenance of community infrastructure and services, which in turn would enhance the value of their property, the quality of their neighborhoods, and the fiscal integrity of their municipality.[32] The California Supreme Court in the *Miller* case, for example, echoed this belief:

> The establishment of single family residence districts offers inducements, not only to the wealthy, but to those of moderate means to own their own homes. With ownership comes stability, the welding together of family ties, and better attention to the rearing of children. With ownership comes increased interest in the promotion of public agencies, such as church and school, which have for their purpose a desired development of the moral and mental make-up of the citizenry of the country. With ownership of one's home comes recognition of the individual's responsibility for his share in the safeguarding of the welfare of the community and increased pride in personal achievement which must come from personal participation in projects looking toward community betterment.[33]

The connection between home ownership and single-family houses in the United States goes back to the early nineteenth century democratic movements among small farmers, who at the time constituted the bulk of the population; and home ownership still retains the notion that personal connection to the soil is a basic requirement of citizenship. In part because of this tradition, there was little effort to develop a system of air-rights ownership when farming declined and urban settlement became predominant during the industrial revolution. Air-rights ownership would have permitted fractionalized owner-occupancy in multiple-unit buildings, encouraged more higher density housing among the middle-classes in American cities, and might have restricted the growth of single-family home ownership.

City planners and the courts agreed that encouraging home ownership would

promote neighborhoods composed of families with an abiding financial and social stake in their immediate surroundings and in the broader community. Exclusive single-family districts would thus exert a positive influence over civic life in
general, and the more such districts a city had, the greater the benefits of this influence. However, given the institutional impediment to fractionalized owner occupancy of residential buildings, the only way to ensure that a majority of the
homes in a neighborhood would be owner-occupied would be to require that all
buildings in a district be single-family dwelling units. Until a system of air-rights
ownership could be developed as in the condominium, the primary form of residential owner occupancy would be single-family housing.

The single-family house, however, was an expensive form of shelter. Thomas
Adams, in his book *The Design of Residential Areas* (1932), argued that zoning
and subdivision controls were devices that could bring home ownership within
reach of millions of American families who were renters and otherwise could not
afford to own. The chief obstacle was the high rate of depreciation of single-
family houses. This forced up financing costs and subjected home owners of
modest means to unbearable losses.

The chief problem, as Adams saw it, was that the unregulated land market in
many American metropolitan areas during the first quarter of this century was
driven by expectations of endless growth, a continuous increase in population
densities and constantly rising property values. Much land, even at the periphery
of the city, was zoned for far more intensive uses (commercial and apartment
buildings) than prevailed at the time or ever would in the future.[34]

Whereas most real estate investors believed that zoning should follow land
values, Adams argued just the opposite: land values should follow zoning. He
contended that once the density of a district was established by zoning, land
prices would adjust themselves in rough proportion to the ability of the land to
produce income as determined by market forces:

> The land prices largely determine the type of development, and where local
> regulations permit an intensive use of the land, the land costs, together with
> the taxes, rise to a point where comparatively high density is necessary to
> make development profitable. On the other hand, were an area zoned so
> that the density of buildings is restricted in such a way as to insure plenty of
> public and private open space without unnecessarily penalizing the land
> owners, land values would adjust themselves and become stabilized, while
> speculation based on anti-social use would be prevented.[35]

Adams believed that exclusive single-family zoning would stabilize property
values by excluding higher-density residential uses on a relatively permanent
basis. This would force land values to adjust to the income levels of home buyers
and make ownership more affordable. The exclusion of higher-density uses from
single-family home districts would also reduce the threat of land-use change,

extend the economic life of single-family houses, and keep special assessments and local property taxes low enough to protect the value of home equities:

> Rapid and indiscriminate changes of use and density cause the premature depreciation of property that lessens security of investment and creates blighted conditions. When land is not planned and zoned to suit the density and character of the buildings first erected, the tendency is to increase the density and change the character of the development long before the buildings, street, sewers, etc., would have required reconstruction if maintained for their original uses. And it should be remarked that the need of combining planning and zoning is greatest in the areas where the smallest houses are erected because such houses show the smallest margin of profit and are least able to bear the losses due to depreciative changes.[36]

By reducing the risk of locational obsolescence zoning would also reduce the risk of loss for both home owners and lenders. Insofar as it guaranteed neighborhood stability for the single-family home as a building type, residential zoning was in fact a crucial pre-condition for the introduction of the long-term, fixed-rate, fully amortizing mortgages introduced by the Federal Housing Administration during the 1930s. With the prospect of stable property values, discount rates on mortgages could be lowered, maturities extended, and loan-to-value ratios for first mortgages raised beyond the traditional 60 percent to 80 percent and higher. By the early 1940s the widespread use of zoning and subdivision controls in combination with this new approach to home financing had revolutionized the American housing sector and paved the way for a massive expansion of home ownership in the following decades.[37]

The Unresolved Problem of the Two-Family Dwelling

The United States Supreme Court's decision in *Euclid v. Ambler* was important in city planning history not only because the court gave legitimacy to municipal zoning as an expansion of the police power, but also because it affirmed the principle of zoning by building type. The case dealt with the question of whether the power to zone included the power to create and maintain separate residential districts "from which business and trade of every sort, including hotels and apartment houses, are excluded." (Apartment houses meant any residential structure containing three or more dwelling units.) In a famous paragraph, the Court summarized the rationales for the exclusion of apartments from residential districts which had been developed by almost a decade of state court rulings:

> With particular reference to apartment houses, it is pointed out that the development of *detached house sections* is greatly retarded by the coming of

apartment houses, which has sometimes resulted in destroying the entire section for *private house purposes;* that in such sections very often the apartment house is a mere parasite, constructed in order to take advantage of the open spaces and attractive surroundings created by the residential character of the district. Moreover, the coming of one apartment house is followed by others, interfering by their height and bulk with the free circulation of air and monopolizing the rays of the sun which otherwise would fall upon the *smaller homes,* and bringing, as their necessary accompaniments, the disturbing noise incident to the increased traffic and business, and the occupation, by means of moving and parked automobiles, of larger portions of the streets, thus detracting from their safety and depriving children of the privilege of quiet and open spaces for play, enjoyed by those in more favored localities, until, finally, the residential character of the neighborhood and its desirability as a place of *detached residences* are utterly destroyed. Under these circumstances, apartment houses, which in a different environment would be not only entirely unobjectionable but highly desirable, come very near to being nuisances. If these reasons, thus summarized, do not demonstrate the wisdom or sound policy in all respects of those restrictions which we have indicated as pertinent to the inquiry, at least, the reasons are sufficiently cogent to preclude us from saying, as it must be said before the ordinance can be declared unconstitutional, that such provisions are clearly arbitrary and unreasonable, having no substantial relation to the public health, safety, morals or general welfare. (Emphasis added.)[38]

Although *Euclid v. Ambler* affirmed the power of local governments to zone in general, it left one very important question unresolved: was the creation of exclusive single-family residential districts a valid exercise of the power to zone?

The central question in the case was whether a municipality had the power to create residential districts that excluded apartment buildings as well as commercial and industrial uses. Single-family districts were not at issue: as the Court said, it was "unnecessary to consider the effect of the restrictions in respect of U-1 [single-family] districts, since none of [Ambler Realty's] land falls within that class."[39]

Nevertheless, Alfred Bettman, who argued before the court in support of the city's power to zone, believed, as did all his colleagues and most commentators since then, that the *Euclid* decision established the validity of exclusive single-family districts. He said:

As none of the realty company's land lay in a single-family zone, the Court did not treat the validity of the establishment of exclusively detached-dwelling districts as involved in the issues of the case. The opinion did, however, go far beyond a mere intimation of the validity of such districts;

for it contains an exceedingly able and clear statement of the social justification of such districts, ending with the sentence: "Under these circumstances, apartment houses which in a different environment would be not only entirely unobjectionable but highly desirable, come very near to being nuisances." The logic of the decision quite clearly includes the single-family district; for all the considerations adduced by the Court in support of the validity of exclusively residential districts apply equally to the validity of the exclusively single-family district; and the ordinance, which was sustained and held to be constitutional, allotted a large percentage of the territory to this class of district.[40]

Bettman's inference, however, is not valid. Although the ordinance under review did include an exclusive single-family zone, Justice Sutherland's opinion makes no reference to single-family housing in its key sections on the constitutionality of the power to zone, nor does it do so in those sections where apartment houses are compared to nuisances. Sutherland speaks only of "detached residences" and "private house purposes," and there is no reason to assume that these terms refer strictly and solely to "single-family" structures. In summarizing the city's zoning ordinance, the Court noted that the ordinance defined a two-family dwelling as "a *detached* dwelling for the occupation of two families, one having its principal living rooms on the first floor and the other on the second floor." Although the *Euclid* decision affirmed that municipalities had the authority under their zoning powers to establish density standards and to exclude apartment houses from low density zones, it did not uphold their authority to exclude two-family houses, for the court did not class these with apartment buildings as coming close to being "nuisances."[41]

The state court decisions on zoning left the matter just as murky. Norman Williams has examined the nearly 600 decisions by state courts that involved the classification of building types for purposes of districting. The vast majority of these cases discuss only the validity of mapping these districts, and of variances, special permits, and the interpretation of regulations based on such a districting principle. Only about 50 decisions have dealt directly with the validity of excluding specific residential building types as a basis for districting, and not more than 20 cases have actually attempted to provide a rational basis for such exclusion. Of these, none drew any serious distinction between the building-types excluded—i.e., between the exclusion of multiple dwellings and of two-family houses (or row houses) from single-family districts, nor between these and the exclusion of multiple dwellings (or row houses) from two-family districts.[42] Ironically, the two state court decisions which have ruled to uphold the exclusion of two-family dwellings from single-family neighborhoods have cited *Euclid* as precedent, ignoring its broad definition of "detached dwellings." They have instead pronounced two-family dwellings to be apartment buildings in form, function, and effect.[43] One in Illinois declared that such districting was valid as a means to control congestion and inconvenience.[44] And another in Kentucky upheld on similar grounds a prohibition against the use of former servants' quarters located over a rear garage as a separate dwelling unit.[45]

The one major exception was the *Miller* case, which has been quoted frequently because of its impassioned justification of exclusive single-family districts. In this 1925 ruling, the California Supreme Court upheld local government zoning as a valid use of the police power. The case involved the issue of whether a city had the authority to prevent a landowner from putting up a four-unit building in a district zoned for both one- and two-family houses. In the majority decision, the court spoke at length about the rationale for the "establishment of single-family residence districts" and contended that "single-family homes" were more "desirable" than apartment buildings "for the promotion and the perpetuation of family life." In its conclusion, however, the California court spoke directly to the issue at hand and declared that two-family dwellings were permissible in "strictly residential districts":

> What has been said about the desirability of encouraging home life in single family dwellings as an element in the promotion of the general welfare of a community may not apply with equal force to a regulation which relates to two-family dwellings. Nevertheless the reasoning in that behalf is not wholly inapplicable to zoning regulations, having as their basis the general welfare of the community, which permit the two-family dwellings in strictly residential districts. A two-family dwelling requires no radical change of architectural design and does not entail any added burdens over the single-family residences in the way of fire or health protection or the exercise of those civic safeguards on the part of the body politic which become necessary in localities where many large apartment houses are permitted to prevail. Moreover, the permitting of two-family dwellings does not radically change the character of the neighborhood, which by proper zoning regulations may be devoted to residential purposes. It should require no argument to show the clear distinction between permitting a two-family dwelling and permitting a 20 or even 10 family apartment house or a number of either in a residential neighborhood.[46]

According to the *Miller* decision, the exclusion of apartment buildings from residential districts composed of small houses was a valid form of regulation by which a community could promote family life and home ownership. Although the court in *Miller* intimated that there might be good reasons for separating two-family buildings from neighborhoods of single-family houses, it failed to indicate what they were. Instead, the court went on to argue that two-family houses were comparable to one-family buildings in terms of architectural form and fiscal impact and were a type of housing that did not "change the character" of a neighborhood "devoted to residential purposes." Hence there could be no valid reason for excluding two-family dwellings from one-family districts so long as the size of lots with the former was sufficient to meet prevailing open-space standards of the district and a measure of architectural control was provided to insure that the two-unit buildings were in harmony with surrounding structures.

This lack of clarity in early court decisions on the issue of exclusion of two-family dwellings from single-family districts is in some ways not surprising. The two-family house was a common feature of the residential landscape of turn of the century suburbia.[47] Exclusive single-family neighborhoods, on the other hand, were quite rare until the 1940s. In an examination of zoning maps drawn between 1910 and 1940 in three major cities, Los Angeles, Chicago and St. Louis, Barbara Flint found few exclusive single-family districts. The majority of single-family houses were located in districts zoned for both one- and two-family dwellings. Exclusive single-family neighborhoods could only be found in "estate" districts where the very rich lived.[48]

It may seem strange that the constitutionality of the exclusive single-family zone has never been settled by the courts, especially in view of its centrality to Euclidean zoning and the American system of residential land-use. The explanation for this quandary lies in the peculiarities of the legal evolution of zoning regulation in the United States. Prior to the *Euclid* case, any exercise of the police power which interfered with property rights was subject to constitutional limitations. Although legislatures were acknowledged as having great discretion as to what constituted a proper exercise of the police power the difficulty of defining the content of the police power meant that such discretion had to be subject to judicial review. The Supreme Court in particular perceived any enactment of the police power as imposing some deprivation of life, liberty, or property and as therefore potentially subject to invalidation under the due process clause. Hence, the burden of proof as to the desirability of any enactment of the police power fell upon the legislature which proposed it. The courts thus functioned as a conduct-limiting institution vis-à-vis the legislature, which had to demonstrate that any particular law or ordinance regulating the activity of private individuals or groups was substantially related to the public health, safety, morals, or welfare.

The *Euclid* decision began not only the gradual disengagement of zoning from nuisance doctrine but also from serious judicial review. This shift in attitude of the courts was expressed by greater judicial deference to legislative decisions as to what constituted the public interest or general welfare. In the period after *Euclid*, the court increasingly gave to legislative enactments under the police power a "presumption of validity." The burden of proof as to the arbitrariness or irrationality of a legislative enactment was henceforth shifted to affected parties.[49]

The shift in the presumption of validity at the same time brought an end to attempts by the courts to articulate a rational basis for single-family zoning. Once this shift had occurred, the rationale for exclusive single-family districts was taken to be self-evident. As Bassett noted in 1936, although there were fears among zoning lawyers during the 1920s that the courts "might not recognize a difference so far as health and safety were concerned between a detached one-family house and a detached two-family house . . . the courts after the *Euclid* decision were so inclined to uphold [single-family] zoning that minor distinctions were swept aside.''[50] From that point on, the courts made no serious effort at judicial review of the relationship between regulatory goals and regulatory instruments in single-family zoning.

The innovations of the Federal Housing Administration (FHA) in real estate appraisal and mortgage underwriting during the 1930s played a decisive role here also. FHA mortgage underwriting procedures discouraged the development of two-family houses. FHA appraisers believed that two-family houses were riskier than one family houses. This belief was based on the assumption that a major depression like that of the 1930s would occur on average every 12 to 15 years. This meant that the rental income stream from a two-unit house was likely to decline at least once and possibly twice during the lifetime of a 25-year mortgage, and that those owner-occupiers with two-family houses would likely have difficulty servicing their mortgages even if they retained their jobs and suffered no decline in family income. This conclusion was supported by the experiences of the Home Owners Loan Corporation during the 1930s with these kinds of properties.[51] As a result, not only did the FHA charge two-family buyers higher insurance premiums, but the greater presumed risk of foreclosure associated with two-family dwellings led the FHA to discourage the mixing of one- and two-family houses together in new subdivisions to minimize potential neighborhood risks as these houses aged.[52]

Another axiom of appraisal theory also led the FHA to promote the widespread use of exclusive single-family zoning. The FHA openly encouraged racial segregation because of its belief that social and racial mixing brought on rapid depreciation of property values. Neighborhoods that were racially and economically homogeneous were supposed to have stable property values. FHA appraisers extended the concept to the physical character of neighborhoods and drew the same conclusion about neighborhoods with buildings of similar type and architectural style. Those neighborhoods with mixes of one- and two-family dwellings were likewise considered as less stable and more subject to incipient depreciation than neighborhoods of "homogeneous physical development."[53]

The precise influence of these practices upon residential zoning has never been demonstrated. Nevertheless, these analyses, based on the accumulated experiences of appraisers and mortgage lenders, provided a strictly economic rationale—the preservation of property values—for the practice of separating one- and two-family dwellings, a practice which city planners and the courts had already come to accept as an essential principle for the ordering of residential land-use in modern cities.

Changing Definitions of Home and Family

As a regulatory device, exclusive single-family zoning was supposed to promote home ownership and to encourage neighborhood environments suitable for families with children. Since the 1960s, however, innovations in property law and changes in family structure have diminished the importance of exclusive single-family zoning as a method of achieving these social goals.

Because owner occupancy was considered to be a superior form of tenure on both social and economic grounds, R-1 zoning was originally justified as a method of promoting the public welfare because it increased the supply of ownership opportunities for all classes of people. This regulatory logic was uniquely a product of the institutional limitations of our system of property laws in the early twentieth century. When residential zoning was first established, American real estate law had not developed a set of rules for regulating ownership of air rights. Without such a framework, fractionalized owner occupancy was not possible. The only exception was the cooperative—a form of owner occupancy that was most successful among the wealthy who wanted large dwellings adjacent to the downtown areas of large cities. For most people, however, owner occupancy of residential buildings was limited to forms of undivided ownership of land and improvements by a single person, and this was most readily available in the form of the single-family house.

The perfection of condominium ownership in the 1960s made possible for the first time on a broad scale fractionalized owner occupancy of multiple unit buildings. The development of the condominium has severed the link between home ownership and single-family dwelling. This makes home ownership possible in all types of buildings from duplexes to large apartment buildings. It also makes home ownership possible for a wide variety of households that do not conform to the traditional image of the American family.

American society is now characterized by a much greater diversity of household types than was true in the past. Because of the "attenuation of the family system," more Americans are spending smaller parts of their lives in married-couple families, either as children or adults. Whereas married couples represented 79.1 percent of all households in 1950, they comprised only 60.9 percent in 1980. Today there are more single persons, childless households, and single-parent families. Not only has household composition become more diverse, but considerably fewer families have children present. According to the 1930 Census of Population, 64 percent of owner-occupied households had at least one child 18 years or less residing with them; in 1980, only 41 percent did.

These statistics indicate that much of our single-family housing is no longer being used primarily by families with children in residence. This trend calls into question the emphasis that exclusive single-family zoning has traditionally placed on promoting a life-style built around female domesticity and child-rearing. This emphasis may have made some sense sixty years ago, when almost two-thirds of the households living in single-family houses had children present. But today, when less than half of them do, it is questionable whether promoting homogeneous, family-oriented neighborhoods will produce better residential environments, or even whether it will bolster the family as an institution in contemporary society.

For one thing, families raising children today are less frequently able to afford detached housing in single-family districts. More of them than ever before are single parents. During the 1970s the number of married couples with children fell from 25.5 million to 24.5 million; by contrast, the number of single-parent households rose by 81.8 percent, climbing from 3.3 million to 5.9 million. During the 1980s, the number of one-earner, one-parent households will continue to increase; whereas in 1980 one out of five children lived in single-parent households, by 1990 one out of four is expected to do so.[54]

The changing role of women in our society also implies a new set of housing preferences that are not strictly compatible with exclusive single-family zoning. A number of studies have shown that women are more likely than men to find low-density suburban residential environments unsatisfactory and that this dissatisfaction is significantly greater for women who are single parents and women who must spend a substantial portion of their daytime hours outside the home at work.[55] These studies conclude that higher density, mixed-use residential environments give women more options to combine child-rearing with employment, and that for single parents they can reduce the financial burden of operating and maintaining a home.

The Debate over Restrictive Family Definitions

In the field of zoning itself, conventional notions about family are being revised in ways that portend a redefinition of the social purposes of the exclusive single-family district. In the debate over the legality of restrictive definitions of "family," the courts have gradually begun to distinguish between density control and regulation of life-style as separate, if not conflicting, objectives of residential zoning. This reinterpretation of the purposes of exclusive single-family zoning opens up the possibility of innovative approaches to density control, and this in turn would have tremendous implications for accessory apartments as well as for affordable housing in general.

In the 1920s when the state courts upheld the power of cities to exclude apartment buildings from residential zones in order to encourage home ownership by families, it was generally assumed that the household occupying a dwelling in a family-oriented district would be a nuclear family—a husband and wife with or without children. About 80 percent of all American households fitted this pattern; the other 20 percent varied enormously. In this category one could find a single person living alone, either unmarried or as a widow or widower; an enlarged family, with married children living at home, or several relatives or other related subfamilies; several related persons or even families living together in as one household in a single dwelling unit, temporarily or on a seasonal basis, or even permanently; common-law marriages; and foster children, living as part of a normal family. In addition, a variety of unrelated persons could also share a single-family house. These could include two or more bachelors or women, sharing a house before or after marriage; guests living in the same dwelling unit for extended periods of time; servants living in part of the same dwelling unit; students, nurses, or other similar groups sharing a common interest and living together; fraternities and sororities; and groups of monks, nuns, or other religious persons living together. These exceptions to the norm occurred frequently enough that most cities either left the term "family" undefined or defined it merely as a "single housekeeping unit."[56]

During the 1960s and 1970s the high courts reviewed a series of cases that challenged the power of municipalities to define "family" in so restrictive a manner as to exclude groups of unrelated persons from occupying dwellings in exclusive single-family zones. These cases were important for two reasons. First, they led to a debate over whether the purpose of single-family zoning was to preserve residential areas that would accommodate the needs and values of only traditional families (persons residing together who are related by blood, marriage, or adoption), or whether it might be a legitimate objective of single-family zoning to preserve a "family style of living" regardless of the type of relationships between the members of the household. Second, municipalities that had included restrictive definitions of family in their zoning ordinances also considered them to be a legitimate form of density control.[57]

The most controversial and famous of these cases was *Village of Belle Terre v. Boraas*.[58] This was the first major zoning case to come before the United States Supreme Court in forty-six years. The Village of Belle Terre, a small suburb on New York's Long Island, denied beach passes to two students living in a six-student household inside the village on the grounds that they were illegal residents according to the town's zoning ordinance. The local regulations restricted the 220-home village of 700 people exclusively to one-family dwellings with "family" defined as "one or more persons related by blood, marriage or adoption, living and cooking together as a single housekeeping unit, exclusive of household servants. A number of persons not exceeding two (2) living and cooking together as a single housekeeping unit though not related by blood, adoption, or marriage shall be deemed to constitute a family."

The six student renters sought an injunction against application of the ordinance on the grounds that it interfered with their right to travel and their right to privacy and also violated the equal protection clause of the United States Constitution. The students also alleged that the ordinance was a tool for expressing exclusionary social preferences and unfairly barred people considered uncongenial by the residents. A lower court approved the ordinance's restrictive definition of family. Upon appeal, the Second District Court used the single-housekeeping unit rule as grounds for reversing the lower court's decision and condemned the ordinance as an unnecessary infringement on the constitutional rights of the challenged household.[59]

The United States Supreme Court, however, did not agree. The majority opinion, written by Justice William O. Douglas, rejected the argument that fundamental rights had been violated. The question, then, was whether the zoning provision under review was reasonable and rationally related to a legitimate governmental objective. The Court identified this objective to be "family needs [and] values" and declared that an ordinance differentiating between related and unrelated households was a reasonable method by which to further this objective.[60]

The majority opinion in the *Belle Terre* case is important because it contains the only attempt by the United States Supreme Court to articulate a rational basis for single-family zoning. In a passage that has been widely quoted, Justice Douglas wrote:

> The regimes of boarding houses, fraternity houses, and the like present urban problems. More people occupy a given space; more cars rather continuously pass by; more cars are parked; noise travels with crowds. A quiet place where yards are wide, people few, and motor vehicles restricted are legitimate guidelines in a land-use project addressed to family needs. This goal is a permissible one within *Berman v. Parker*. . . . The police power is not confined to elimination of filth, stench, and unhealthy places. It is ample to lay out zones where family values, youth values, and the blessings of quiet seclusion and clean air make the area a sanctuary for people.[61]

In his dissent, Justice Thurgood Marshall argued that the majority opinion confused density control with life-style regulation in single-family zoning. Justice Marshall contended that an overly restrictive definition of single-family use is both inappropriate and ineffective in controlling population density and its various undesirable effects, such as traffic and noise:

> As I pointed out earlier, these are all legitimate and substantial interests of government. But I think it is clear that the means chosen to accomplish these purposes are both overinclusive and underinclusive, and that the asserted goals could be as effectively achieved by means of an ordinance that did not discriminate on the basis of constitutionally protected choices of life style. The ordinance imposes no restriction whatsoever on the number of persons who may live in a house, as long as they are related by marital or sanguinary bonds—presumably no matter how distant their relationship. Nor does the ordinance restrict the number of automobiles that may be maintained by its occupants. In that sense, the ordinance is underinclusive. On the other hand, the statute restricts the number of unrelated persons who may live in a home to no more than two. It would therefore prevent three unrelated people from occupying a dwelling even if among them they had but one income and no vehicles. While an extended family of a dozen or more might live in a small bungalow, three elderly retired persons could not occupy the large manor house next door. Thus the statute is also grossly overinclusive to accomplish its intended purpose.[62]

Specific regulations that would more directly serve the interests of the community in controlling traffic, noise, and congestion might include "limiting each household to a specified number of adults with no limitation on the number of dependent children . . . rent control, limits on the number of vehicles per household, and so forth." These methods, concluded Marshall, "would surely be better tailored to the goals asserted by the village than the ordinance before us today, for it would more realistically restrict population density and growth and their attendant environmental costs." [63]

Justice Marshall's dissent was important because it distinguished control of specific effects of density from control of the type of occupants of a house and questioned the propriety of doing the latter in the name of achieving the former. Since the *Belle Terre* decision, two states faced with challenges to restrictive definitions of family have followed Marshall's line of argument and ruled that use restrictions on life-style cannot be employed for purposes of density control. [64] In these states, municipalities wishing to regulate population density in R-1 zones must adopt a two-part definition of "family"; the definition must include the old single housekeeping-unit rule and a separate density-control rule, such as a restriction on the number of persons per dwelling unit or a requirement specifying the minimum floor area per person allowed.

This distinction is important in another way also: it may eventually open the way to loosening restrictions on two-family houses in R-1 neighborhoods. Once the idea that single-family housing can be used in a non-family manner is considered legitimate and where the effects of density can be controlled by means other than regulations on type of occupancy, what purpose is served by requiring that unrelated individuals occupy a one-family dwelling jointly as a single household? Why cannot we go one step further and permit single-family housing to be used in a multifamily manner, provided of course that the effects of increased intensity of use are controlled?

Recent rulings of the Supreme Court implicitly acknowledge this distinction between the purposes of density control and life-style regulation in exclusive single-family zoning. The court, however, has moved in this direction by affirming the principle that the promotion of a family life-style can take *precedence* over controls on the intensity of use. In its 1976 decision in *Moore v. East Cleveland*, the court ruled that extended families have the right to live together as a single household no matter how large they may be, and that density regulations cannot prevent them from doing so. This ruling in effect exempts one particular residential life-style from controls regulating the intensity of use. Although the decision in the *Moore* case compounds some of the worst inequities built into exclusive single-family zoning, it also creates an unusual situation: adverse density effects may actually be easier to control in the case of single-family houses with accessory apartments than when single-family houses are occupied in the "normal" fashion by families.

Parking problems offer an excellent illustration of this paradox. Off-street parking requirements in residential districts are usually ineffective because they assume that a universal household type generates "normal" parking demand. Most systems of residential parking control further assume that parking demand increases only as the number of households per lot increases. In reality, parking demand also depends on household composition and household size. Where households vary considerably in size and composition within a single type of district, traditional parking standards are inefficient as a method to prevent congestion resulting from excessive on-street parking.

For example, off-street parking regulations in many communities require a minimum of two off-street spaces per dwelling in single-family zones, on the assumption that the average dwelling will be occupied by a two-adult, two-car family. This practice often leads to inadequate provision for parking. For example, zoning laws would not stop a married coupled with two grown-up children from living in a house in a single-family neighborhood even though the family had four vehicles—two more than the number of required off-street spaces; nor would the zoning law force them to give up two of the cars. Under *Moore*, zoning officials also could not stop a married couple with two children and several aunts and uncles from living together in the same house with five or more vehicles. In places where restrictive definitions of family have been struck down by the courts, zoning could not stop four or more unrelated individuals, each with an automobile, from occupying the same house as a single household, even though again the number of automobiles exceeded the two-space requirement.

However, in each of these neighborhoods zoning would prohibit four people with two cars from living in the same house if one of the four were an unrelated individual living in an accessory apartment built over the garage. This arrangement involves fewer persons and fewer cars, but it would still be prohibited because the property is not occupied by a single housekeeping unit. The inconsistencies and contradictions of single-family zoning become even more apparent when one realizes that under the traditional density measure of units per lot the addition of an accessory apartment would require the installation of additional off-street parking. In the example cited above, where the number of adult users of the house increases but the degree of multiple household occupancy does not, zoning officials cannot require that additional off-street parking spaces be added to the property. If the single-housekeeping unit rule were struck down and accessory apartments were legalized in single-family districts, a city could nevertheless require owners to install additional off-street parking space as a condition of permitting addition of a second unit.

Conclusion

The changing economic environment of housing and changes in family structure have made the traditional goal of home ownership more difficult to achieve today. The climbers up the ladder of life have themselves changed. Some attain ownership of the detached house, but without the family that is supposed to go with it. The top rung of the ladder is also higher up. Many of the institutional arrangements devised by government to help people achieve ownership of single-family homes no longer exist. With many of the housing finance aids gone and the income tax system gradually becoming less supportive, the ladder is becoming more like a pyramid. Less prestigious but affordable substitutes, such as condominiums and townhouses, are now available lower down, and can be cordoned off in new subdivisions to preserve some social distance and the integrity of the older standards of housing and neighborhood. Another substitute, however, the single-family home with an accessory apartment, now appears at the very apex of the pyramid, where according to law and propriety it should not be.

All these changes indicate that a reordering of the hierarchy of land uses is now under way. The traditional relationships between building types, lifestyles, and tenures are unravelling. It would be a mistake to view the adjustment occurring in single-family housing as simply a reduction in living standards—or what Patrick Hare has called the "carving up of the American Dream." The creation of accessory apartments in single-family homes is less a downgrading of this cherished ideal than an adaptation to new dimensions of family, of householding, and of housing need.

As part of this reordering of the land-use hierarchy, the traditional meaning of the word "home" itself should be redefined. This chapter has shown that the word "home" was given a more inclusive meaning in early zoning practice than it is today. It was broad enough that some of the nation's high courts could not find sufficient grounds for excluding the two-family dwelling from "low-rise districts of detached homes." Even the theoretical fountainhead of the entire system of traditional zoning—the *Euclid* decision—provided no explicit rationale for exclusive single-family districts. The court in *Euclid* left the issue unsettled. This earlier and more elastic definition of "home" represents an ignored tradition that deserves greater investigation and research. Its revival could help legitimize current efforts at improving the use of our existing housing stock.

Making multi-family use of single-family housing may not be inconsistent with the fundamental purposes of single-family zoning today. The accessory apartment offers a way to make ownership of existing homes more affordable for the first-time buyer and for long-term owners as well who need the additional income from an apartment to help maintain their properties. This has always been one of the benefits provided by duplex ownership.[65] By creating a mix of housing types in low-density neighborhoods, accessory apartments can also provide a supply of transitional housing arrangements for people when they pass through difficult transitions in life, such as divorce, marital separation, and coming of age. The "extra bedroom" in single-family houses once served this function more often than it does today. For owner-occupiers who live alone, for the widowed, retired, or infirm, or for young families with small children, the opportunity to exchange services with tenants next door offers substitutes for social supports that were provided by the extended family in earlier generations. Differences in life-style between owners and renters have also become less divergent over the years as the proportion of owner-occupants who are single persons, single parents, and unmarried couples has increased.

The principle of exclusive use districts, however, has an inherent defect. As Richard Babcock has put it, "The unstated consequence of the 'principle' of exclusive districts... was that it underscored the differences between uses and discouraged a search for a way to recognize and express in the law the similarities between different uses." [66] This emphasis on differences has discouraged a similar search by specialists in urban design and city planning. If we are serious about finding real solutions to our housing problems, we must begin that search now. Out of it will surely come practical strategies for adapting our existing housing stock to new forms of family living, forms that serve the diverse housing needs of individuals without sacrificing neighborhood livability.

Notes

1. Constance Perin, *Everything in Its Place. Social Order and Land Use in America* (Princeton, NJ: Princeton University Press, 1977), 47.
2. Joel Schwartz, "Evolution of the Suburbs," in Philip C. Dolce, ed, *Suburbia, The American Dream and Dilemma* (Garden City, NY: Doubleday, 1976), 1–36.
3. Harlan Paul Douglass, *The Suburban Trend* (New York: Century, 1925).
4. Robert Walker, *The Planning Function in Urban Government* (Chicago, IL: University of Chicago Press, 1950), 23. Mel Scott, *American City Planning Since 1890* (Berkeley, CA: University of California Press, 1971), 192–98. Seymour Toll, *Zoned American* (New York: Grossman, 1969), 188–210.
5. Stanislaw J. Makielski, Jr., *The Politics of Zoning: The New York Experience* (New York: Columbia University Press, 1966), 7–40.
6. Richard Babcock contends that this practice grew up out of the early "nuisance" concept of zoning. "The owner of land in that zone was no worse off than before zoning. Being a nuisance or potential nuisance himself, there was nothing from which he needed protection. And the misguided or unfortunate person whose home was located in a lower zone had only himself to blame." *The Zoning Game, Municipal Practices and Policies* (Madison, WI: University of Wisconsin Press, 1966), 128.
7. Robert H. Nelson, *Zoning and Property Rights, an Analysis of the American System of Land-Use Regulation* (Cambridge, MA: M.I.T. Press, 1977), 1–12.
8. Scott, *American City Planning Since 1890*. John Delafons, *Land-Use Controls in the United States* (Cambridge, MA: M.I.T. Press, 1969), 85–86. Sam Bass Warner, Jr., *Streetcar Suburbs, The Process of Growth in Boston, 1870–1900* (New York: Atheneum, 1969), 122–23.
9. See Nelson, *Zoning and Property Rights*. A precedent for zoning as a governmental function could be found in the building codes of many American cities which established "fire zones." These districts excluded wood-frame structures and were created in and around the downtown section of a city, where the concentration of population and commercial and industrial facilities made any fire a universal threat to life and property. Except for fire zones, building codes did not vary by location; they established minimum standards which were enforced uniformly across the entire city.
10. Edward M. Bassett, *Zoning: The Laws, Administration and Court Decisions During the First Twenty Years* (New York: Russell Sage Foundation, 1940), 64–66.
11. In the earliest efforts by cities to use zoning to protect single-family neighborhoods, residential zones were established for small groups of blocks with single-family houses scattered throughout the city. The rest of the city was left unzoned. The state courts invalidated most of these ordinances by the early 1920s on the grounds that this type of zoning arbitrarily selected certain districts for protection and did not represent a comprehensive scheme of regulation for the entire

municipality. See Bassett, *Zoning*, 90–91. Also Alfred Bettman, *City and Regional Planning Papers*, Harvard City Planning Studies. Vol. XIII (Cambridge, MA: Harvard University Press, 1946), 158–59.

12. The famous Triangle Shirt Waist Company fire of 1911 in New York City, in which 146 shirtwaist makers, most of them young girls, burned or leaped to their deaths from the ten-story Asch Building near Washington Square at the foot of Fifth Avenue, had tragically dramatized that danger for the entire nation. See Seymour Toll, *Zoned American*, 26.

13. Bassett, *Zoning*, 56–58.

14. Walker, *The Planning Function in Urban Government*, 56–57.

15. Steerman v. Oehmann, *Washington Law Reporter*. 53, 8 (1925): 437.

16. Bettman, *City and Regional Planning Papers*, 168–71.

17. Bassett, *Zoning*, 64.

18. Bassett, *Zoning*, 20, 49.

19. Thomas Adams, "The Character, Bulk & Surroundings of Buildings," in Thomas Adams, dir., *Buildings: Their Uses and the Spaces about Them, Regional Plan of New York and Its Environs*, vol. VI, New York City, 1931, 178.

20. Bassett, *Zoning*, 87.

21. Linda M. Grady, "Single-Family Zoning: Ramifications of State Court Rejection of Belle Terre on Use and Density Control," *The Hastings Law Journal*, 32 (July 1981): 1690–91.

22. Edward M. Bassett, "Control of Building Heights, Densities and Uses by Zoning," in Thomas Adams, dir., *Buildings: Their Uses and the Spaces About Them, Regional Plan of New York and its Environs*, vol. VI, New York City, 1932, 359–61.

23. John Gries and James Ford, eds., *Home Ownership, Income and Types of Dwellings, The President's Conference on Home Building and Home Ownership*, vol. IV, Washington, D.C.: 1932, 203. Clarence A. Perry, *Housing for the Machine Age* (New York: Russell Sage, 1939). Henry Wright, "The Place of the Apartment in the Modern Community," *Architectural Record*, 67 (1930): 206–13, 254–60.

24. Hall v. Leonard, 174 Misc 454, 21 NYS 2d 43 (Sup Ct. Bronx County, 1940), revd 260 App Div 591, 23 NYS 2d 360 (1st Dept. 1940), affd mem 285 NY 719, 34 NE 2d 83 (1941). Cited in Norman Williams, Jr., *American Planning Law: Land Use and the Police Power* (Chicago, IL: Callaghan & Co., 1974), vol. II, 288–90.

25. Barnhart v. Board of Appeals of Scituate, 343 Mass 455, 179 NE 2nd 251 (1962).

26. Paul Boyer, *Urban Masses and Moral Order in America, 1820–1920* (Cambridge, MA: Harvard University Press, 1978), 233–51. Christopher Lasch, *Haven in a Heartless World, The Family Beseiged* (New York: Basic Books, 1978), 29–36. These theories about human development also provided the underlying rationale for child welfare programs, campaigns for parent education, and the movement to eradicate child-labor. See Lawrence K. Frank, "Childhood and Youth," in President's Research Committee on Social Trends, ed., *Recent Social Trends* (New York: McGraw-Hill, 1933), 751–52.

27. John Modell and Tamara K. Hareven, "Urbanization and the Malleable Household: An Examination of Boarding and Lodging in American Families," in Michael Gordon, ed., *The American Family in Social-Historical Perspective*, 2nd ed (New York: St. Martin's Press, 1978), 51–68.

28. State ex rel. Twin City Building & Investment Co. v. Houghton, 144 Minn 1, 174 NW 85 (1919) revd on reh 144 Minn 13, 176 NW 159 (1920); Brett v. Building Commissioner of Brookline, 250 Mass 73, 145 NE 269 (1924); City of Bismarck v. Hughes, 53 ND 838, 208 NW 711 (1926); City of Providence v. Stephens, 47 RI 387, 133A 614 (1926); State ex rel. Morris v. Osborne, 22 Ohio NP(NS) 549, 31 Ohio Dec 197 (Ohio Com Pl 1920); Wulfsohn v. Burden, 241 NY 288, 150 NE 120 (1925).

29. 195 Cal 477, 234 P 381 (1925), app dismd 273 US 781 (1927).

30. Bettman, *City and Regional Planning Papers*, 172–3.

31. Most of the pre-*Euclid* state court decisions upholding zoning stressed the need to make home ownership affordable to "those of moderate means." See, for example, Brett v. Building Commissioner of Brookline, 250 Mass at 78–79, 145 NE at 271.

32. Gries and Ford, *Home Ownership, Income and Types of Dwellings, The President's Conference on Home Building and Home Ownership*, IV, introduction. See also, Thomas Adams, *The Design of Residential Areas: Basic Considerations, Principles, and Methods*, Harvard City Planning Studies, vol. VI (Cambridge, MA: Harvard University Press, 1934), 41–43.

The most ardent and influential advocate of zoning as a vehicle for the promotion of home ownership in the 1920s was Herbert Hoover. In 1921, when Hoover became Secretary of Commerce, he created a Division of Building and Housing, the principal aim of which was to encourage home ownership on a sound economic basis through consumer education and modernization of construction standards. Hoover and his Department organized *Better Homes in America*, an organization whose purpose was "to encourage thrift for home ownership, and to spread knowledge of methods of financing the purchase or building of a home." The organization, which was headed by Hoover, established volunteer committees staffed by local community leaders and civic associations around the country to spread the word. These committees grew from 760 in 1924 to 7,279 by 1930.

Hoover was so impressed with the importance of zoning to the spread of home ownership that he also appointed the Advisory Committee on Zoning to prepare a standard zoning enabling act for adoption by state legislatures. Bassett was named chairman of the committee. Serving with him were members of the National City Planning Institute, including Frederick Law Olmsted, Lawrence Veiller, Morris Knowles and John Ihlder, as well as Irving B. Hiett, former president of the American Association of Real Estate Boards. The act was widely influential in the drafting of state enabling legislation during the 1920s and 1930s. John P. Dean, *Homeownership: Is It Sound?* (New York: Harper & Brothers, 1945), 42–43. Walker, *The Planning Function in Urban Government*, 67. Scott, *American City Planning Since 1890*, 194.

33. Miller v. Los Angeles Board of Public Works, *loc. cit.*
34. Adams, *The Design of Residential Areas*, 37.
35. *The Design of Residential Areas*, 39.
36. *The Design of Residential Areas*, 40–41.
37. Leo Grebler, David Blank and Louis Winnick, *Capital Formation in Residential Real Estate, Trends and Prospects*, National Bureau of Economic Research (Princeton, NJ: Princeton University Press, 1956), 220–37.
38. Village of Euclid v. Ambler Realty Co., 272 US 365 (1926), revg 297 F 307 (ND Ohio 1924).
39. *Ibid.*
40. Bettman, *City and Regional Planning Papers*, 54.
41. For a similar interpretation of the failure of *Euclid* to affirm exclusive single-family districts, see Richard G. Babcock, "The Egregious Invalidity of the Exclusive Single-Family Zone," Conference Paper, Lincoln Institute of Land Policy, University of Southern California, February 12, 1983.
42. Williams, *American Planning Law*, 1974: II, 326.
43. In the 1920s, the Massachusetts courts, for example, declared in favor of their exclusion on the grounds that two-family structures increased the risk of fire to single-family dwellings. "Restriction of the use of land to buildings each to be occupied as a residence for a single family may be . . . regarded as preventive of fire. It seems to us manifest that, other circumstances being the same, there is less danger of a building becoming ignited if occupied by one family than if occupied by *two or more families.* Any increase in the number of persons or of stoves or lights under a single roof increases the risk of fire. A regulation designed to decrease the number of families in one house may reasonably be thought to diminish that risk." (Emphasis added.) Brett v. Building Commissioner at Brookline, 250 Mass at 78, 145 NE at 271 (1924).
44. Wesemann v. Village of LaGrange Park, 407 Ill 81, 87, 94 NE 2d 904-908 (1950).
45. The latter case is discussed by Williams, *American Planning Law*, II, 285, but no citation is provided.
46. Miller v. Los Angeles Board of Public Works, 195 Cal 477, 234 P 381 (1927), app dismd 273 US 781 (1927).
47. Sam Bass Warner, Jr., *Streetcar Suburbs: The Process of Growth in Boston, 1870–1900* (New York: Atheneum, 1969), 73–74. See also Roger D. Simon, *The City Building Process: Housing and Services in New Milwaukee Neighborhoods, 1880–1910* (Philadelphia, PA: American Philosophical Society, 1978), 34.
48. Barbara J. Flint, *Zoning and Residential Segregation, A Social and Physical History, 1910–1940*, Ph.D. Dissertation, University of Chicago, 1977. Harland Bartholomew's studies of urban land uses in American cities at the end of the 1920s revealed a similar pattern. Harland Bartholomew, *Urban Land Uses: Amount of Land Used and Needed for Various Purposes by Typi-*

cal American Cities, Harvard City Planning Studies, vol. IV (Cambridge, MA: Harvard University Press, 1932), 21–32.

49. Norman Williams and Tatyana Doughty, "Studies in Legal Realism: Mount Laurel, Belle Terre, and Berman," *Rutgers Law Review,* 29 (1975): 73–109. Conservative critics of zoning tend to cite *West Coast Hotel v. Parrish* (1937) as marking the full acceptance of this new view of the police power at the Supreme Court level. See Norman Karlin, "Zoning and Other Land Use Controls," in M. Bruce Johnson, ed., *Resolving the Housing Crisis: Government Policy, Decontrol and the Public Interest* (Cambridge, MA: Ballinger, 1982), 42; See also Bernard H. Siegan, "Property, Economic Liberties, and the Constitution," in M. Bruce Johnson, ed., *Resolving the Housing Crisis: Government Policy, Decontrol and the Public Interest* (Cambridge, MA: Ballinger, 1982), 364. Norman Williams argues that the length of the transition period among the states in the field of zoning law varied greatly, with some mid-western states like Illinois still continuing until recent years to place the burden of proof on municipalities. See Williams, *American Planning Law,* 1974, 106-7.

50. Bassett, *Zoning,* 192.

51. Clement Lowell Harriss, *History and Policies of the Home Owners Loan Corporation,* Financial Research Project: Studies in Urban Mortgage Financing (Princeton, NJ: National Bureau of Economic Research, Princeton University Press, 1951).

52. Frederick N. Babcock, *Valuation of Real Estate* (New York: McGraw-Hill, 1932), 75–78. Mortimer Kaplan and Samuel A. Miller, "Government Insurance and Economic Risk," *Kyklos,* 8 (1955): 252–274.

53. Frederick Babcock, *Valuation of Real Estate,* 82–88. See also, Frederick N. Babcock, Maurice R. Massett, Jr., and Walter L. Greene, "Technique of Residential Location Rating," *Journal of the American Institute of Real Estate Appraisers,* 5 (April 1938), 133–40.

54. Sar A. Levitan and Richard S. Belous, *What's Happening to the American Family?* (Baltimore, MD: The Johns Hopkins Press, 1981).

55. William Michelson, "The Place of Time in the Longitudinal Evaluation of Spatial Structures by Women" (Toronto: University of Toronto, Center for Urban and Community Studies, 1973). David Popenoe, *The Suburban Environment: Sweden and the United States* (Chicago, IL: University of Chicago Press, 1977). Donald N. Rothblatt, Daniel J. Garr, and Jo Sprague, *The Suburban Environment and Women* (New York: Praeger Publishers, 1979). Susan Saegert, "Masculine Cities and Feminine Suburbs: Polarized Ideas, Contradictory Realities," in Catharine R. Stimpson, Elsa Dixler, Martha J. Nelson and Kathryn B. Yatrakis, eds., *Women and the American City* (Chicago, IL: University of Chicago Press, 1982), 93–108.

56. Williams, *American Planning Law,* 1974: II, 350. See also Arden H. Rathkopf, *The Law of Zoning and Planning* (New York: Clark Boardman aCo. 1979). By definition this meant that there could be only one building on each lot, in which there could be only one dwelling unit to be occupied by only one household.

57. City of Des Plaines v. Trottner 34 ILL. 2d 432, 216 NE 2d 116 (1966). State courts in California, New Jersey and New York have similarly struck down restrictive definitions of family. See Brady v. Superior Court, 200 Cal. App 2d, 19 Cal. Rptr. 242 (1962); Kirsch Holding Co. v Borough of Manasquan, 59 NJ 241, 281, A 2d 513 (1971); City of White Plains v. Ferraioli, 34 NY 2d 300, 357 NYS 23 449, 313 NE 2d 256, 71 ALR 3d 687 (1974). For an excellent summary of these cases, see Marsha Brown Ritzdorf-Brozovsky, *The Impact of Family Definitions in American Municipal Zoning Ordinances* (Seattle, WA: University of Washington, 1983). Ph.D. Dissertation.

58. 416 US 10, 94 S. Ct. 1536 (1974).

59. The district court ruling, which the United States Supreme Court overturned, argued that the restrictive family definition regulated land-users, not land-uses and therefore was unconstitutional: "We start by examination of the sole ground upon which it was upheld by the district court, namely the interest of the local community in the protection and maintenance of the prevailing traditional family pattern, which consists of occupancy of one-family houses by families based on consanguinity or legal affinity. In our view such a goal fails to fall within the proper exercise of state police power. It can hardly be disputed—and the district court so found—that the ordinance has the purpose and effect of permitting existing inhabitants to compel all others who would take up residence in the community to conform to its prevailing ideas of life-style, thus

insuring that the community will be structured socially on a fairly homogeneous basis. Such social preferences, however, while permissable in a private club, have no relevance to public health, safety, welfare. . . ." 19. 476 F. 2d at 815-16 (2d Cir. 1973).

60. *Ibid.*, 1541.
61. *Ibid.*, 1541.
62. *Ibid.*, 1546.
63. *Ibid.*, 1546.
64. State v. Baker, 81 NJ 99. 405 A 2d 368 (1979). City of Santa Barbara v. Adamson, 27 Cal. 3d 123 (1980).
65. Albert Sukoff, "In Praise of the Duplex," Berkeley, CA, 1981. Unpublished paper.
66. *The Zoning Game*, 1966, 30.

5

Neighborhood and Environmental Impacts of Accessory Apartment Conversions

Although the cultural meaning of exclusive single-family zoning is probably the greatest obstacle to accessory apartment conversions, certain "objective" physical and environmental problems also deserve attention. Conversions mean more people, and more people mean more cars, more parking, and sometimes the need for more public services. Conversions also involve the physical alteration of houses, which can disrupt the architectural integrity of a single-family neighborhood. Increased cars and room additions together can affect perceived densities. To the extent that this occurs, the quality of life in the neighborhood and property values as well may be affected. This chapter discusses these impacts, describes how they affect neighborhood quality, and suggests ways in which they can be mitigated.

The case studies in this chapter were conducted while California cities were responding to a measure by the state legislature to promote the development of accessory apartment conversions. In September 1982 the California legislature passed SB 1534, sponsored by Senator Henry Mello of Monterey County. It stated: "The Legislature finds and declares that California's existing housing resources are vastly underutilized due in large part to changes in social patterns. The improved utilization of this state's existing housing resources offers an innovative and cost-effective solution to California's housing crisis."[1] This enabling legislation set guidelines for local government regulation of accessory apartments in all residential zoning districts in California, including exclusive single-family districts. It stipulated that a local jurisdiction could not prohibit accessory apartment conversions in single-family zones unless it could present a set of findings showing that conversions would endanger the public health, safety, or welfare of residents in the community. If any local jurisdiction could not present such findings, the bill stipulated that it had to adopt zoning regulations and procedures to be used for approving applications by property owners who wished to install secondary units in their houses. The law also contained a set of exemplary guidelines which were the most restrictive that the state would allow local ordinances to be; cities could, however, establish requirements that were less restrictive if they wished to. The law also gave cities and counties up to a year to comply.

Senate Bill 1534 led to a debate within many California suburbs like San Leandro over two issues: whether to permit accessory apartments in single family zones; and if they were to be permitted, how restrictive controls on them should be. The outcome of this debate depended not only upon the attitudes and opinions of individual home owners and home owner associations, but also upon an objective appraisal by the local planning department of the neighborhood impacts which conversions might produce. The following case studies were undertaken to throw some light on this question.

San Leandro, California

Located southeast of Oakland across the bay from San Francisco (see Exhibit 5.1), San Leandro is an older industrial suburb that was first settled in the 1870s. The northern sections of the town were subdivided prior to 1914 but were not developed until the 1920s. Following World War II, which brought industry to the city for the first time, the southern section of the city was subdivided and transformed into tracts of modern, suburban ranch homes.

EXHIBIT 5.1

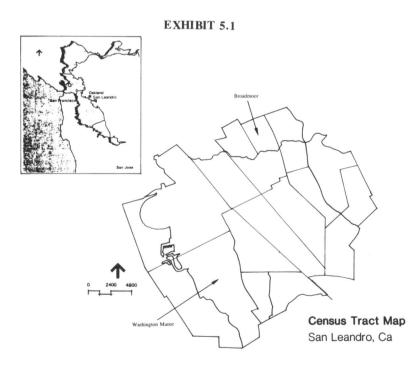

Census Tract Map
San Leandro, Ca

EXHIBIT 5.2
Change in Population by Age, San Leandro, California, 1960–1980.

Age	1960	Percent	1980	Percent	Change
<20	25,476	38.62	14,122	22.1	–11,354
20–24	2,629	3.99	5,136	8.0	2,507
25–34	8,438	12.79	9,253	14.5	815
35–44	11,655	17.67	6,543	10.2	–5,112
45–59	11,161	16.92	13,472	21.1	2,311
60+	6,603	10.01	15,426	24.1	8,823
Total	65,962	100.00	63,952	100.1	–2,010
Median age		31.1		40.1	
Children under 19 per household		1.27		.52	
Adults over 45 per household		.89		1.06	

Source: 1980 *Census of Population and Housing*, Summary Tape File 1.

San Leandro is a classic example of an aging suburb, precisely the kind of suburban community at which the Mello Bill was directed. In 1960, the median age of the city's residents was 31.1 years, slightly above the national median of 29.2. By 1980, however, the median age was 40.1 years, whereas nationally it was only 30.1.

Between 1960 and 1980, the number of households in the city rose by 7,135, or more than a third. Population, however, declined by 2,010, or just over 3 percent. Most of this decline was attributable to a drop in the number of persons 19 years of age or younger, as the children of the families who had settled here in the 1950s and 1960s grew up and moved away (see Exhibit 5.2). In 1960 the number of children per household was 1.27; by 1980 the ratio had fallen by 60 percent to .52 per household. Despite its self-image as a family oriented community, only 22 percent of the city's households in 1980 had children 19 or younger present in them. By contrast, 35 percent of the households in the nine-county San Francisco Bay Area had children under 20 present; nationally 39 percent of all households did.

This aging process is clearly reflected in the changed age composition of San Leandro's population. From 1960 to 1980 the proportion of adults between 35 and 44 years also fell, while the number of adults over 60 years of age more than doubled. A modest net increase in adults in the 25–34 age group also occurred as young couples replaced some older families. The increase in the population between 20 and 24 years was largely attributable to young adults who grew up in the community but have remained living at home. Social aging in the city has also affected the distribition of household sizes. Households with four or more persons decreased between 1960 and 1980, and those with one and two persons

EXHIBIT 5.3
Change in the Distribution of Households by Size,
San Leandro, California, 1960–1980.

	1960	Percent	1980	Percent	Change
Number of Persons per Household					
1 person	1,923	9.58	7,814	28.72	5,891
2 persons	5,697	28.39	10,325	37.95	4,628
3 persons	3,987	19.87	4,181	15.37	194
4 persons	4,433	22.09	2,945	10.83	–1,488
5 persons	2,390	11.91	1,222	4.49	–1,168
6 persons+	1,639	8.17	717	2.64	–922
Total	20,069	100.00	27,204	100.00	7,135
Median household size		3.11		2.06	
Average household size		3.29		2.34	

Source: 1980 *Census of Population and Housing,* Summary Tape File 1.

rose. Median household size fell from 3.11 to 2.06, a decline of 33 percent. By 1980 almost two-thirds of the households in the city consisted of either one or two persons (see Exhibit 5.3).

As an aging suburb San Leandro is not unique in the San Francisco–Oakland metropolitan area (SMSA). Eight other cities in the metro have a median age of 40 years or more. An analysis of 1980 census tapes revealed that, out of 477 census tracts in the SMSA with owner-occupancy rates in excess of 50 percent, half had populations with a median age between 34.0 and 37.9 years. In another 96, the median age of the population exceeded 38.0 years; seven of these 96 tracts were located in San Leandro.[2]

Case Studies

Two neighborhoods in the city were selected for an intensive examination of the potential demand for accessory apartment conversions and probable neighborhood impacts: Washington Manor in the southern part of the city and Broadmoor in the northern part. These two neighborhoods were selected because they were broadly representative of the population and housing stock of the city. Broadmoor is an older neighborhood with large houses and deep lots. Most of its housing stock was built between 1920 and 1950. Washington Manor is a quintessential 1950s subdivision with modern ranch-style homes placed on 6000-square-foot lots. Both areas have aging populations and reflect the range of neighborhood conditions and standards which can be found in older suburbs

EXHIBIT 5.4
Percentage Distribution of Total Population by Age, Washington Manor, San Leandro, California, 1960–1980.

	1960	1980
Total population	4,829	4,086
Age		
<20	48.1	27.0
20–24	2.9	7.3
25–34	20.9	12.4
35–44	18.7	11.4
45–59	6.9	26.4
60+	2.6	15.5
Median age (yrs.)	22.3	36.9
Children 19 and under per household	1.9	0.7
Adults 45 and over per household	0.4	1.2

Sources: 1960 *Census of Population.* 1980 *Census of Population and Housing,* Summary Tape File 1.

throughout the United States. Washington Manor will receive relatively more attention in this chapter because it is the more environmentally constrained of the two neighborhoods.

Washington Manor

Washington Manor, or the "Manor," as local people call it, was selected from among five alternative case study areas in the southern part of the city because its housing stock was almost entirely single-family, and because its boundaries as a neighborhood were well defined by major man-made features—a park and a drainage canal. Washington Manor is one of several large post-war subdivisions located in the southern part of San Leandro. These districts are far more homogeneous in terms of type of construction, architectural style, site plan and visual character than neighborhoods elsewhere in the city.

The Manor was developed and entirely built out in 1958. It was subdivided with lots of 5,000 to 7,000 square feet fronting curvilinear streets and several cul-de-sacs. The Manor covers about 30 acres and includes about 200 homes. Gross dwelling density (total number of residential units divided by total acreage, including streets, non-residential uses, and public facilities) is 6.5 units per acre.

Compared to the city as a whole, Washington Manor has a higher percentage of married persons, lower proportions of divorced, separated and widowed persons, more households with children under 19 (40.0 percent) and fewer owner-

EXHIBIT 5.5
Percentage Distribution of Dwellings and Households by Size, Washington Manor, San Leandro, California, 1960–1980.

	Year			Year	
	1960	**1980**		**1960**	**1980**
Total Dwellings	1,224	1,429	**Total Households**	1,202	1,413
Percent	100.0	100.0	Percent	100.0	100.0
1 room	.0	.1	1 person	0.8	10.7
2 rooms	.0	.2	2 persons	13.6	37.2
3 rooms	.0	2.4	3 persons	20.7	21.5
4 rooms	.1	6.4	4 persons	32.0	18.1
5 rooms	67.7	39.5	5 persons	20.5	6.9
6 rooms+	32.3	51.4	6 persons+	12.4	5.7
Median number of rooms	5.2	5.6	Median household size	4.0	2.6

Sources: 1960 *Census of Population.* 1980 *Census of Population.* 1980 *Census of Population and Housing*, Summary Tape File 1.

occupied households with heads 65 years or older. The generation that settled here in the 1950s produced the baby boom. The families were larger and the children more numerous than in any other part of the city. In 1960, median age of the residents was only 22.3 years; by 1980 it had climbed to 36.9 (see Exhibit 5.4).

The departure of children from the area has been striking. In 1960, the average household contained two children 19 years or younger; half the population consisted of persons under the age of 20. By 1980 the ratio of children per household dropped below 1.0. Adults over 45 now outnumber children. Median household size has also declined sharply. In 1960 its size was 4.0 persons; by 1980 it had dropped to 2.6—a decline of over 35 percent in household density (see Exhibit 5.5).

Whereas household size has been falling, houses in the neighborhood have become larger. Room additions in existing structures account for close to four-fifths of the increase in median dwelling size since 1960. This combination of falling household size and enlarged dwellings also led to a 46 percent increase in the average number of rooms per person—from 1.31 in 1960 to about 2.0 in 1980.

For this case study we selected a specific section of the Manor containing 87 single-family homes covering approximately 13 acres. According to 1980 block group statistics, 95 percent of the dwellings in this part of the Manor were owner-occupied and 94 percent of the households were families—primarily married couples with or without children. About 35 percent of the area's residents had lived in their homes since 1960, and 36 percent had moved in since 1970.

Although 45 percent of the homes contained two persons or less, the Manor still has many families with children; however, 76 percent of the children in the neighborhood are between 13 and 19.

Hence, the case study area in Washington Manor contains three distinct groups of homeowners: 1) "empty nesters" who have lived in their homes since they were built in 1958, 2) middle-aged home owners with teenaged children who have lived in their homes since the 1960s, and 3) young couples who have moved into the neighborhood since the early 1970s. Although the median household size for the area is 2.67—which is significantly higher than the city median of 2.34—it is likely to fall by the end of this decade when the teenagers who are still present become adults and move away.

The Attitudes of Home Owners Towards Conversions

The ambivalent attitude of the Washington Manor Homeowners Association (WMHA) toward accessory apartment conversions is indicative of the divisions on this issue throughout the city. The WMHA is composed primarily of older residents, many of whom have lived in the neighborhood since its creation in the 1950s. During field surveys in the Manor, two prominent members of the WMHA were interviewed.

Although officially the organization opposes conversions, one of the respondents (a man) indicated that some home owners in the neighborhood are interested in converting parts of their homes. He believed that for the elderly among these, the need for additional income was not the only reason; many, especially widows, are lonely and would like to have people living with them for companionship and security. Some younger couples, he said, are having difficulty making their house payments and have a strong desire to rent out sections of their homes to "keep afloat." He knew of several couples who in fact were doing so. He said that "empty nesters" like himself who have large homes which are almost paid for are not interested in conversion.

> But for people under 35 it's a different story. They have to make high mortgage payments. The economy is the culprit. If housing were available at reasonable market rates, people wouldn't even consider conversion.

The opponents of legalized conversions, on the other hand, are fearful of change, especially the introduction of renters into the neighborhood. "People are afraid the standard here would be lowered if we had renters in the neighborhood. There would be more absentee landlords, and there would be shabby homes." Both of the WMHA members that were interviewed agreed that the lots and houses in the Manor were fairly small and that one could not create very large apartments out of them. Second-story additions were acceptable, but building backyard cottages or relaxing lot coverage requirements was strictly out of the question. Both respondents were opposed to garage conversions unless the garage was located in a rear yard. The Association has received complaints about a few garage conversions that neighbors felt had led to increased curb parking.

WMHA members believe that curb parking in general should be discouraged because it destroys the quality of the neighborhood and makes it "feel more dense." If property owners are to be permitted to install accessory apartments, the WMHA contends, they should be required to add at least one independently accessible off-street parking space to their properties. There are a lot of cars already in the neighborhood. One of the respondents argued that permitting conversions only on parcels with frontages in excess of 55 feet would be a way to ensure that sufficient off-street parking would be available.

Suitability for Conversion: Old Homes Versus New Homes

What about these fears and concern? How real are they? How many houses in this neighborhood have the capacity to accept accessory apartment conversions? And if conversions were permitted, how many would occur? To what extent would accessory conversions change the physical appearance of the neighborhood?

The layout of most modern three-bedroom homes precludes internal conversion, so that creating an accessory apartment requires an addition to the existing structure. Modern houses were designed with an "open-door" concept that affords little privacy. The rooms in a modern house all open onto each other and provide no avenues for the divisions of space that exist in Victorian homes, for example. Junior bedrooms are much smaller in modern homes than in older houses. Children were only supposed to sleep in them; the rest of the time they would play under their mother's thumb in the kitchen or backyard patio.[3] The Victorian home also had servants, so the kitchen was usually set off at the rear of the house along with a maid's room. This made the creation of a small living unit out of part of the kitchen and maid's room a simple task. Because most older houses had two stories, one could easily divide them into flats.

In a modern home, however, installing an accessory apartment requires adding a room at the rear of the house or adding a second story. Additions have two drawbacks. First, they are more expensive than internal conversions because of the added cost of framing, flooring, and foundation work.[4] Second, most additions are also readily visible to neighbors.

For the Manor's ranch-style homes of 1950s vintage, these objections may not be valid. Many ranch-style homes have been altered by their owners in countless ways for purposes other than accessory apartment conversion. New master bedrooms or guestrooms have been added, often with a separate bath. Frequently these additions are set off in a separate wing of the house to make them more private. In other cases, second stories have been added, again including bedrooms with separate baths. Garages and basements have also been remodeled and turned into family rooms or recreation rooms.

Modern ranch-style houses are in fact easy to alter and expand. Almost any room is available for change. The construction materials are generally lightweight and based on a simple technology that is familiar to residents who spend time maintaining their homes. The space around each house provides direct light and ventilation to all sides of the building, but it also provides opportunities for easy access to all sides for the construction of alterations and rooms.

Studies of postwar suburbs like San Leandro have documented the popularity of home expansion projects. Wachtel's essay on the first Levittown (in Nassau County, Long Island, New York) noted that within six years after the completion of the last home in the giant subdivision,

> ... the community finds itself in the midst of a home improvement boom. The pressure of expanding families has forced many families staying in Levittown to finish the expansion attic or even to add an extra bedroom by expanding the house on the ground level. Improvements have not been limited, however, to bedrooms and attic dormers; construction of garages, dining rooms, dens, expanded living rooms, cellars, and porches have provided a basis for a growing home improvement industry in Levittown.[5]

Popenoe's study of Levittown, Pennsylvania, the second of the communities planned and built by the Levitts, noted that twenty years after completion, 25 percent of the houses had major additions or alterations, and over 50 percent had remodeled interiors.[6]

Although this practice has been common in suburban subdivisions of the 1950s, it is not characteristic of tracts of the 1960s which contain much larger homes. Most of these were built for second- and third-time buyers who already had several children. A study of several neighborhoods of 1960s vintage in San Jose, California found that only about 4 percent of the structures had alterations or additions. Because of their greater size and larger lots, the additions that had been made were also far less noticeable to passersby on the street.[7]

This finding has several important implications. First, many room additions can be converted into accessory apartments cheaply and easily. Second, as additions or modifications to existing structures, conversions would be consistent with the continuous process of physical adaptation which many single-family neighborhoods have undergone. Third, in neighborhoods where additions and alterations to homes are common, visual disruption from accessory conversions would be negligible. On the other hand, in subdivisions with newer, larger homes, accessory apartments conversions will likely not require external additions and will therefore not affect the appearance of the building.

Conversion Potential of Houses in the Manor

The Manor was a product of the very last years of the postwar housing boom.

EXHIBIT 5.6
Typical Single-Family Homes,
Washington Manor, San Leandro, California

Photographs courtesy of Clare Watsky

All of the houses were either one-floor rectangular or L-shaped homes placed at the center of 50-foot by 110-foot lots. Front yards are set back an average of 30 feet, and rear yards are generally 25 feet deep. Average lot coverage is about 40 to 50 percent. Height limits in the area allow second stories, although none of the houses were originally built with them. Originally, the typical house in the Manor contained two or three bedrooms, two baths, and a two-car, single-door garage (see Exhibit 5.6). Today about 20 percent have four or more bedrooms. Most of these and many of the three-bedroom units are the product of room additions undertaken by owners since the 1950s.

These houses have been continuously changing since their construction. Building permits for the period 1958–1982 show that 43 of the homes (50 percent) have gained additional living space since they were built. This includes 13 second-story additions and 32 ground-floor room additions. Three permits were also recorded in the study area for garage conversions (see Exhibit 5.7). Some modifications have also occurred without permits. A field survey in the area found five garage conversions for which no building permit had been recorded. Two second-story additions also lacked building permits. The field survey also identified four houses that had accessory apartments.

Many houses in the Manor—especially those that have already been enlarged by ground-floor additions, second-story additions, and garage conversions—

EXHIBIT 5.7
Additions and Alterations, Washington Manor,
San Leandro, California

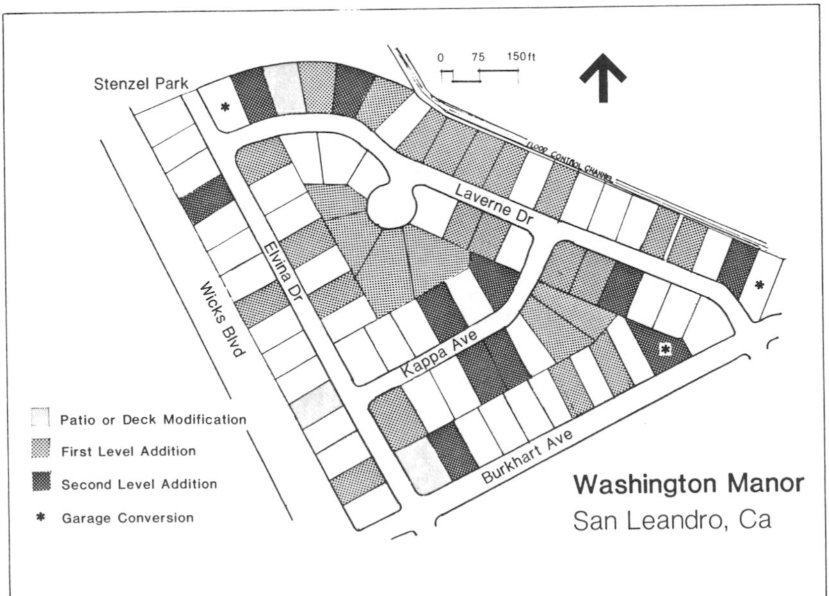

Map by Clare Watsky

EXHIBIT 5.8
Accessory Conversion Site Plans,
Washington Manor, San Leandro, California

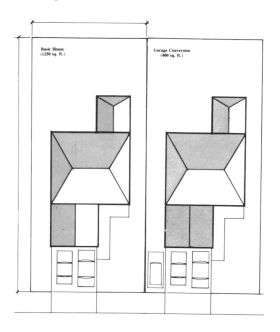

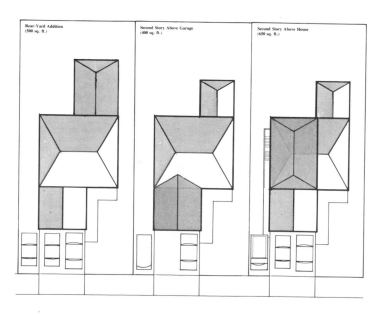

Source: Sandborn Maps, City of San Leandro

EXHIBIT 5.9
Second-Story Additions, Washington Manor,
San Leandro, California

Photographs courtesy of Clare Watsky

have the potential for accessory conversions. Exhibit 5.8 displays alternative site plans for accessory apartment conversions that would fit the typical house and lot configuration of the neighborhood. Each case also shows where and how an additional vehicle could be given its own independently accessible off-street parking space along the side yard adjacent to the driveway apron.

In cases where the rear of a house was previously extended in order to add a fourth bedroom and a second bath, an accessory unit of anywhere from 450 to as much as 600 square feet can be created out of these rooms if another 200 square feet can be added to the extension. Access to the secondary unit can be provided at the side of the house or at the rear. Because of the large number of ground-floor additions that have been made here, this alternative is probably the most compatible with the general character of house alterations in the neighborhood.

Conversion of existing second stories or the addition of new ones is also a way to create accessory apartments. Fifteen of the homes in the Manor already have second stories, and almost all those that do not could easily accommodate one (see Exhibit 5.9). Most of the homes built during the 1950s in San Leandro were framed so that the ground floor structure could support a second story. In several neighborhoods in the northern part of the city, close to half of all homes were originally built with some kind of second story, and another 20 percent have added second stories since their construction. Although they can be costly, planning approval for them is easier to obtain than for ground-floor extensions because second stories are not affected by lot coverage requirements. The height limit in the city's single-family zones is 30 feet. This is common practice throughout the state. Single-family districts in California suburbs sometimes have height limits of 40 feet.

The placement of the second story depends on the configuration of the house. In some cases, it can be placed above the garage, in others above the primary living area. A ticklish problem in either case is where to install an entry door and staircase. Tradeoffs are involved. If the door and stairway are placed at the front, the single-family image of the house is destroyed. If placed at the rear, the intimacy of a garden and patio suffers. Quite often the best solution is to place the door and stairs at the side of the house. Another approach is to take advantage of the service door to the garage and install a spiral staircase inside the garage leading up to the unit. This was the solution of one owner in the Manor who added a second story to her house expressly for the purpose of creating an accessory apartment. The owner of the house in Exhibit 5.10, on the other hand, decided to place the door and stairway to his secondary unit at the very front of the building. The owner lives in the upstairs unit, which also has a rear deck overlooking a garden. Despite the popular myth that duplexing leads to lower maintenance and creates a blight on the neighborhood, this particular one was by far the best maintained property in the entire study area.

The garage is an obvious candidate for an accessory apartment. It is the simplest and cheapest of all conversions to design and execute. Many family

EXHIBIT 5.10
Duplex Addition, Washington Manor,
San Leandro, California

Photograph courtesy of Clare Watsky

rooms that were originally garages can be turned into studio apartments. Providing access to the street is not a problem if there is a service door where the garage is attached to the front of the house. Most of the attached garages in the Manor have such a service door, which does not directly face the street and cannot be seen by pedestrians.

Garage conversions, however, raise some serious questions about the compliance of illegal conversions with health and safety codes. The Manor has a tradition of garage conversion that goes back to the 1960s; in that decade many families with growing children found themselves pressed for living space in their five- and six-room houses, and some began converting their garages illegally to create family rooms or extra bedrooms. Although there were complaints about whether this was appropriate in a single-family neighborhood, city officials were more concerned with building code violations, particularly faulty wiring that could lead to fires. They decided that public safety was much more important than "image." Conversions also appeared to serve a genuine need for families hard pressed for space; they were popular not only in the Manor but in other parts of the city also. Planning commissioners recognized that forcing residents to remove their illegal conversions would encounter stiff resistance.

The planning code was consequently amended to permit a relaxation of the off-street parking requirement for single-family dwellings "where the property owner is able to demonstrate that [conversion] is necessary for the beneficial use

EXHIBIT 5.11
Garage Conversions, Washington Manor,
San Leandro, California

Photographs courtesy of Clare Watsky

and development of a [single-family] property and will not be detrimental to neighboring properties or to the public health, safety, and welfare.''[8] The commission required property owners who converted their garages to use the driveway apron, the adjacent side yard, or the front yard as a replacement for one or both spaces removed. The city then urged owners to come forward and legalize their converted garages, which quite a few of them did. In the case of houses with frontages wider than 60 feet, where the garage was attached to the side of the house, owners could replace off-street parking spaces by adding a carport at the side of the garage. These houses with wider-than-normal frontages are found primarily on corner lots. The top photograph in Exhibit 5.11 represents one of the better conversions of this type. A replacement garage has been added on the left and the driveway apron widened to accommodate three vehicles. Because of its location at the side of the house, the new garage would be an excellent candidate for an accessory apartment conversion. An entrance could easily be placed at the rear or on the side.

Exhibit 5.12 illustrates a case where the garage and the entire front yard were remodelled. Here the owner first added an extra bedroom and a bath by building a second story. Later a room with a separate entrance was added on the ground floor at the rear. Finally, the garage was rebuilt as a combination guest-room and family room. The old driveway was taken out and a new one cut through the right-hand side of the lot. The house now has seven rooms and the current driveway provides uncovered parking for three vehicles.

EXHIBIT 5.12
Converted House, Washington Manor,
San Leandro, California

Photograph courtesy of Clare Watsky

Although the city permits garage conversions for family use, it is unlikely that they would ever be allowed for use as accessory apartments. The loss of two off-street parking spaces would probably put more cars on the street. In addition, the Washington Manor Homeowners' Association opposes accessory apartment conversions in attached garages because of their visibility from the street.

Impacts of Increased Population Density

Accessory conversions in the Manor would cause population density to rise, but it is unlikely that the increase would cause congestion or health hazards. In the first place, average household size has declined in the neighborhood and with it so has population density. Most suburbs like San Leandro had considerably higher population densities when they were younger. When Washington Manor was developed between 1958 and 1960 with its gross dwelling density of 6.6 units per acre, it had an average household size of 4.0 persons and a gross population density of 26.4 persons per acre. This was high for a neighborhood composed primarily of two- and three-bedroom dwellings; the addition of extra bedrooms and family rooms was a way in which the inventory eventually adjusted to this population squeeze. By 1980 population aging had reduced average household size to 2.9 persons per household and gross population density to 19.3 persons per acre.

The numerical increases in population that would occur with accessory apartment conversions would be small. Accessory apartments ordinarily provide accommodation for single persons rather than families with children. This presumption is consistent with United States Bureau of the Census *Components of Inventory Change* reports on occupants of converted dwellings.[9] It is also consistent with the widely documented growth of single-person households as the leading component of household formation today.[10] In the past, by contrast, conversions were a response to the demand for family housing and did in fact cause substantial increases in population density in the neighborhoods where they occurred.[11]

There is also little chance that more than 20 or 25 percent of the houses in the Manor would ever have accessory apartments. There are no universities, hospitals or large government facilities in the area that would generate a strong demand for small apartments. Most of the rental demand in the area comes from families looking for three- and four-bedroom houses. Renters of accessory apartments in the Manor would probably belong to the social networks of residents—they would be friends or relatives of those living in the primary units or of their neighbors.

On the supply-side, considerations of economic feasibility would also limit the number of accessory apartment conversions. Some second-story additions might be feasible; but they would have to be quite large in order to yield a rent high enough to justify the capital cost of conversion, and this would make them more like the duplex conversion in Exhibit 5.10. The same would be true of ground-floor additions, which would be even more expensive. Windshield surveys and inspections of plans showed that no more than 15 of the houses that have already been expanded by alteration (10 ground-floor and 5 second-story additions) are large enough to be converted easily and cheaply into accessory apartments. Another 7 accessory units could be created by adding new ground floor rooms or second story additions. Hence accessory apartments could be cheaply and successfully added to only between 18 to 22 of the 86 houses in the Manor. Assuming that 20 percent of them would be vacant at any one time and that average household size would be the same as for apartments elsewhere in the city (1.25), conversions would probably raise population density no higher than 21 persons per acre.

For these reasons, the effects of increased population density on public facilities such as schools and playgrounds would be negligible. So would the effects on water supply and sewage disposal, although in some cases increased density might absorb underutilized capacity and allow these services to be provided more efficiently. Cars and parking, however, are another matter.

Cars and Parking

Just as accessory units can push population density in an aging single-family neighborhood back up toward historic levels, they can also raise vehicular densities, though usually not beyond the peak levels that prevailed when the population of the neighborhood was younger. There will certainly be additional cars; but in neighborhoods undergoing population aging like the Manor, vehicular densities will also have a tendency to fall. Vehicle ownership per household tends to rise and fall over the family life cycle. It varies with the age of the head of household, rising to a peak between ages 40 to 54, and then declining.[12] During middle age, when household income is at its maximum, so is household size and vehicle ownership. Some of the additional vehicles are used by teenagers, and some are recreational vehicles. During vehicle counts conducted in the Manor, about 12 were observed parked in driveways.

Insofar as vehicular density is a function of household size, it falls as families age and their average size declines. This implies a simple recursive model of vehicle density in neighborhoods that explains population density (persons per lot) and vehicular density (vehicles per lot). The model was estimated by using Ordinary Least Squares (OLS) on data from 38 census blocks in San Leandro. Only block groups with owner-occupancy rates above 50 percent were used. The results of the model were then used to project vehicular densities as population density increases with the introduction of accessory apartments. A specification of the model along with an explanation of the estimating procedures used and the OLS results are included in an appendix at the end of this chapter.

Exhibit 5.13 presents the projection results. Both population and vehicular

EXHIBIT 5.13
Projected Incidence of Vehicles Under Varying Density Assumptions,
Washington Manor, San Leandro, California.

	Income per Capita	Persons per Lot	Estimated Vehicles per Lot	Actual Vehicles per Lot
1980	$9,407	3.16	2.30	2.34
1990 Percent of buildings with accessory conversions				
0	$10,391	2.74	2.03	—
10	$10,395	2.84	2.13	—
20	$10,343	2.94	2.22	—
30	$10,288	2.94	2.32	—
40	$10,212	3.14	2.41	—
50	$10,098	3.24	2.50	—
60	$9,956	3.31	2.60	—
70	$9,689	3.44	2.69	—

density were expressed on a per-lot basis. Vehicle ownership in the Manor has risen during the past decade, as small children have grown into teenagers and more families have acquired recreational vehicles. In 1970 there were approximately 1.76 vehicles per lot in the Manor. By 1980 the figure had climbed to 2.34 vehicles per lot. The second row displays the values for average household size and vehicular density in 1990 assuming no conversions. At that time, the neighborhood should contain about 2.74 persons and 2.03 vehicles per lot. Vehicular densities rise as the percentage of houses with accessory apartments increases. As the proportion of conversions approaches 30 percent, vehicular density reaches 2.32—the 1980 level estimated by the model.

It was noted earlier that the demand for small apartments in the area would probably support conversions in no more than 25 percent of existing houses. Assuming a 20 percent vacancy factor, the number of vehicles per lot at this percentage would be 2.22. This is about 5 percent less than current vehicular density in the Manor and about 9 percent greater than the density expected in 1990 if there were no accessory conversions in the neighborhood. The resulting increase in trip generation would probably be on the same order—about 10 percent. This small an increment in traffic would have no perceptible impact on the neighborhood in terms of noise, accidents, noxious fumes, or the like. Traffic volume must increase by a much greater margin for the perceived quality of life to be affected.[13]

Parking, however, may present a problem. The Manor has the highest rate of vehicle ownership of any single-family neighborhood in the city, and also the highest incidence of curb parking: about 35 percent of the curb spaces are filled during peak hours of 7 p.m. to 7 a.m. In other neighborhoods, only 15 to 20 percent of the spaces are ever occupied during peak hours. In the hills where lots are 10,000 square feet or more, only about 10 percent of the curb spaces are ever occupied during these peak hours.[14] If accessory units were added to 20 percent of the houses in the Manor and all additional cars were parked on the street at peak hours, approximately 42 percent of the parkable curb spaces would be occupied. By current standards, this would be excessive.

There is a great deal of concern in the Manor these days over curb parking. To the members of the WMHA who were interviewed for this case study, the neighborhood seems jammed with cars, and residents would like to see fewer vehicles on their streets than are there today. Most residents view the streets in their neighborhood not as places to keep cars but as open space. The representatives from the WMHA noted that streets with lots of cars parked at the curbs convey a sense of congestion and high density. Heavy curb parking is also associated with poor, low-status neighborhoods. The more fashionable upper-middle income neighborhoods in the city do not have much curb parking, and the WMHA wants to apply that standard to their own district.

The city's fire department also wants fewer cars parked at curbs. The inner streets in the Manor are only 45 feet wide, which makes access by fire vehicles

EXHIBIT 5.14
Off-Street Parking Capacity, Washington Manor,
San Leandro, California

Map by Clare Watsky

difficult. The fewer the number of vehicles parked at curbs on residential access streets, the easier and quicker it is for firemen to bring their trucks and equipment right up to the front of a house. The difference in time might be only a few minutes, but that could mean a loss of thousands of dollars for someone whose home is on fire, as one fire official noted.[15]

On the other hand, off-street parking spaces could be added to many parcels in the Manor despite the constraints of the standard 50-foot frontage. The Manor contains seven irregularly shaped parcels with 60-foot frontages. Some driveways are already large enough to accommodate three vehicles side by side and others could be expanded. Although 52 of the homes have driveways that can hold only two cars, 30 of these are wide enough to hold up to three or four cars if part of the side yard is used. Another four lots have driveways that could hold as many as five cars (see Exhibit 5.14). Converting the side yard between the driveway and the adjoining property to a parking pad is not unusual. Some home owners in the Manor have already done this to accommodate an extra car or recreation vehicle (see Exhibit 5.15).

Broadmoor District

Because of its physical constraints, Washington Manor has only limited ca-

EXHIBIT 5.15
Front-Yard Parking Pads, Washington Manor,
San Leandro, California

Photograph by Clare Watsky

EXHIBIT 5.16
Demographic Composition of Households, Broadmoor District, San Leandro, 1980.

	Broadmoor District	San Leandro City	San Francisco Bay Area
Percent owner-occupied households	64.0	66.2	56.0
Median household size (owners)	1.9	2.3	2.5
Percent married persons	55.1	58.0	41.9
Percent divorced and separated	11.0	10.7	12.1
Percent widowed	14.3	9.6	7.1
Percent of households with children under 19 years	23.9	26.0	35.2
Percent of owner-occupied households with head 65 years and older	38.2	28.0	19.2

Source: 1980 *Census of Population and Housing*, Summary Tape File 1.

pacity to absorb accessory apartment conversions. Other neighborhoods in San Leandro, particularly those in the northern part of the city, are less constrained and have much greater potential.

Broadmoor is a case in point. One of the oldest subdivisions in the city, it contains large lots with expansive front yards, a mix of architectural styles and lush landscaping. The district covers an area of about 24 square blocks. Two curvilinear collector streets, Broadmoor and Dowling Avenues, run through it from east to west and define an inner neighborhood of four blocks which provided the subject of this case study.

Broadmoor houses a much older population than Washington Manor. It has more widowed persons, fewer households with children under 19 years of age, and more heads of household over 65 than any other of the city's residential districts. About 38 percent of all owner-occupant households are headed by persons 65 years or older. At the same time only about 24 percent of all households have children 19 years of age or younger present and over 24 percent of the population is either widowed, separated, or divorced (see Exhibit 5.16).

Broadmoor's population has been aging for quite some time. The median age of the population living there in 1960 was 43.7 years, while for the city as a whole it was 30.1 years. In 1980, the median age of its residents had fallen to 40.6 years, largely because younger couples had begun to buy homes in the neighborhood. Few of them had children. The result was that the median household size fell from 2.4 persons in 1960 to 1.9 persons in 1980.

The district is subdivided into relatively large lots; two-thirds of them measure

EXHIBIT 5.17
Lot and Building Sizes, Broadmoor District, San Leandro, California

Lot Size (square feet)	Number of Lots	Percent of Total Lots	Average Living Area of Building	Average Lot Coverage (percent)
10,000 and above	44	73	2,300	20
5,000–10,000	13	22	1,900	30
5,000 and below	3	5	1,500	40
Total lots	60	100	2,173	23

Source: City of San Leandro, Sanborn Maps and 1974 Aerial Survey.

50 feet by 200 feet (see Exhibit 5.17). The typical Broadmoor house sits 40 feet back from the front lot line, which makes for spacious front yards. A driveway runs along one side yard from 40 to as much as 80 feet back to a detached garage at the rear. Rear yards are frequently 100 feet deep; greenhouses, carriage houses or other types of accessory structures are common in back yards, especially on the larger corner lots (see Exhibit 5.18). The area is zoned R-1-B-1—this provides for single-family use, but front yards must be at least 40 feet deep and maximum permitted lot coverage is 50 percent.

Three types of housing predominate in Broadmoor. The most common is the one-story cottage which dates back to the 1920s and 1930s. Larger two-story houses from that era are scattered throughout the neighborhood (see Exhibit 5.19 A and B). The next most predominant house type is the ranch-style home built during the 1950s; these are substantially larger than the ranch homes in the southern part of the city (see Exhibit 5.19 C).

Broadmoor's houses are spacious. Median dwelling size is 5.9 rooms, and about half the houses in the district contain three bedrooms or more. As average household size in the district has fallen over the years, space consumption per capita has climbed from 1.9 rooms per person in 1960 to 2.5 in 1980.

The area could accommodate a variety of different types of accessory apartments, including conversions of parts of existing houses; conversions of accessory structures already in place, such as carriage houses, green houses and the like; second-story additions on top of garages; and ground-floor additions at the rear or side of existing houses. Close to 80 percent of the properties in the study area have some kind of potential for accessory apartments.

Many structures already have these kinds of additions, which could be easily adapted for use as accessory apartments. Some of the older homes have garages with accessory structures added on the ground floor at the side or on top as a second story. Exhibit 5.20 displays an example of each. The second-story addition above the garage in this exhibit is currently being used as living quarters.

In other cases, where the house is large enough, a part of it could be easily

EXHIBIT 5.18
Subdivision Plan, Broadmoor,
San Leandro, California

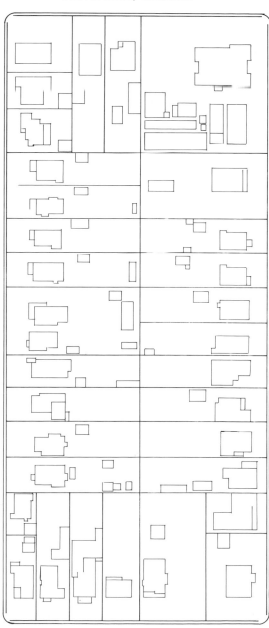

Source: Sanborn Maps, City of San Leandro

EXHIBIT 5.19A
Typical Single-Family Homes, Broadmoor,
San Leandro, California

Single-Family Cottage

EXHIBIT 5.19B

Two-Story House

EXHIBIT 5.19C

Modern Ranch Home

Photographs courtesy of Clare Watsky

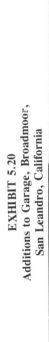

EXHIBIT 5.20
Additions to Garage, Broadmoor,
San Leandro, California

EXHIBIT 5.20 (continued)

Photographs courtesy of Clare Watsky

converted into an accessory apartment. A good example is represented by the first frame in Exhibit 5.21. This is a three-bedroom house with one of the bedrooms located above a garage-basement combination. Because the garage and bedroom are at the rear of the house, a separate entrance could be tucked away behind the house or near the service entrance to the left of the garage door.

A major addition on the ground floor with a second story was made at the rear of the house in the second frame of Exhibit 5.21. The location and size of this addition make the rear of this structure an excellent candidate for an accessory conversion.

Exhibit 5.22 is also an interesting case. Here, a kitchen door at the side became the entrance to an attic apartment added to the top of the house. The dormer was created at the time the conversion occurred.

Because of their long, wide driveways, the lots in Broadmoor could easily accommodate the additional cars that might come with accessory apartments. Almost all driveways can handle three cars parked in tandem, and many are wide enough to hold two cars parked either in tandem or side-by-side while still providing garage access for a third vehicle (see Exhibit 5.23). Property owners have widened their driveways by paving over part of the front yard near the house or near the adjacent property (see Exhibit 5.24). Long driveways and large rear yards also mean that additional off-street parking could be provided at the side of the house in a carport or possibly an extension to the existing garage.

Because of its long, wide driveways, large lots, and small households, Broadmoor, unlike Washington Manor, has no perceptible parking problem. Currently there are 1.6 vehicles per lot, and only about 18 percent of the curb spaces are occupied at peak hours. Exhibit 5.25 projects the vehicular densities which would occur under different conversion rates in 1990. A computational procedure similar to the one in the Washington Manor case was used. Average household size is projected to rise because young families are expected to continue moving into the neighborhood during the 1980s and some will eventually have children. At a 20 percent conversion rate in 1990, the vehicular density would rise to 1.97. This would add about 19 more cars to the neighborhood than are there today. Broadmoor's 10,000 square-foot lots however would easily accommodate the additional vehicles in rear yards and driveways. Use of driveways might be preferable in some cases to the addition of another garage or carport at the rear of the main structure in order to preserve the rustic quality of the area's deep, lush back yards.

Unlike the WMHA, the Broadmoor Homeowners Association (BHA) does not categorically oppose accessory apartments. The BHA President, who was interviewed for this case study, acknowledged the need for low-cost housing as well as for ways to make the homes in the area affordable for young families who would like to move into the area. While she believes that there would be little demand for accessory apartments in the neighborhood, she pointed out that the ones which already exist, including some converted guest houses and second

EXHIBIT 5.21
Additions to Existing Housing,
Broadmoor, San Leandro, California

EXHIBIT 5.21 (continued)

Photographs courtesy of Clare Watsky

EXHIBIT 5.22
Accessory Apartment Attic Conversion,
Broadmoor, San Leandro, California

Photograph courtesy of Clare Watsky

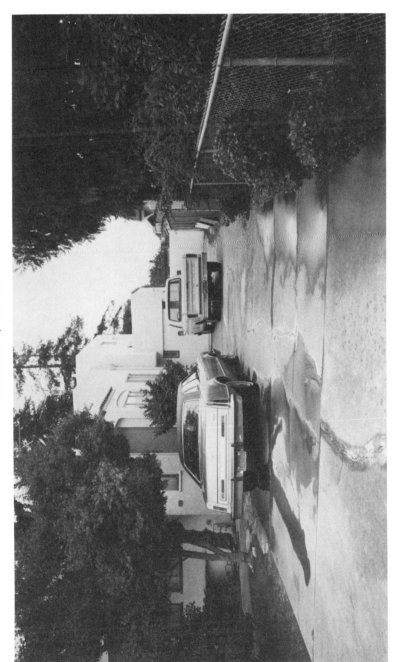

EXHIBIT 5.23
Double-Wide Driveway, Broadmoor,
San Leandro, California

Photograph courtesy of Clare Watsky

EXHIBIT 5.24
Double-Wide Driveway with Extension,
Broadmoor, San Leandro, California

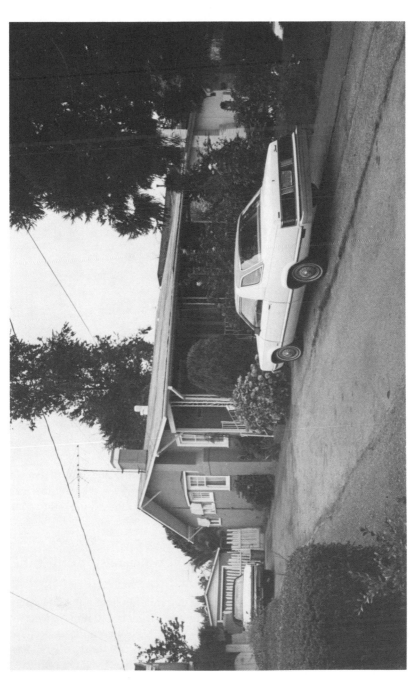

Photographs courtesy of Clare Watsky

EXHIBIT 5.25
Projected Vehicular Densities Under Varying Conversion Rates, Broadmoor
District, San Leandro, California.

	Income per Capita	Persons per Lot	Estimated Vehicles per Lot	Actual Vehicles per Lot
1980	$9,607	2.33	1.64	1.66
1990 Percent of structures with accessory apartments				
0	$10,416	2.42	1.77	—
10	$10,419	2.52	1.87	—
20	$10,352	2.62	1.97	—
30	$10,268	2.72	2.06	—
40	$10,149	2.82	2.15	—
50	$10,013	2.92	2.24	—
60	$9,891	2.99	2.34	—
70	$9,804	3.12	2.43	—

stories above garages, have stirred no controversy. The BHA is more concerned about home owners who operate businesses out of their garages, such as printing shops or nurseries. BHA members, she added, want to retain their neighborhood's attractive single-family character, and this means that adequate off-street parking must be provided to prevent congestion on the streets. Consequently, the BHA has proposed that accessory apartments only be permitted on sufficiently large lots (10,000 square feet or more) and that lot coverage requirements not be compromised.

While the BHA clearly recognizes a need for affordable housing, it also wants to prevent decline and deterioration which might occur given the neighborhood's advanced age. The BHA believes that carefully framed regulations might address both of these concerns.

The Accessory Apartment Ordinance

During the first half of 1983, the planning commission held public hearings on legalizing accessory apartments. Most of the city officials and home owners who testified agreed that San Leandro's housing stock was underutilized because of population aging. They also agreed that accessory apartments should be permitted in the city. Accessory apartments would not only make for more efficient use of the housing stock but would also help those retired homeowners who could not keep up their properties. The city, in fact, proposed that Community Block Grant Funds be used to assist this group. Although representatives of the local homeowner improvement associations supported the legalization of accessory apartments, they opposed garage conversions and duplexing. They also argued that the ordinance should require that additional off-street parking be provided by property owners who install accessory apartments and that the added parking should not be in front yards.

After six months of hearings and city planning staff review of alternative proposals, the commission finally approved an ordinance which the city council adopted on September 8, 1983. According to the ordinance, an accessory apartment can be created in a single-family house in an R-1 district, if it meets certain requirements. It must be no larger than 450 and no smaller than 300 square feet. It must be attached to the primary unit, but it cannot be an attached garage. One of the units must be owner-occupied and both units together must have three off-street parking spaces. Front-yard setbacks and driveways will not qualify as off-street parking. On lots with extra-wide frontages, side yards over nine feet wide may be converted to parking pads. For parking in side yards narrower than this, the owner must apply for a variance. The city council also indicated that if experience with the ordinance was favorable, some of the restrictions might be relaxed in the future.[16]

Under this ordinance, few home owners in the Manor will be able to install accessory units because of the difficulty they will have complying with the parking standard. The houses in the northern part of the city with their wider, deeper lots and long driveways leading back to detached garages are more likely candidates under the ordinance. These neighborhoods in older subdivisions, like Broadmoor, where the lots are frequently 10,000 square feet or larger are also better situated with respect to shopping and services and closer to the sections of the city that have traditionally supported a rental market. Experience to date bears this out. In the year following adoption of the ordinance, the planning department received 120 enquiries from interested home owners in all parts of San Leandro, but only five applications for accessory conversions had been approved, all of which were in the northern section of the city.

Conclusion

Neighborhoods vary dramatically in their capacity to absorb accessory apartment conversions. Accessory apartments may involve external alterations, but these will rarely change the single-family image of a neighborhood; in many single-family neighborhoods external alterations are normal. Where they do affect the image of neighborhood, simple design controls can be devised to deal with them.[17]

Parking is a much more serious problem. The extent to which parking becomes a "problem," however, will depend on the lot configuration and subdivision design of the neighborhood as well as on neighborhood standards of aesthetics, safety, and convenience. In some neighborhoods, cars are always parked off-street in covered spaces hidden from view. In others, cars are also parked off-street, but no one cares if they are uncovered and visible. And in still others, curb parking is the accepted rule.

Planning for accessory apartments must reconcile the prevailing standards of each neighborhood with the kinds of parking effects that conversions would produce. Clearly some neighborhoods will not be able to handle the increased parking demand that accessory conversions would generate unless prevailing standards of what constitutes a "liveable" neighborhood are lowered. The same amount of conversion in another neighborhood might induce negligible parking impacts. The approach to controlling parking impacts must therefore be flexible enough to encompass the variety of conditions and standards to be found in any community.

This suggests the need for *performance* standards rather than *prescriptive* standards. A *prescriptive* standard dictates a specific method for achieving some objective. A *performance* standard is based on the idea that many different methods can be used to achieve the same objective. The objective of residential parking controls is to maintain safe and accessible streets; however, the method of achieving this varies among neighborhoods. Under a performance standard approach, parking requirements for accessory conversions would depend on the prevailing parking standards and parking conditions of the neighborhood under question. Thus in some neighborhoods, any additional off-street parking must be garaged where it is customary to do so; in others, tandem parking in driveways might be acceptable; and in others, side-yard parking pads could be used. In still others, a limited amount of curb parking could be permitted where this is normal and customary.

Performance standards can also be applied to the aesthetic problem of visual impacts. The visual effects of building alterations on neighborhood character are negligible in places like Washington Manor where external alterations are common. In neighborhoods with larger houses, or where covenants regulating external appearance are customary, the incidence of room additions and visible alterations would be much lower. The larger the average house, of course, the more likely that conversion will require only minor external alterations. Again, no single standard is appropriate.

To encourage accessory apartment conversions in single-family neighborhoods without sacrificing neighborhood liveability, a simple ordinance with a single standard may not suffice. In places where housing needs warrant the promotion of accessory apartments, a broader, more comprehensive effort at neighborhood planning involving the formulation of performance standards would be appropriate, even though this may be administratively more complicated than a system of prescriptive standards. To be effective, a performance-standard approach requires that city planners develop some inexpensive yet accurate procedures for assessing parking and housing conditions and identifying prevailing building and use standards in different neighborhoods. These might include neighborhood building permit histories, comparisons of actual and theoretical lot coverage, measurement of vehicular density, and analysis of off-street parking utilization. Some of the methods of quantitative and qualitative analysis used in this chapter might serve as models.

Notes

1. Senate Bill No. 1534, September 27, 1982.
2. United States Bureau of the Census, 1980 *Census of Population and Housing*, Summary Tape File 1.
3. Kate E. Rogers, *The Modern House, U.S.A.* (New York: Harper & Row, 1962), 102–7.
4. Martin Gellen, "A House in Every Garage: The Economics of Secondary Unit Conversions," Working Paper. Center for Real Estate and Urban Economics (Berkeley, CA: University of California, 1982).
5. Harold Wachtel, "Levittown: A Suburban Community," in William M. Dobriner, ed., *The Suburban Community* (New York: G.P. Putnam and Sons, 1958), 300.
6. David Popenoe, *The Suburban Environment: Sweden and the United States* (Chicago, IL. University of Chicago Press, 1977), 118.
7. Bert Verrips, *Seconds Units an Emerging Housing Resource* (San Francisco, CA: People For Open Space, 1983), 60–61.
8. City of San Leandro, Planning Code, Title 7, chapter 3, section 521.6.
9. United States Bureau of the Census, 1980 *Census of Housing, Components of Inventory Change*, vol. 4, table 2.
10. United States Bureau of the Census, "Households, Families, Marital Status and Living Arrangements," *Current Population Reports*, Series P-20, no. 382, 1983.
11. Planning Advisory Service, *Conversions of Large Single-Family Dwellings to Multiple-Family Dwellings* (Chicago, IL: American Society of Planning Officials. Report No. 5, 1949).
12. Automobile Association of America, *Transportation Conservation Data Book*, Oak Ridge National Laboratory, Edition No. 4, 1976. Brian V. Martin, Frederick W. Memmott, III, and Alexander J. Bone, *Principles and Techniques of Predicting Future Demand for Urban Area Transportation* (Cambridge, MA: M.I.T. Press, 1961), 71–75.
13. Donald Appleyard, *Liveable Steets* (Berkeley, CA: University of California Press, 1981), 61–77.
14. Kathy Livermore, "An Assessment of the Physical Potential for Accessory Unit Development In San Leandro," Department of City & Regional Planning, University of California, Berkeley, 1983. Prepared for the Department of Planning, San Leandro, California. Unpublished.
15. City Planning Commission meeting February 10, 1983, San Leandro.
16. Telephone interview with Martin Vitz, Senior Planner, City of San Leandro, August 2, 1984.
17. Tri-State Regional Planning Commission, *Legalizing Single-Family Conversions* (New York: Tri-State Regional Planning Commission, 1981).

Appendix 5-A
Recursive Model of Vehicular Density, San Leandro, California

The model consists of two equations. The first explains the average number of persons per household (P/H) in the neighborhood as a negative function of the median age (A) of the residents and as a positive function of the owner-occupancy rate expressed as a percentage (0). The second equation explains vehicular density, or vehicles per household (V/H), as a positive function of average household size (P/H) and per capita income (Y).

$$P/H = a_0 + a_1A + a_20$$

$$V/H = b_0 + b_1(P/H) + b_2(Y)$$

where: a_0, a_1, a_2, b_0, b_1, and b_2 are parameters.

The model was estimated by using Ordinary Least Squares (OLS) on data from 38 census blocks in San Leandro. Only block groups with owner-occupancy rates above 50 percent were used. The block groups included neighborhoods at different stages of the population aging process; the youngest was 30.1 and the oldest 54.2. Vehicles per household was computed from 1980 census tabulations of vehicles available to households. These include automobiles, trucks, and recreational vehicles owned or leased by household members. The fit achieved in both equations was excellent. All the signs were as expected (see Exhibit 5A.1).

The parameters from this model can be used to project vehicular densities so long as we can assume that cross-sectional variation in household size and vehicular density reflect neighborhoods at different stages of the population-aging process. On this assumption, we would expect both population and vehicular density in single-family neighborhoods to fall as their populations age. This may not be quite true because of cohort effects. The city contains at least three generations of home owners whose incomes and family sizes were determined in part by conditions that prevailed during the era when they entered the labor market and formed families. It is almost impossible to isolate these cohort effects statistically. But even if it were possible, it is not clear that this adjustment would significantly alter the forecast results for a specific neighborhood.

Per capita income was discounted by a percentage factor that varied with the amount of conversion in the neighborhood. This was done in the belief that the need for additional income would be an important factor inducing home owners to convert part of their dwellings. Hence, higher amounts of conversion in the neighborhood would be associated with lower per capita income.

Projections of vehicular densities were computed in the following manner. First, the average household size for Washington Manor was projected for 1990 on the assumption that the owner-occupancy rate would remain the same and the median age of the residents would rise to 41.0 years; for Broadmoor it was as-

EXHIBIT 5A.1
Multiple Regression Model of Vehicle Density, San Leandro, California, 1980

Variable	Coefficient	T-Statistic
Persons per household regressed on median age and owner-occupancy rate		
Percentage of owner-occupied dwellings	.012335	7.563
Median age of population	−.028061	−6.910
Constant	2.719910	4.774
R-squared	.856	
F-test	56.499	
N of Cases	38	
Vehicles per household regressed on income per capita and average household size		
Income per capita (in 1000's)	.071498	5.406
Persons per household	.811364	15.557
Constant	−.940842	5.462
R-squared	.932	
F-test	130.705	
N of cases	38	

sumed that the owner-occupancy would also remain unchanged and that the median age of residents would fall as more younger couples move into the neighborhood and those already there have children. Real per capita income in 1990 was projected by compounding 1980 per capita income at 1.5 percent a year for ten years. Using these projections, vehicular density for 1990 was calculated on the assumption of no accessory conversions in the neighborhood.

Finally, average household size was converted into an expression of lot density—persons per lot. This model assumes that the average household size of occupied accessory apartments would be 1.25. If both the apartments and the persons occupying them were included in the calculation, average household size in the neighborhood would appear to decline as the percentage of houses with conversions increases.

A similar adjustment procedure was used for vehicles. Projected vehicles per lot was computed using the parameters of the regression equation and then adding the additional cars per lot generated by the assumed number of accessory conversions. This number of conversions was adjusted by a vacancy factor of 20 percent. It was assumed that there would be an average of 1.25 vehicles per occupied accessory apartment.

6

Promotion and Control of Accessory Apartment Conversions

When proposed by local planning commissions, legalization of accessory apartment conversions has often generated vocal opposition from home owners. A public hearing, however, is one of the least effective methods of measuring the full range of public sentiment on any issue. It provides a self-selected sample that indicates only who has the most intense concern about an issue and which groups in the community are the best organized. The "silent majority" invariably stays home.

Although public officials and housing activists have been the primary advocates of accessory apartment conversions, survey research studies indicate that widespread support for the legalization in single-family neighborhoods exists among home owners and renters alike. For example, Exhibit 6.1 displays the results of a poll on housing and land-use from the San Francisco Bay Area that sought to measure the political support for legalization of accessory apartments.[1] A majority of those surveyed indicated that they favored the legalization of "in-law" apartments; their support did not vary significantly by either housing tenure or income.

It could be argued that these findings reflect unique conditions of the San Francisco Bay Area. Residential construction has lagged behind household formation since 1975. Home prices and rents have risen faster than incomes, and faster also than home prices and rents elsewhere in the country. One would thus expect support for accessory apartments to be highly correlated with attitudes toward the need for housing development in general. Exhibit 6.2 shows that in fact this is the case: acceptance of in-law conversions declines as support for housing development in general decreases. But the table also shows that even a majority of those who believe that housing development should be discouraged nevertheless support the legalization of accessory conversions.[2]

This is not to disregard the political significance of the impassioned opposition. The opponents of accessory apartment conversions articulate concerns that prevail to some degree among supporters, many of whom believe that making more efficient use of space in the existing housing stock should be encouraged,

EXHIBIT 6.1
San Francisco Bay Area Poll on Legalizing Accessory Apartments,
November 1983

Question: Another kind of law has been proposed to allow home owners to have mother-in-law apartments in single-family homes. Do you favor or oppose a law allowing mother-in-law apartments in single-family homes in your neighborhood?

| | Percent | | | Number of Cases |
	Favor	Oppose	Undecided	
Grand Total	73.10	19.20	7.70	632
Tenure				
Owner	72.50	19.30	8.20	354
Renter	74.00	19.20	6.80	276
Income				
<$15,000	75.50	18.40	6.20	102
$15,000-29,999	74.00	19.30	6.70	213
$30,000+	73.10	19.40	7.50	263
Ethnicity				
White	62.80	17.30	19.90	492
Black	78.30	17.40	4.40	46
Hispanic	62.50	25.00	12.50	48
Asian	58.10	35.50	6.50	31
Gender				
Male	68.40	21.20	10.50	316
Female	77.90	17.10	5.10	316

Source: Field Research Poll—Project No. 803-005, November, 1983.

but not at the expense of neighborhood liveability. Although a majority of home owners do favor legalizing accessory apartment conversions in single-family neighborhoods, even these supporters are concerned about how many are needed, where they should be located, and their physical and social effects on neighborhoods.

Housing Policy and Accessory Apartments

All housing policy involves promotion and control. *Promotion* in the case of accessory apartments means efforts or actions intended to increase the supply of this type of housing. *Control* means efforts to prescribe what accessory apartments should be like and to limit their numbers where they may be inappropriate. How much promotion and how much control is needed will depend on market forces, political judgments about housing needs, and public sector resource constraints, and these will vary considerably from community to community.

The kinds of policy and program adopted at the local level will vary depending on supply and demand conditions. In some places, the market already may be producing accessory apartments in sufficient quantity as illegal units. Where this

EXHIBIT 6.2
Attitudes Toward Housing Development of Respondents to
Poll on Legalizing Accessory Apartments,
San Francisco Bay Area, 1983

Question: Should new housing be encouraged in the Bay Area?

Attitude Toward Legalizing Mother-in-Law Apartments	Strongly Encouraged	Somewhat Encouraged	Somewhat Discouraged	Strongly Discouraged
Favor	79.3	73.4	63.2	59.5
Oppose	13.7	18.8	28.4	29.0
Undecided	7.1	7.8	8.4	11.5
Total	100.0	100.0	100.0	100.0
Number of Cases	241	218	95	37

Chi-Square = 14.412
Sig.   =   0.036

Source: Field Research Poll—Project No. 803-005, November, 1983.

kind of indigenous movement exists it may be best to do nothing, unless the effects on neighborhood liveability clearly warrant measures to control them. In other places the demand may exceed the supply, and some type of promotional effort may be necessary. In still other places, the potential supply of conversions may exceed the demand because of a high incidence of large houses with surplus space. In these places no effort need be made to promote, but controls may be necessary simply to stabilize the market.

The evaluation of costs and benefits also determines how much promotion and control are required. This evaluation itself is a political process that is shaped by the structure of interest groups in any particular community. In places where environmental groups and neighborhood improvement associations are better organized and more vocal than housing development interests, concern for maintaining neighborhood quality will outweigh consideration of housing needs. In other communities, where housing needs are given greater weight in the political process, the benefits of accessory apartment conversions will be valued more than the costs. In these communities, a policy of more promotion and less control will carry the day.

Housing policy, however, is not just a local affair. Its formulation has traditionally been an activity of state and federal governments which have in the past assumed responsibility for leading the way and encouraging innovative solutions to housing problems. Because of their ultimate authority over local land-use regulation, state governments in particular can provide leadership in promoting accessory apartment conversions in the single-family housing stock. The California legislature set a shining example of such leadership in 1982 when it passed Senate Bill 1534. This was enabling legislation which gave cities the right to legalize accessory apartment conversions and which also set limits on the type of restrictions that local governments could impose on conversions.[3] More recently, the California legislature directed state agencies to revise underwriting guidelines of all state home mortgage assistance programs to make homes with accessory apartments eligible for these programs; the legislature also directed the California Housing Finance Agency to develop an accessory apartment financing program to be funded by tax-exempt mortgage revenue bonds.[4] Similar steps could be taken by Congress to make accessory apartment conversions eligible for federal mortgage loan and housing assistance programs and financing demonstration projects.

The Instruments of Promotion and Control

There are two basic instruments the public sector can use to promote and control the development of housing: specialized financing programs and land-use regulations and building codes. The two are usually applied independently, but they can be combined in imaginative and effective ways.

Financing programs offer mortgage credit for the purchase and construction of housing at a subsidized interest rate or with an extended amortization term. Specialized financing programs are basically a promotional device; they provide incentives for builders and landowners to develop housing of desired types or in desired locations. Specialized financing programs can also be used as a control device depending on the standards and qualifying criteria employed. Land-use regulations and building codes, on the other hand, are primarily control devices, and restrictive by nature. They limit the types and amounts of housing that can be produced.

Regulations can sometimes be promotional when they are relaxed. This can be done formally as a process of *deregulation*. Deregulation removes restrictions on the types of housing and the quality of housing that property owners and developers can choose to produce. The effect can be promotional when there is a market demand for certain prohibited types of housing. An alternative to formal deregulation is *non-enforcement*. Non-enforcement leaves a regulation in place should it be needed in the future or to respond temporary needs. However, non-enforcement is of questionable legality and may raise serious problems of equal treatment before the law.[5]

Let us look more closely at how each of these instruments may be used for purposes of both promotion and control.

Financing Accessory Apartment Conversion

In any given area, the financing instruments most suitable for promoting accessory conversions will depend on the characteristics of the population and housing market. More specifically, the frequency of turnover in single-family homes and the strength of the demand for home ownership will determine the best type of financing mechanism.

Much of the popular lore on accessory apartments emphasizes the potential for conversion by senior citizens and "empty nesters" living in the spacious houses they bought when their families were much larger. The need for additional income and increased security are frequently cited as motivations.[6] But the research in this book suggests that while some middle-aged and retired owners may want to convert parts of their houses into accessory apartments, the vast majority probably do not. Because of fixed-payment mortgages and various forms of property-tax relief, these home owners enjoy a standard of space consumption and privacy they are unlikely to give up unless forced to do so by deteriorating finances.

On the other hand, young adults, who represent a large share of the home-buying market today, face a considerably higher real cost of ownership, over both the short- and long-run. To own a home, many of them must incur extraordinarily high housing expenses. Consequently, they have a greater incentive to install accessory apartments than do middle-aged empty nesters. The young families of today are also smaller than those who bought large houses in the 1950s and 1960s, and they are likely to be more willing to adjust their space standards in the short-run in order to secure the benefits of home ownership over the long-run. This is especially true of single parents who must both work and care for children. Even if they have the income to afford a big house, few single parents have the time to maintain large houses with large yards. In addition, single parents also tend to depend more upon neighbors for assistance and favors than do married-couple parents; consequently, duplexes, townhouses and other kinds of low-rise, moderate density housing are much more popular among them than detached single-family homes.[7]

For these reasons, I suspect that the greatest potential for accessory apartment conversion exists in houses owned by young couples, individuals, and single parents. The United States Census Bureau's *Components of Inventory Change* also provides evidence that accessory conversions in single-family houses are becoming more popular among younger home owners. Of owner-occupiers living in single-family dwellings that had been changed by conversion between 1973 and 1980, 46 percent were over the age of 45, while 59 percent were over 45 during the decade between 1960 and 1970.[8]

In any promotional effort, which group should be targeted depends on the characteristics of the local housing market. In some communities there may be little turnover of large homes. Their occupants, although aging, have no incentive to move. A few may die, but even when they do, surviving spouses usually stay on in these houses which are owned free and clear. Many widows and retired couples, however, may not have sufficient savings to maintain their unencumbered homes and still meet other living expenses, and they may not want to risk their savings on a conversion. In this type of situation, some kind of second mortgage equity loan or a "reverse mortgage" instrument would be appropriate solutions for them.

Equity loans are probably already being used in this way. They are most appropriate for middle-aged borrowers whose earnings are at peak levels and will remain so for ten years or more. The equity withdrawn can be used to finance the conversion. These loans usually have short maturities, often from seven to ten years. Once the loan is paid off, the accessory apartment can provide an excellent income stream for the home owner upon retirement.

Reverse mortgages are specifically designed for home owners who are on the verge of retirement, have little savings, but are rich in equity accumulated through both appreciation and payments on the principal. The loan is secured by the appraised equity value of the house. The amount borrowed is used to buy an annuity, the payments from which cover interest due on the reverse mortgage and provide an income stream to the home owner to meet living expenses. When the home owner dies or moves away, the net proceeds from the sale of the house are used to pay off the outstanding balance.

Although the reverse mortgage is employed today to finance an annuity, there is no reason why it cannot also be used to finance the development of accessory apartments in single-family homes. Because reverse mortgages are interest-only loans, monthly payments are lower than they would be for fully amortizing mortgages. The underwriting costs of financing accessory apartment conversions might be higher than normal because of the construction component of the loan and variability in the projected income stream from the accessory unit. This problem can be dealt with by using a portion of the loan proceeds to set up a reserve fund to guarantee interest payments during any extended period of vacancy.

On the other hand, in markets where older couples and widows move away or die more frequently, the perfect time to create accessory apartments is when the houses are sold to younger families and individuals. Young buyers usually cannot undertake conversion themselves because most of their savings must be used to purchase a house and make needed improvements on it. This capital constraint could be overcome by using a combination purchase and construction loan to both acquire the house and cover the cost of conversion.

Whereas the reverse mortgage is still experimental, financing instruments like this combined-purpose loan have been in use for years, particularly in inner city housing revitalization programs. These programs allow a qualified buyer to fold the total costs of rehabilitation and modernization into the first mortgage when purchasing a house in a targeted location. The below-market interest rate is achieved by using tax-exempt mortgage revenue bonds or "blending" low-interest public funds with market-rate financing. Lenders prefer purchase-rehab loans to small add-on second mortgages for rehabilitation. The additional underwriting and administrative costs associated with the rehabilitation can be more easily recaptured from fees calculated on the much larger base amount of the purchase loan. Both state and municipal housing finance agencies and private lenders have had substantial experience with these programs.[9] Adapting them for programs to promote house conversions would be relatively simple.

Financing programs could be used not only to promote but also to control accessory apartment conversions. The incentives provided by financing programs would reduce the out-of-pocket costs of code compliance for property owners, thereby removing a significant motive for illegal conversion. Purchase-conversion loans could be used to upgrade existing illegal units when the homes that contain them come onto the market. Special financing programs could also be targeted to neighborhoods where there is widespread public acceptance of accessory apartment conversions. Channelling demand into some neighborhoods but not others might help stem illegal conversions in those neighborhoods where parking and street congestion are problems and environmental degradation is a genuine concern.

Regulatory Strategies

Land-use regulations and building codes as instruments of control have three objectives: (1) to limit the quantity of accessory conversions in order to prevent neighborhood change, (2) to uphold prevailing standards of housing and neighborhood quality, and (3) to protect public health and safety. Sometimes these objectives are served by the same instrument. The quantity of conversions need not be controlled directly; parking and building code standards can achieve the same end by making many conversions economically unfeasible.

How much control is necessary depends in part on the supply and demand balance and the community evaluation of costs and benefits. There are also limits to how much control can be exercised. The existence of illegal conversions, which can be found in almost any community, attests to this. Any effort to control the quantity or quality of accessory conversions cannot avoid dealing with the problem of illegal units.

The two most common strategies of control are the *laissez-faire* and the *conditional-use* approach. The laissez-faire approach is basically a "do-nothing" method of control: public officials simply do not enforce regulations against conversions unless neighbors make specific complaints. The conditional-use approach, on the other hand, legally permits conversions provided they meet a set of specific conditions, usually occupancy and design requirements.

Under the laissez-faire approach the instrument of control is the enforcement mechanism. In neighborhoods where conversions are tolerated, they will be left alone. In other neighborhoods, where residents do not want them and protest at city hall to this effect, abatement proceedings against them can be initiated. Selective enforcement also minimizes the resources that must be spent on control efforts. In an era of fiscal constraints, this has doubtless seemed an attractive option for many public officials.

The laissez-faire approach also depends upon informal social controls and is therefore self-regulating. By threatening to complain to city hall, neighbors can pressure owners of illegal units into complying with neighborhood standards of maintenance, parking, and so forth. The threat of discovery and abatement also forces the owner of an illegal unit to select tenants who will fit into the neighborhood well and not give neighbors cause to complain.

Laissez-faire works well in places where the homeowning population is relatively tolerant of accessory conversions, where there is a strong demand for them, and where there is an indigenous market for them that some home owners are willing to serve. In these cases, promotion may be unnecessary. A limited form of enforcement may be required, however, to ensure that conversions do not get out of hand. In these situations, the laissez-faire approach is ideal, because the community retains the right to clamp down whenever conversions begin causing traffic, parking, or other problems. It may also work well in situations where there is little demand for accessory conversions and home owners are willing to tolerate a few illegal units.

This approach has two main drawbacks. First, it cannot be an officially recognized policy because it creates serious legal problems of equal protection under the law. In most cities where selective enforcement is practiced, local officials will insist that limited manpower resources and fiscal constraints leave them no other choice. They will enforce when only called upon to do so. If the housing market is tight, officials will also claim that uniform and active enforcement would lead to evictions and displacement and exacerbate community housing problems. Second, it permits illegal units to flourish, and some of them may pose health and safety problems for occupants and neighbors alike. Without direct regulation, there is no way to ensure that converted units will not threaten the physical well-being of the community. This issue will be discussed at greater length below.

The second approach, legalization of accessory apartment conversions that meet certain specified requirements, is becoming more popular throughout the country today as the idea of accessory apartments is being legitimized. Accessory apartments are now permitted on a conditional-use basis in many parts of the nation, even in exclusive suburbs such as Westchester County in New York, Fairfax County in Virginia, Montclair County in New Jersey, and Marin County in California.[10]

Fear of a change and a desire to protect the social character of single-family neighborhoods has led most communities to adopt this approach. A 1980 survey of local government officials in the New Jersey–New York–Connecticut region showed that more than half of the communities that said they would permit accessory apartment conversions favored special-use permits, variances, or case-by-case approval by the local planning board. Out of 186 respondents, only two officials indicated that their communities would allow accessory apartments "by-right"—as a permitted and unconditional use requiring only a valid building permit.[11] A 1983 California survey of city and county officials reported similar findings. Out of 426 cities and counties reporting, slightly more than 75 percent indicated that they employed conditional-use permits for accessory apartments, and only 16 percent allow them "by-right."[12]

Under the conditional-use approach, the home owner who wishes to install an accessory apartment on his or her property must file an application and notify all neighbors who wish to protest to come forward. In addition, the home owner must submit to a public hearing and explain his or her need to create the accessory unit. The decision then rests with the planning commission and interested neighbors who might object.

Under the conditional-use approach, the method of control is a political one and the decision criteria used are not always clear. Public hearings can be expensive and time-consuming. They also force the home owner who wishes a conditional use permit to give up his or her privacy. The more onerous the process, the more likely it is that persons who wish to add accessory apartments to their homes will be discouraged from doing so. This, of course, may be a desirable outcome for those who oppose legalization of accessory apartment conversions.

Most cities that adopt the conditional-use method of approval do so in order to severely restrict the types of properties that can have legal accessory apartment conversions. As conditions for permitting the conversion, a community can require that the owner live on the property. Owner-occupancy provisions are usually enforced by requiring a deed of restriction to be filed. Many cities also restrict occupancy of accessory apartments in R-1 zones to relatives of the owners or more frequently to persons 60 years of age or older. Planning commissions reserve the right to impose other restrictions that might seem appropriate as a result of findings presented at the hearing.

Many of the restrictions imposed through the conditional-use process cannot be enforced unless a city resorts to police-state methods. For example, Sunnyvale, California, located in the heart of the "Silicon Valley," wanted to permit accessory apartments in single-family districts only for occupancy by senior citizens. One city official responded:

> The City can easily control the structural components of adding a second unit. But it is next to impossible to actually enforce the social-oriented ideas for creating a second unit. For example, it's been suggested that the units be permitted only for senior citizens. . . . I would not like the City to get into a position where it has to ask the age of every person who lives in a second unit. In theory, the socially oriented reasons for establishing a second unit as affordable housing for the elderly sound great. However, in the real world it is totally unenforceable. No one is going to throw out a single 55-year old woman from her home for the sole reason that she is not technically a senior citizen.[13]

The 1983 California survey of accessory apartment ordinances found that almost two-thirds of all communities in the state had ordinances which were re-

strictive in intent or effect. Ordinances were classified as restrictive or not restrictive depending on the types of provisions they contained.[14] *Unrestrictive* ordinances were those which (1) required no increase in lot size over the minimum
for the zoning district; (2) reduced or waived off-street parking requirements; (3)
allowed the second unit to be attached or detached; (4) set no maximum size limit
on the secondary unit; and (5) did not require the occupants of the secondary unit
to be related by blood, marriage, or adoption to those living in the primary unit.
The *moderately restrictive* ordinances were the same except that they required
the secondary unit to be attached to the main part of the house and stipulated a
maximum size. *Restrictive* ordinances required (1) that the lot size be larger than
the minimum for the zoning district, (2) that the same amount of off-street parking be provided for the secondary unit as for a regular single-family unit, (3) that
the second unit be attached, *or* (4) that the occupants of the secondary unit be related by blood, marriage, or adoption to those living in the primary unit. *Very restrictive* ordinances required (1) that the lot be twice the minimum size for the
zoning district, and (2) that it be a corner or deep lot. Of all the jurisdictions reporting, the California survey found that only 3 percent of all ordinances were
unrestrictive, 33 percent were moderately restrictive, 40 percent were restrictive
and 24 percent were very restrictive.

The California study also found that most of the jurisdictions with "restrictive" requirements employed the conditional-use method approval, whereas
those with the "least restrictive" requirements employed administrative permits.
An administrative permit is a use permit issued on a conditional basis, but the approval process involves no public hearing, only a planning department review.
Although only 5 percent of all reporting jurisdictions in the California survey issued administrative permits for accessory conversions, they had the highest rates
of both applications and approvals. Ironically, jurisdictions which allowed
"by-right" approvals had the lowest rates of applications and approvals. These
jurisdictions passed very restrictive ordinances and adopted a "by-right" approach in apparent anticipation of few or no applications.

Because of the tremendous difficulties of enforcing complex special restrictions and the personal and monetary costs the approval process imposes upon ap-
plicants, the conditional-use process may achieve little control and instead encourage illegal conversions. Corte Madera, a small city in Marin County California, allows accessory apartment conversions only under conditions that are very
restrictive; as a result, seven applications were approved under the current ordinance between 1980 and 1982, but the city estimates that several dozen illegal
conversions occurred in the same period.[15] The Tri-State Regional Planning
Commission study in the New York–New Jersey–Connecticut area also revealed
that the more restrictive the local ordinance, the lower the number of legal conversions. In municipalities that had adopted accessory apartment ordinances,
substantially fewer home owners than anticipated came forward to legalize their
conversions. The local officials interviewed believed that the low response rates

were due to the restrictiveness of the ordinances and that the majority of single-family conversions continued to be done illegally.[16] In one Connecticut town the zoning enforcement officer estimated that for each conversion approved by the Board of Zoning Appeals, there were nine illegal ones.[17] On the other hand, in 1982, Daly City, a suburb of about 12,000 households located south of San Francisco, adopted a relatively permissive ordinance legalizing accessory apartment conversions which employed an administrative review procedure. During 1983, the city received 85 applications and approved all but five. Daly City planning officials estimate that the city has close to 1500 illegal units, but that because of the ordinance fewer are being installed illegally.[18]

Regulation and the Problem of Illegal Conversions

It would be more accurate to speak of illegal accessory apartment conversions in single-family zones as "nonconforming" uses rather than "illegal" units. Some nonconforming uses are illegal units but some are not. The legal ones were installed prior to the formal adoption of zoning. Marin County, California, for example, has about 4,000 nonconforming accessory apartments in single-family zones. About 600 were in place before the adoption of zoning laws in the 1950s; the rest are illegal.

Illegal conversions are common in places where there is excess demand for rental apartments, where zoning laws prohibit or tightly restrict accessory apartments in single-family districts, and where enforcement procedures are slow and ineffective. As long as the cost of enforcement and full legal compliance is high, and as long as the probability of discovery and cost of punishment is low, the incentive for illegal conversion is substantial. In communities where illegal conversions are widespread, public officials are usually unwilling to absorb the political and agency costs of a crackdown. Most efforts to enforce zoning regulations against illegal units grow out of complaints made by neighbors or from code inspections of unrelated renovation work in the same building. In either case, enforcement is difficult and often ineffective.

Building inspectors usually do not have the power to enforce the planning code, except perhaps in small towns. They can, if they choose, report zoning violations discovered in the process of their work to the zoning enforcement officials, who can then initiate enforcement proceedings. An order for removal of the illegal improvements can then be issued; failure to comply is subject to coercive administrative and judicial remedies and fines. It must be kept in mind, however, that administrative follow-up on notices to desist is usually inadequate, and many such notices are never recorded. But even when enforcement officials resort to sanctions, these may not be sufficient to bring about compliance. Zoning violations in most communities are misdemeanors, and the courts are usually reluctant to mete out punishment more severe than small fines.

Where zoning prohibits accessory apartments, a property owner can sometimes "bootleg" an accessory apartment conversion as a recreation room, guest room, studio-workshop or office. Hence the unit may comply with the building code but not with the planning code. Whether or not the illegal apartment is reported depends upon the type of improvements that are "bootlegged" and the discretion of the building inspector.[19]

The existence of a second unit in a single-family house is usually indicated by the presence of a second kitchen; for purposes of inspection, this is generally defined to mean the presence of a second stove in a room other than the kitchen. In most communities, an order to remove a second kitchen can be complied with simply by removing the stove. Nothing prevents the owner from reinstalling the stove, or replacing it with a micro-wave oven or hotplate, and then continuing to use the premises as an accessory apartment. In some places, a deed of restriction can be recorded against the property to prevent sale or refinancing of the structure as a two-unit dwelling; but this by itself will not prevent current or even future owners from renting out the accessory apartment.[20]

Zoning restrictions may not be the only reason for illegal units. This is clear from the limited success of municipalities in getting owners of illegal units to come forward and register them even when offered amnesty. For example, when the City of San Francisco rewrote its zoning ordinance in 1960, an effort was made to bring all illegal and nonconforming units under the new code. San Francisco's housing stock consists primarily of row houses with high basements. The high basements are easily adaptable and have been widely converted to extra bedrooms and accessory apartments as far back as anyone can remember; thousands were created during the housing shortages of World War II and the immediate post-war years. The implementation of the 1960 zoning ordinance provided an opportunity to upgrade these units. City officials declared that they would grant immunity from prosecution to all owners of illegal units for single-family (R-1) and two-family (R-2) zones who would come forward to register their units and submit them to code inspection. As an incentive, the city offered to waive all permit and review fees. Less than 60 property owners came forward to take advantage of the offer.[21] Weston, Connecticut, was similarly unsuccessful in its efforts to get owners of illegal units to come forward when it legalized accessory apartments in single-family zones.[22]

Owners of illegal conversions may prefer to keep their accessory apartments secret in order to avoid paying property taxes on them.[23] Some evidence suggests that home owners who convert illegally are trying to avoid not only paying property taxes on the accessory apartment but also paying the higher taxes that would follow from reassessment of the rest of property if the accessory apartment were installed legally.[24] In many cities, issuance of a building permit automatically triggers reassessment of the entire property if the improvements exceed a certain minimum amount. In states that allow differential assessments, effective rates for two-unit buildings may be higher than for single-family homes.[25] The additional tax liability can greatly reduce cash flow from the extra unit.

A more significant motivation may be the desire to avoid income taxes. The amount of residential rental income in the United States that is legally subject to income taxation but goes "unreported" is substantial. "Unreported" income represents "off-the-books" income earned but not declared by those who file income tax returns. According to Simon and Witte, from 35 percent to 50 percent of rental income is not reported to the Internal Revenue Service (IRS).[26] The only published empirical study of tax compliance found that rental income was relatively well reported for most multiple-unit rental buildings (86 percent) but was less so for rented rooms (68 percent), rented single-family homes (65 percent), rented garages and parts of single-family dwellings (35 percent), and sublet lodgings (30 percent).[27] An accessory apartment with no building permit and no entry on the property tax rolls leaves no "paper trail" that could be used to prove tax evasion in the event of an IRS investigation.

Even when zoning is not a constraint, property owners may choose to convert without a valid building permit in order to avoid the costs of compliance with building codes. Two reasons for avoidance are involved here: it may be cheaper to convert if various code provisions are not followed; and owners who convert may fear that an inspection might turn up other violations in the rest of the building that would be expensive to remedy.

Many of the provisions of building codes have little to do with health and safety per se. One well-recognized role of local building ordinances is the promotion of job security and employment opportunities in the building trades. This is presumably the reason for the "excessive" requirements of local codes, about which both professional and "do-it-yourself" builders frequently complain. Some local electrical codes, for example, will not recognize as legal any work that is not performed by a licensed electrician even if the work otherwise conforms with all safety specifications.[28] Other examples include required use of special procedures or materials.[29] Other "excessive" requirements of building codes are the product of aesthetic and cultural preferences, such as window and ceiling-height standards. Estimates of the reduction in construction costs from elimination of these provisions range from 2 percent to as high as 15 percent.[30]

"Excessive requirements" aside, indirect evidence suggests that the incidence of serious safety hazards in illegal units is not as great as one might suppose. Michael O'Hare has shown that owner-resident landlords who undertake improvements without building permits in order to save money do in fact follow safety provisions of fire and electrical codes. It is in their interest to do so, because they live adjacent to the unit and are at risk themselves. This means that deliberate chiseling, use of substandard materials, and corner-cutting rarely occur in owner-occupied rental housing, although incompetence and ignorance remain possible risks of "do-it-yourself" work.[31]

Fire risk does not appear to be greater for illegal than for legal units. The three largest casualty and fire insurers in California indicate that they have observed no instances of fires involving homes with illegal conversions in either Marin and

San Francisco Counties—or anywhere else in northern California, for that matter. About 10 percent of the single-family dwellings in both of these counties contain illegal accessory apartments.[32] In addition, studies on fire prevention and control in residential dwellings indicate that very few fires occur as a result of the kinds of code violations one would expect to find in illegal units. The single greatest cause of residential fires is smoking in bed. Other major causes include the use of kitchen stoves for heating, the malfunctioning of hot water heaters, and the storage of combustible materials near furnaces in basements.[33]

If illegal conversions do in fact contain genuine safety hazards, and if the cost of compliance with codes involves financial hardship or loss for homeowners, the appropriate response by the public sector would be to develop a special set of "life-safety" standards for accessory apartments. These standards would require compliance only with code provisions specifically designed to avoid life-threatening hazards, particularly those related to fire. This procedure has been used in housing rehabilitation programs. For years, building and fire officials applied new construction standards to older residential structures. This made rehabilitation prohibitively expensive and led to code enforcement efforts that ended in evictions and demolitions. During the 1960s neighborhood preservation programs began developing special rehabilitation standards for buildings constructed prior to World War II. These standards lowered the cost of rehabilitation substantially, saved many old but still habitable units, and reduced the risk of fire and other hazards to those who occupied them.[34]

This same approach has been used in efforts to rehabilitate low-income residential hotels. For example, under a state law designed to preserve and rehabilitate low-income residential hotels for senior citizens, the state of California has developed a model building code that establishes a minimum state standard for earthquake and fire safety. The code is intended to provide a rehabilitation standard that will protect life and health to the greatest extent possible and yet make preservation of residential hotels economically feasible. Any materials or methods of construction that will achieve specified performance standards in the model code may be used. The Division of Codes and Standards of the California Department of Housing and Community Development also offers technical assistance to local inspectors on request as part of the program.[35]

Special standards that minimize the costs of code compliance have also been developed for loft conversions in New York City, Chicago, and Boston. Alternative standards have been formulated for mechanical systems such as elevators, as well as for wiring and plumbing, and a degree of flexibility has been introduced by several "as-of-right optional standards for light, air, egress, and other factors."[36]

Following the model of rehabilitation programs, the provision of financial assistance to owners who wish to install accessory apartments would probably help to discourage some illegal conversions. Combining minimum "life-safety" standards with special loan assistance would also help to encourage more upgrading of existing illegal units. Assistance of this type could be made available to buyers of those properties at the time of turnover. Again, purchase-rehabilitation loan programs offer some instructive examples that can be applied to correcting code problems in house conversions.[37]

Zoning by Building Envelope

Most of the regulatory approaches discussed so far are interim strategies. They represent incremental adjustments to broad, fundamental changes occurring in the housing sector and family structure. They are also the products of political compromise. As experiments and efforts to test the waters, however, they are also learning experiences for citizens, property owners, and public officials alike, and out of such experiences bolder innovations might come.

One such innovation might be "zoning by building envelope." The new dimensions of family and housing tenure which are emerging today suggest the desirability of a system of residential zoning that regulates *intensity of use* instead of *population density*. This type of regulation would be accomplished by zoning districts according to desired maximum building envelope rather than by specifying a maximum density standard, such as units per lot. Zoning by building envelope would control only bulk, height, yard setbacks, and parking standards. There would be no control on the degree of multiple occupancy. The purpose of this type of zoning would be to preserve low-density neighborhood form, to control parking and traffic, and to prevent the demolition of existing buildings and their replacement by much larger multiple-unit structures. No effort would be made to dictate a lifestyle or type of occupant. In effect, the form of a residential building could be regulated independently and separated from its traditionally perceived associations with households of a certain type and size.

Zoning by building envelope would work as follows. There would be no regulation of building type—that is, no explicit restriction on the number of units in a structure. Intensity of use would be controlled by a "floor-area ratio." This would limit the total amount of permitted habitable floor space in a residential building to a certain proportion of the total lot area. Height regulations and yard controls would be included, and some limits on the bulk of second stories could also be established to preserve skylines.

Under this sort of zoning, residential districts would be differentiated *not* by the maximum permitted number of units per lot but rather by the maximum permitted size of and shape of the building envelope. Buildings in what were single-family districts would retain their existing envelopes. The same structure, for example, could contain *either* one dwelling unit with seven rooms for occupancy by a family of four or five persons, *or* two-dwelling units with four rooms each to accommodate two separate households of two persons. A control on minimum dwelling-unit size might be included to ensure a level of housing accommodation that is consistent with minimum standards of public health and safety. The minimum size regulations of local housing codes could be used for this purpose.

The minimum amount of off-street parking to be required would be determined by the amount of habitable floor area in the structure. For example, for every 500 square feet of living area one off-street parking space would be provided on the site. This would make the number of off-street parking spaces independent of the number of units in the structure. One family in a 1500 square-foot house would be required to have as many parking spaces as three individuals each occupying a separate 500 square-foot unit in the same building envelope.

Zoning by building envelope would represent a genuine performance standard approach to the control of population density. So long as sufficient off-street parking and open space are provided, the number of dwelling units and the number of persons could be increased. Because the number of dwelling units in any structure could vary within a range constrained only by off-street parking and minimum dwelling-size requirements, the actual number of units could change as the character of market demand changes. In single-family districts where there is little demand for small dwellings, houses would probably remain unchanged. In districts where there are single-family houses with surplus space and a strong demand for small economical units, large numbers of conversions could take place.

Zoning by building envelope would also allow all types of conversions to occur. Accessory apartments would be permitted as of right. Only a valid building permit and a plan-review would be required. Because this would be a much simpler procedure than going through the conditional-use process, there would probably be fewer illegal conversions. Some very large houses, which because of their size might be difficult to sell and therefore likely candidates for rental occupancy, could be duplexed and converted to condominiums. In suburbs where there is little or no rental demand, the majority of conversions might take this form. Depending on how the height limitations and yard requirements are set, this type of zoning might also cause some existing buildings to be demolished and replaced by new structures more suitable for flexible conversions or by small, high-quality duplex condominiums.

This approach to the control of conversions would clearly be less restrictive and more promotional in nature than any of the approaches discussed so far. In some situations, this type of zoning would create opportunities for entrepreneurs to become involved in the business of house conversions. These opportunities for profit would probably be limited to foreclosed properties for sale at deep discounts, old mansions, and "white elephants"—large houses in neighborhoods of smaller dwellings. In some cases, small houses on lots where a larger building envelope is allowed could be demolished and profitably replaced with a larger duplex.

Zoning by building envelope is not new. It has been used since the early 1960s to regulate multi-family housing development in many central cities—including Boston, Chicago, Philadelphia, Denver, and Washington, D.C.—where its purpose has been to encourage high density housing while ensuring adequate provision of open space and mitigating the impact of development on surrounding areas.[39] The experiences of central cities in this regard also demonstrate the biggest drawback of this method of residential zoning. Restrictions on the total amount of floor space tend to encourage an increased supply of small units whether through new construction or conversion.[40] The reason for this is that for any given amount of total floor space in a building, more rent can be obtained if the area available is divided up into more smaller apartments rather than fewer larger units.

Hence, zoning by building envelope is not strictly neutral with respect to dwelling size. This means that if exclusive single-family zoning were replaced by a system of zoning by building envelope, there would be fewer units for large households, particularly families with children who rent. They would have to pay a premium to bid dwellings away from smaller households. Low- and moderate-income families seeking to live in large units would be at an even greater disadvantage because of their relatively weaker competitive position in the housing market, and overcrowding among some of them would probably occur. To prevent this from occurring in places where small households can pay a higher price per square foot than larger households can, government might have to provide some type of non-zoning incentive to ensure an adequate supply of large units.

Zoning by building envelope would also allow neighborhoods to become more diverse in terms of life-style, while the physical form of neighborhoods would remain fixed. Social composition and density would, however, vary more than they do today and might conceivably change more frequently as well. It is important to recognize, however, that this increased diversity is inevitable. Because of increased divorce, delayed marriage and child bearing, longer life expectancy, and alternative sexual life-styles, more people today spend greater parts of their lives than did earlier generations living in household arrangements other than a married-couple family. The course of the family life cycle at all income levels has also become more discontinuous and less predictable than it was in the past. The country now abounds with single people, single parents, childless couples and various new pairings of unmarried individuals. The traditional nuclear family no longer reigns as the dominant form of householding in American society, and we should expect to see as a result an eventual diminution of the exclusive single-family districts as a dominant form of residential land use also.

Zoning by building envelope represents thus a more complete and conscious adaptation of our system of residential land-use to these new lifestyles and householding arrangements than do the incremental adjustments discussed earlier in this chapter. The nuclear family system has become "attenuated" in large part because life-styles in our society have become more a matter of choice than compulsion. Zoning by building envelope would be a way of coming to terms with that fact. It would be a way to build more flexibility and choice into our housing stock while at the same time preserving the environmental values associated with low-density residential neighborhoods and the forms of ownership that in our culture are regarded as essential to the quality of life.

Notes

1. San Francisco Bay Area Council, "Annual Regional Planning Poll," 1983. Unpublished. Conducted by Field Research Institute for the San Francisco Bay Area Council (a private, business supported regional planning organization), the poll used a random sample of 632 households stratified to reflect the age and sex distribution of household heads in the region.
2. Another poll conducted by the Research & Decisions Corporation in 1984 for the San Francisco Chamber of Commerce similarly found widespread support for legalization of accessory apartments. A sample of 760 names were drawn at random from the county voter registration rolls. The respondents were phoned and asked a number of questions about development and planning issues in San Francisco. One of the questions was: "Should home owners in single family neighborhoods be allowed to have small second units or 'in-law' apartments in their homes?" 85 percent answered "yes," 10 percent "no," and 4 percent were undecided. Of the 266 home owners in the sample, 80 percent answered "yes," 15 percent "no," and 5 percent were undecided.
3. California Government Code, Section 65852.2.
4. Senate Bill 2161, Chapter 1630, Statutes of 1984.
5. For a discussion of the theory of deregulation as well as "non-enforcement as an alternative to deregulation," see Barry M. Mitnick, *The Political Economy of Regulation: Creating, Designing, and Removing Regulatory Forms* (New York: Columbia University Press, 1980), 417–45.
6. Tri-State Regional Planning Commission, *Single-Family Conversions: A Survey of Local Officials in the Tri-State Region.* Interim Technical Report 3112, 1981. See also Patrick Hare, "Rethinking Single-Family Zoning: Growing Old in American Neighborhoods," *New England Journal of Human Services,* (Summer, 1981).
7. Donald N. Rathblatt, Daniel J. Garr, and Jo Sprague, eds., *The Suburban Environment and Women* (New York: Praeger Publishers, 1979), 179, 220.
8. United States Bureau of the Census. *Census of Housing, Components of Inventory Change, U.S. & Regions,* vol. 4, 1970, 1980.
9. George Peterson, *The Use of Mortgage Revenue Bonds* (Washington, D.C.: Urban Institute, 1979).
10. Hare, Connors and Merriam, *Accessory Apartments: Using Surplus Space in Single-Family Houses,* Planning and Advisory Service Report, no. 365 (Chicago, IL: American Planning Association, 1982), 2.
11. Tri-State Regional Planning Commission, *Single-Family Conversions: A Survey of Local Officials in the Tri-State Region,* Interim Technical Report 3112, 1981.
12. California Department of Housing and Community Development, *1983 Survey of Second-Unit Ordinances in California,* Sacramento, California, 1984.
13. Ann Draper, Planning Officer, City of Sunnyvale. Quoted in California Department of Housing and Community Development, *1982 Survey of Second-Unit Ordinances in California,* 1983, 42.
14. California Department of Housing and Community Development, *ibid.*; 426 (87 percent) of all city and county governments in the state responded to the survey.
15. Interview with Jana Haehl, City Councilwoman, Corte Madera, December 8, 1982.
16. Hare, Conners and Merriam, *Accessory Apartments: Using Surplus Space in Single-Family Houses,* 5.
17. Central Naugatuck Valley Regional Planning Agency, 1982, 43.
18. Telephone interview with Terry Sedig, Daly City Planning Department, December 11, 1983.
19. Interview with Robert Levy, Superintendent, Department of Public Works, City of San Francisco, September 28, 1981.
20. Interview with Bernard Cummings, Chief of Bureau of Building Inspection, City of San Francisco, California, September 22, 1980. Interview with Daniel J. Sullivan, Director of Plan Review, Department of City Planning, San Francisco, California, July 15, 1982. Similar practices are followed in other California localities. See Donald Hagman, *Urban Planning,* 1975, chapter 8.

21. Memo, Robert Feldman, Department of City Planning to City Attorney, City of San Francisco, 1980.
22. Phyllis Ann-Santry, "Legalizing Single Family Conversions," *Planning: 1981*. Proceedings of the National Planning Conference (Washington, D.C.: American Planning Association, 1982), 177–78.
23. For a review of the literature on tax avoidance and illegal production, see Rodney T. Smith, "The Legal and Illegal Markets for Taxed Goods: Pure Theory and an Application to State Government Taxation of Distilled Spirits," *Journal of Law & Economics*, 19 (1976): 393–429.
24. Phyllis Ann-Santry, "Legalizing Single Family Conversions." *Planning: 1981*. Proceedings of the National Planning Conference, 176. Jana Haehl, a city councilwoman from Corte Madera, California also cites property tax reassessment as a major fear among owners of single family homes with accessory apartments in her community. Other public officials in California also believe that the fear of reassessment discourages home owners from converting legally who would otherwise prefer to do so. See Bert Verrips, *Second Units: An Emerging Housing Resource* (San Francisco: People for Open Space, 1983), 44–45.
25. In California, this practice became common in the late 1960s when the entire property assessment system was modernized. Interview with Carl Gustafson, Chief Appraiser, Alameda County, March 13, 1979.
26. Carl P. Simon and Ann D. Witte, *Beating the System: The Underground Economy* (Boston: Auburn House, 1982).
27. H.M. Groves, "Empirical Studies of Tax Compliance," *The National Tax Journal*, 11 (1958). 291–301.
28. Charles G. Field and Steven R. Rivkin, *The Building Code Burden* (Lexington, MA: D.C. Heath & Co., 1975), 22.
29. See Leland S. Burns and Frank Mittlebach, "Efficiency in the Housing Industry," from *The Report of the President's Committee on Urban Housing*. Technical Studies, vol. II (Washington, D.C.: United States Government Printing Office, 1968), 98–102.
30. For a review of these studies, see John Quigley, "Residential Construction and Public Policy: A Progress Report," in Richard R. Nelson, ed., *Government and Technical Progress: A Cross-Industry Analysis* (New York: Pergamon Press Inc., 1982), 387–91.
31. Michael O'Hare, "Improvement of Owner-Occupied Rental Housing: A Game-Theoretic Study of the Decision to Invest," *Journal of the American Real Estate and Urban Economics Association*, 9 (1981): 60–61. See also by the same author "Structural Inadequacies in Urban Environment Management," *Regional and Urban Economics*, 3 (1978): 139–43.
32. Phone interviews with claims adjustment and investigation divisions at Allstate Insurance Co., Fireman's Fund, and Transamerica, Inc. September 5–12, 1982.
33. William H. McLain, "The Role of Fire Prevention and Control in Building Construction and Regulation," in Patrick W. Cooke, ed., *Regulatory Concerns of Building Rehabilitation* (Washington, D.C.: National Bureau of Standards, 1979). See also, C.H. Yuill, "Fire Losses: A Needless Waste," in Chester Rapkin, ed., *The Social and Economic Consequences of Residential Fires* (Lexington, MA: Lexington Press), 27–42.
34. Roger S. Alhbrandt, *Flexible Code Enforcement: A Key Ingredient in Neighborhood Preservation Programming* (Washington, D.C.: National Association of Housing and Redevelopment Officials, 1976).
35. California Department of Housing and Community Development, "Residential Hotel Rehabilitation Demonstration: A Progress Summary—June 1981," Sacramento, California. Memorandum.
36. Richard J. Roddewig, *Loft Conversions: Planning Issues, Problems and Prospects*, Planning Advisory Service Report No. 362 (Chicago, IL: American Planning Association, 1981), 12–13.
37. Alhbrandt, *Flexible Code Enforcement: A Key Ingredient in Neighborhood Preservation Programming*, 4.
38. Property owners could establish covenants to restrict conversions and to maintain single-family use in their neighborhoods. This method would not work well unless it was accompanied by the establishment of a home owners association with the power to levy assessments and fines.
39. Norman Williams, Jr., *American Planning Law: Land Use and the Police Power* (Chicago, IL: Callaghan & Co.), II, 665–66.
40. Norman Williams, *ibid.*, 687–88.

Conclusion

The central premise of this book is that the housing needs of our society today are quite different from those that gave rise to the land-use practices and housing policies of the last thirty years, and that accessory apartments represent one of the more tangible forms in which social change is leading to new practices and policies. Accessory apartment conversions make more efficient use of the existing stock through better space utilization. They also can generate additional rental housing in areas where development is restricted and new apartments are too expensive to build by conventional means. But even where rental housing supply is not so constrained, accessory apartment conversions have attracted widespread public interest as a way to create low- and moderate-income housing for both owners and renters that requires little or no public subsidy. At the same time, accessory apartments also provide affordable owner and renter housing for small households—young marrieds, elderly and single persons, and single parents—the most rapidly growing segment of our population today.

The need to utilize our housing stock better stems from the perception that changes in family structure have reduced the average size of households and that many persons consequently have more space in their dwellings than they reasonably might need. As this book has argued, zoning regulations, financing instruments, and the income tax treatment of home ownership have encouraged underutilization and discouraged the recycling of surplus space into additional housing units. The effectiveness of future efforts to promote and control accessory apartments will depend in part on our knowledge of the incidence of underutilization in the single-family inventory and on our understanding of how altering zoning and these institutional arrangements will influence space consumption decisions of households.

Although this book has addressed these issues, more research and investigation of these matters is needed. The last systematic study of space utilization in American housing—*American Housing and Its Use, The Demand for Shelter* by Louis Winnick and Ned Shilling—was conducted over thirty years ago. Updating of this study is long overdue. The place to start is with the Department of Hous-

197

ing and Urban Development's *Annual Housing Survey*. It offers a rich source of information about housing consumption which can be used to investigate the determinants of space utilization in both owner and renter housing. Also needed is more original survey research which investigates the behavioral determinants of space utilization in single-family housing, including the perceptions of home owners about space standards and alternative uses of surplus space. Such surveys can be used to develop a more accurate measure of space utilization than the *rooms-per-person ratio*, which, as indicated in Chapter 3, measures household density more than it does actual space utilization. Survey research can also shed light on the potential of extra bedrooms, basements, attics, and garages in single-family houses for accessory apartment development, about which census data tell us nothing.

The development of accessory apartments is one facet of the "densification" of single-family neighborhoods which occurs not only by means of house conversions but also by room additions and the in-filling of empty lots. As single-family neighborhoods age, they are used more intensively as owners improve their properties by adding various facilities (workshops, storage rooms, greenhouses, etc.) or expanding the amount of living space. Empty lots are filled in and accessory apartments created during times when housing demand rises.

This building up of the physical fabric of a neighborhood usually occurs through an incremental process as individuals adapt their dwellings and property in response to changes in their personal fortunes as well as market forces. However, the kinds of structural change in the family and the housing economy discussed in this book imply a much more conscious effort to adapt maturing single-family neighborhoods to new housing needs. Communities that encourage conversions and in-fill development as a housing policy will need to engage in some degree of physical planning, if not to protect the quality of neighborhood environment, then at least to adapt streets and service delivery systems to greater densities for purposes of convenience and efficiency. Planners need, therefore, to understand the process of densification better and to develop methods for analyzing how land uses, buildings, property subdivision, landscaping, access, and service distribution in neighborhoods can change over time. Such methods could be used for planning and evaluating the future of single-family neighborhoods. An important step in this direction has been taken by Anne Vernez-Moudon, of the University of Washington, and Chester Sprague, of the Massachusetts Institute of Technology, in their research on consolidation of single-family neighborhoods in central cities. More work in this area needs to be done, particularly about the process of densification and in-fill as it has occurred in post-war suburbs.

Physical and social change in single-family neighborhoods in the past was rarely if ever managed with the conscious intention of adapting the single-family housing stock to new housing needs; instead, mature neighborhoods were often allowed to languish and decay while new communities were created on an ever-expanding suburban frontier. We can no longer afford to do this. If we can master the methods of adaptive residential reuse and learn how to redesign neighborhoods without incurring huge demolition, displacement, and rebuilding costs—which conventional redevelopment so frequently involves—we can achieve a tremendous social and private saving in capital and infrastructure while continuing to ensure every American "a decent home and suitable living environment."

Index

Abu-Lughod, Janet, 77, 78

accessory apartment: and "baby boom," 57; as blight indicator, 104; California ordinances about, 185-186; candidates for conversion to, 8-9, 149, 163; and cars, 163, 171-172, 175; conversion rate of, 42-43; defined, 3-4, 7, 36; and "densification," 198; and dwelling-unit size, 45; as external addition, 140; and family life cycle, 48, 53; financing of, 180-183, 190-191; from garage conversion, 146-147; and household size, 4, 7; and housing policy, 178-180; incentives to install, 96, 181; incidence of, 36-37, 41, 47, 171; as "in-law" apartment, 4-7, 53, 177; legal status of, 5-6, 170-171, 177-178, 184, 187-188, 190, 194n2; level of rent, 53; merger, 43-47, 53; neighborhood impact, 171; opposition to, 177; origins of, 7; and population density, 150; potential number of, 93, 96; problems of, 103; regulation of, 170, 184-185; safety of, 189-190; in single-family homes, 4, 127, 134; site plans, 146; size, 5; and social change, 197; and state governments, 179; substandard, 57; support for, 163, 172-173, 177; as "swing" supply, 46; and taxes, 188-189, 195n24; types of, 156; and zoning, 126, 133, 192. *See also* conversion; parking; zoning

Adams, Thomas, 114

Advisory Committee on Zoning, 130n32

American Association of Real Estate Boards, 130n32

American Housing and Its Use, the Demand for Shelter, 197

American Public Health Association (APHA), 73

Annual Housing Survey (AHS), 46, 55n11, 81, 99n29

Babcock, Richard, 128

Baer, William C., 86

Bane, Jo, 71

Bassett, Edward M., 107, 108, 109, 119

Beresford, John, 69

Better Homes in America, 130n32

Bettman, Alfred, 112, 116, 117

Blank, David M., 33

Breuer, Mercel, 17

Broadmoor (CA) and Broadmoor Homeowners Association, 136, 155-156, 163, 170-171

Burglin, Lisa, 55n19

California, 82, 133

California Department of Housing and Community Development, Division of Codes and Standards, 190

California Housing Finance Agency, 180

California Supreme Court, 112, 113, 118

Chesapeake Bay cities, 50

Chicago (IL), 119

CINCH, (Components of Inventory Change) 8, 29, 31, 33, 35-37, 41, 45-47, 55n15, 93, 96, 150, 181

Community Block Grant Funds, 171

Components of Inventory Change. *See* CINCH

Consumer Expenditure Survey of 1972-73, 81

conversion: and age of home owner, 47-48; of attic, 14; of basement, 14, 140, 188; in cities, 38-39, 41, 49-50, 52; defined, 1, 35-36; and family cycle, 7, 17, 19, 26; of family dwellings, 39; of garage, 14, 140, 143, 146-147, 149-150; and Great Depression, 31, 54n5; of group dwellings, 2; and house design, 140-141; and household composition, 4, 45, 47-48; and housing inventory, 30-36; incidence of, 29-31, 33, 46-47; legal status of,

conversion (continued)
29, 42, 53, 143, 147, 149, 183, 184, 186; neighborhood impact of, 133; in nonmetropolitan places, 35; by owner-occupant, 38-39, 45, 47; potential extent of, 179; regulation of, 183-184, 192; of rental dwellings, 33-34, 49; substandard, 49-50; suburbs, 8, 34, 39, 41-42, 49-50, 52; suitability for, 140; types of, 2-3, 14; and unit size, 49, 60

Corte Madera (CA), 186, 195n24

Daly City (CA), 187
Design of Residential Areas, 114
Diamond, Douglas, 80, 81
Doling, John, 80
Douglas, William O., 123, 124
Downs, Anthony, 58, 96

Ellis, J.R., 80
"empty nesters," 63, 65, 86-87, 181
Euclid v. Ambler Realty, 112, 115-117, 119, 120, 127, 130n41
Exhibition House (Breuer), 17-18

family: attentuation of, 67-69, 71, 121; defined, 98n21, 125, 131n59
Federal Housing Administration (FHA), 73, 115, 120
Fischer, Claude, 83
Flexabilt House (Robertson), 26
Flint, Barbara, 119
Foley, Marian M., 77, 78
Follain, James R., Jr., 81

Gans, Herbert, 105
Glick, Paul, 7, 8, 67
Grebler, L., 33, 81, 87
Gutheim, Frederick, 19

Hare, Patrick, 41, 55n18, 127
Hareven, Tamara, 8, 97n3
Harvard-MIT Joint Center for Urban Studies, 71
Hiett, Irving B., 130n32
Hillestad, Carol E., 81
home ownership: and condominiums, 121; factors encouraging, 113-114; versus renting, 78
Home Owners Loan Corporation, 120
Hoover, Herbert, 130n32
household: and "baby boom," 67, 71, 98n25, 138; composition, 61-62, 65-66, 121; doubling up, 67; and dwelling size, 71-73, 76; formation rate, 57; headship rate, 61-62, 67,

69, 71; income, 99n29; instability, 69; in 19th-century Boston, 8; non-family, 67, 69, 71; one-parent, 122; single-person, 67, 71, 150; size, 49, 60-64, 66-67, 71, 97n3, 109; two-person, 65, 69, 71; "undoubling" of, 62, 66-67. *See also* conversion.

housing: affordability crisis, 57-58; censuses and surveys, 31, 83, 87; as commodity, 61; demand for, 71, 74, 77; design, 9-10, 14-19, 23, 25-26, 140-141; in mobile homes, 36, 46; policy, 58, 179-180; prices, 73, 82; rental, 58; and taxes, 79-80, 127; and technology, 6, 9, 14, 19, 23, 98n19, 99n32; two-family, 117, 119; units defined, 5; unit size, 59-65. *See also* single-family housing

Ihlder, John, 130n32
Illinois, 117-118

Kain, John F., 73
Kentucky, 118
kitchen, 5-6, 50, 188
Knowles, Morris, 130n32
Koch, Carl, 19, 23

Levitt houses, 14, 19, 141
Lincoln (MA), 55n19
Lipstein, Benjamin, 50
Los Angeles (CA), 119
Lowry, Ira S., 81

McCarthy, Kevin, F., 80
McGough, Duane, 36
MacLeod, P.B., 80
Marin County (CA), 187, 189
Marshall, Thurgood, 124, 125
Masnick, George, 71
Mello, Henry, 133
Miller v. Board of Public Works of the City of Los Angeles, 112-114, 118
Mittlebach, Frank G., 81, 87
Modell, John, 8, 97n3
Moore v. East Cleveland, 125-126
Myers, Dowell, 90

National Association of Home Builders, 42, 53
National City Planning Institute, 130n32
New York City, 86, 108
New York City Planning Commission, 110
Niebanch, Paul, 86
Northern California Community Survey, 83, 87
Norton, Eliot, 67
Noto, Nonna, 81

O'Hare, Michael, 189
Olmsted, Frederick Law, 130n32
overhead capital, 74

Panel Study of Income Dynamics, 81
parking: and household size, 151; off-street, 147, 149, 154, 170, 186, 191-192; problems, 125, 152-153, 163, 172; regulations, 126; and vehicular density, 151, 174-176
Perin, Constance, 103
Popenoe, David, 141
population: census of, 31, 121; structure, 61-63, 69, 74, 98n25
Primary Sampling Units (PSU), 54n3
Public Works Administration, 31

Quigley, John M., 73

Real Property Survey (1934), 31
reverse mortgage, 182
Rivlin, Alice, 69
Robertson, Frank, 26
rooms, defined, 55nn15, 16

St. Louis (MO), 73, 119
San Anselmo (CA), 55n19
San Francisco and Bay area (CA), 177, 188, 190
San Francisco-Oakland-Sacramento (SMSA), 101n58, 136
San Jose (CA), 141
San Leandro (CA), 134-137, 141, 146, 151, 155, 170-171
Sarma, Syam, 81
Schilling, Ned, 66, 197
Senate Bill 1534 (CA), 179-180
Simon, Carl P., 189
single-family housing: adaptability of, 8-9, 26; "expandable," 9-10, 14; two- and three-zone, 17
single-family residential areas, 8, 10, 106-107, 113, 118-119, 198-199. *See also* zoning
space: and family cycle, 23, 76-78, 89, 193; overhead, 87, 91; per capita consumption of, 71, 80-81; persons-per-room ratio (PPRR), 71; "reserve," 86-87; in single-family housing, 198; standards of, 75, 86-87; surplus, 58-59, 61, 74-76, 83-85, 87, 90-91, 93, 96, 179, 197; underutilization, 74-75, 78, 82, 85, 87, 89, 91-93, 197
Sprague, Chester, 198
Standard Metropolitan Statistical Area (SMSA), 54n3, 55n11, 55n22, 101n58, 136
Sunnyvale (CA), 185

Survey of Consumer Finances (1955), 78
Sutherland, 117

Techbuilt House, 19, 23, 25-26
Thibodeau, Thomas, 41
Triangle Shirt Waist Company fire, 128n12
Tri-State Regional Planning Commission (NY-NJ-CT), 42, 186

Urban Institute, 41
U.S. Bureau of the Census, 5, 8, 33, 36, 41, 46, 85, 90, 150, 181
U.S. Bureau of Labor Statistics (BLS), 31, 33
U.S. Department of Housing and Urban Development (HUD), 46, 81, 198
U.S. Housing Authority, 31
U.S. Supreme Court, 112, 115, 117, 119, 123-125, 131nn49, 59

Veiller, Lawrence, 130n32
Vernez-Moudon, Anne, 198
Village of Belle Terre v. Boraas, 123-125

Wachtel, Harold, 141
Washington Manor (CA) and Washington Manor Homeowners Association (WMHA), 136-141, 143, 146, 150, 152-154, 163, 171-172
West Coast Hotel v. Parrish, 131n49
Weston (CT), 188
Williams, Norman, 117
Winnick, Louis, 33, 66, 71-72, 78, 197
Witte, Ann D., 189
Woodruff, A.M., 50
YMCA and YWCA, 66
Young, Arthur, 41

zoning: for apartments, 111, 115, 117-118, 122; by building envelope, 191-193; by building type, 115; bulk-control, 105; constitutionality of, 117, 119; and conversion, 3; critics, 131n49; and definition of dwelling unit, 6; and definition of family, 122-123; enforcement, 187; evolution of, 107, 128n11; expense of complying with, 190; and family life-styles, 110; and FHA mortgages, 115, 120; and home ownership, 130n32; and housing design, 10; and land values, 114; modern, 108; New York City law about (1916), 108; "nuisance" concept of, 128n6; and population density, 108-110; purposes of, 104-105, 110-113, 183; residential, 103; and role of women, 122; single-family, 82, 104-

zoning (continued)
105, 108-109, 114, 120-121, 126-127; and social diversity, 193; and "stage theory of neighborhood evolution," 106; and underutilization, 82, 89; and urban change, 105, 193; "use" and "area" controls, 106-109, 128; validity of, 117-119. *See also* accessory apartment: legal status of; conversion: legal status of